The Culture of Redemption

The Culture of Redemption

Leo Bersani

Harvard University Press
Cambridge, Massachusetts, and London, England   1990

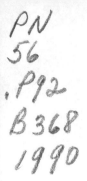

This book is printed on acid-free paper, and its binding
materials have been chosen for strength and durability.

Library of Congress Cataloging-in-Publication Data

Bersani, Leo.
   The culture of redemption / Leo Bersani.
      p.   cm.
   Includes index.
   ISBN 0-674-17977-3
   1. Psychoanalysis and literature.   2. Literature,
Modern—History and criticism.   3. Aesthetics.   I. Title.
PN56.P92B368   1990
809'.93353—dc19   89-15304
                                                            CIP

Contents

The Culture of Redemption

Prologue

This book is a frankly polemical study of claims made in the modern period for the authoritative, even redemptive virtues of literature. Chapter 1 lays out the main lines of my argument; but it may be useful if, in a prefatory note, I both define the boundaries of the argument and alert the reader to a certain conceptual mobility in its elaboration. The generically and historically heterogeneous essays that follow will make it clear that I am not interested in a thorough, and thoroughly scholarly, tracing of the genealogy of the culture of redemption. Were I to have written that sort of book, I would, for example, have studied the relation of modern ideas of art as redemptive to earlier notions of art as preserving otherwise perishable experience, or as expressing the universal through the particular; and within the modern period the redemptive aesthetic would have to be distinguished from the willed isolation and alienation of art from the rest of life in the art-for-art's-sake credo. Indeed, the aesthetic morality I will be studying frequently includes the project of art's faithful adherence to experience; it may even be consistent with an ideal of nearly literal realism. A crucial assumption in the culture of redemption is that a certain type of repetition of experience in art repairs inherently damaged or valueless experience. Experience may be overwhelming, practically impossible to absorb, but it is assumed—and this is especially evident in much encyclopedic fiction—that the work of art has the authority to master the presumed raw material of experience in a manner that uniquely gives value to, perhaps even redeems, that material. This may sound like an unattackable truism, and yet I want to show that such apparently acceptable views of art's beneficently reconstructive function in culture depend on a devaluation of historical experience and of art. The catastrophes of history matter much less if they are somehow compensated for in art, and art itself gets reduced to a kind of superior patching function, is enslaved to those very materials to which it presumably imparts value.

The culture of redemption might be thought of as the creation of what Nietzsche called the theoretical man—who Nietzsche claimed first appeared in the West in the person of Socrates—the man who attributes to thought the power to "correct" existence. Although it is true that no one would seem more securely exempt than Socrates from promoting the notion of art as redemptive, that notion is itself, as I have just suggested, antiartistic. The redemptive aesthetic asks us to consider art as a correction of life, but *the corrective virtue of works of art depends on a misreading of art as philosophy.* Art, as Plato rightly saw, cannot have the unity, the identity, the stability of truth; it does not belong to the world of perfectly intelligible ideas. A redemptive aesthetic based on the negation of life (in Nietzschean terms, on a nihilism that invents a "true world" as an alternative to an inferior and depreciated world of mere appearance) must also negate art.

In the culture of redemption, this negation is never explicit, but it can be seen with particular clarity within the very works that make the redemptive claim for art. Thus the extraordinary value that Proust's narrator learns to attribute to art is evidenced in his own work by a strong (but happily unsuccessful) movement away from novelizing and by a depreciation of his own fictions. As the Proustian novel progresses, it comes more and more to be dominated by the enunciation of general laws, and the narrator's life is subordinated to those laws and given the status of a heuristic lie. This life, and the dramatic fictions that constitute it, would be nothing more than what art adds to philosophy: the degradation of laws into vivid exemplary illustrations of laws. The Proustian novel almost (we will see the full importance of this qualification) realizes a dream in Western thought of literature as *serving* philosophy, as providing an addendum of examples to a purer (if perhaps inherently unreadable) discourse on and of truth. *A la Recherche du temps perdu* moves toward, but never reaches, an ideal limit where the novel itself would be freed from its exemplifying function, would no longer be burdened with the impurities of novelizing. Ideally, art would be truth liberated from phenomena. The stretching of the Proustian novel toward this extreme limit (where art would become its own philosophical criticism) even gives to the later volumes their austere beauty, the beauty of a novel that has nearly abstracted itself from its fables.

The shapes of a literature *without* redemptive authority are most carefully investigated in my discussions of Baudelaire, Nietzsche, Bataille, and Pynchon. The book doesn't "lead up" to Baudelaire and Nietzsche, but the reader might like to know that Chapter 3 was the last chapter to be written, that it is probably something like the conceptual center of the work. This, I should add, I find all the more surprising in that Chapter 3 ends by leaning heavily on a work that at once proposes an aesthetic of redemption and yet so radically redefines the notion as to become a powerful argument against it: Nietzsche's *The Birth of Tragedy*. But even as I write this I feel inclined to displace this center, to move it back to the discussion of narcissism in Chapter 2. In my previous work on Freud, I have been interested in tracing the collapse of theoretical authority in his work, the discursive moves by which arguments are at once elaborated and disformulated, and I have argued that those moments of collapse—the antisystemic moments in Freud—provide us with the most authentically psychoanalytic events in his writing. For these events confirm the necessary implication of psychoanalytic theorizing itself in disturbances that, while ostensibly the subject of its discourse, more profoundly *agitate* that discourse. Chapter 2 attempts to locate that area of Freudian theory most likely to provide us with a satisfactory account both of the collapse of theory and of attempts at theoretical and systemic recovery. The reaffirmation of system—by which I also mean the reaffirmation of authority—takes place in Freud primarily by way of reinforcements in the theory of the ego as, precisely, the instance of authority in the self with respect to both the inner and the outer worlds. Freud's 1914 essay "On Narcissism" is a startling demonstration of just such an exercise in recovery, an exercise all the more unexpected because the discussion begins by suggesting that the ego is born as an already shattered totality, as an agency seduced into being by the very prospect of being shattered.

The conceptual mobility I referred to at the start can perhaps best be located in a move from the somewhat limited vocabulary of redemption to the theoretical centering of the question of authoritative selfhood. This shift corresponds to a growing conviction on my part that the culture of redemption itself depends on even more fundamental assumptions about authoritative identities, about identity *as* authority. I recognize that, in saying all this, I also confirm a slightly dispiriting consistency in my own work. I have perhaps been less restlessly self-dismissive in my criticism than my work suggests I should be, and, just as concentric circles are constituted by movements at once amplifying and replicative, I have for some years now repeatedly circled around the question of the relation between cultural authority, selfhood, and sexuality. To say this should be taken as a confession that the questions I ask in reading literary texts (or visual art) constitute a kind of moral criticism, and that this involves a certain indifference to criticism anxious to teach us the difference between the literary and the nonliterary.

The aesthetic of narcissism adumbrated in certain chapters of this book is in line with this more general ethical-erotic project. The narcissism pointed to in the first pages of Freud's essay on narcissism is a self-*jouissance* that dissolves the person and thereby, at least temporarily, erases the sacrosanct value of selfhood, a value that may account for human beings' extraordinary willingness to kill in order to protect the seriousness of their statements. The self is a practical convenience; promoted to the status of an ethical ideal, it is a sanction for violence. If sexuality is socially dysfunctional in that it brings people together only to plunge them into a self-shattering and solipsistic jouissance that drives them apart (a jouissance somehow "figured" in writers as different as Baudelaire, Bataille, and Flaubert), it can also be thought of as our primary, hygienic practice of nonviolence, and even as a kind of biological protection against our continuously renewed efforts to disguise and to exercise the tyranny of the self in the prestigious form of legitimate cultural authority. To trace some of the narcissistic retreats and intensities of literature may at least help us to think of art, and teach us to want an art, unavailable for any such legitimizing plots.

PART I

The Corrective Will

CHAPTER 1

Death and Literary Authority:
Marcel Proust and Melanie Klein

What is the redemptive power of art? More fundamentally, what are the assumptions that make it seem natural to think of art as having such a power? In attempting to answer these questions, I will first be turning to Proust, who embodies perhaps more clearly—in a sense, even more crudely—than any other major artist a tendency to think of cultural symbolizations as essentially reparative. This tendency, which had already been sanctified as a more or less explicit dogma of modern high culture by Proust's time, persists in our own time as the enabling morality of a humanistic criticism. I will argue that the notion of art as salvaging somehow damaged experience has, furthermore, been served by psychoanalysis—more specifically, by a certain view of sublimation first proposed rather disconnectedly by Freud and later developed more coherently and forcefully by Melanie Klein. The psychoanalytic theory I refer to makes normative—both for an individual and for a culture—the mortuary aesthetic of *A la Recherche du temps perdu*.

As everyone knows, involuntary memories play a crucial role in the Proustian narrator's discovery of his vocation as a writer. Let us begin with a somewhat untypical example of the genre, the passage in *Sodome et Gomorrhe* describing the "resurrection" of Marcel's grandmother on the first evening of his second visit to Balbec. This passage reformulates the importance of memory for art in terms of another relation about which the theoretical passages concluding *Le Temps retrouvé* will be at once prolific and evasive: the dependence of art on death.

This dependence is obliquely defined in two very different ways, and the difference is first pointed to by what the narrator describes as the painful contradiction inherent in his involuntary memory. On the one hand, the possession of others is possible only when they are dead; only then is nothing opposed to our image of them. Biological death accomplishes, or literalizes, the annihilation of others that Proust tirelessly proposes as the aim of our interest in others. "The living reality" of his grandmother at the moment of involuntary memory is exactly equivalent to her ideal penetrability. At such moments, the narrator writes, nothing remains of past joy and past suffering other than "the self that originally lived them."[1] The posthumous possession of others is always an unprecedented self-possession.

And yet there is of course a real loss. It is, however, by no means certain that it is the grandmother herself who has been lost, since her death is seen primarily as having deprived Marcel of himself. When the narrator speaks of "that contradiction of survival and annihilation so strangely intertwined within me *(cette contradiction si étrange de la survivance et du néant entre-croisés en moi),*" he means, first of all, that his grandmother has suddenly been resurrected in him and, second, that death has erased his image from her tenderness ("un néant qui avait effacé mon image de cette tendresse").[2] In a sense, then—and quite bizarrely—it is Marcel's grandmother who has survived her death and Marcel himself who has disappeared. Nothingness, as the narrator strikingly puts it, had made of his grandmother "at the moment when I had found her again as in a mirror, a mere stranger whom chance had allowed to spend a few years with me . . . but to whom, before and after those years, I was and would be nothing" (2:785–786; 2:758–759). In these boxes of survival and nothingness placed one within the other, the living grandson sees an image of his grandmother contained within his own image; but her image—although it can now be nowhere but in him—no longer contains him. Hidden within this strangely specular relation to his grandmother's renewed presence is Marcel's own absence. The unprecedented self-possession I referred to is identical to an irremediable loss of self.

Who, finally, is that "mere stranger" now seen for the first time? More significant, I think, than the posthumous porousness of the other is the fact that the grandmother is only now authentically *other*. It could perhaps be said that the only way we ever experience death (as distinct from dying) is in a change in the mode of a relation. Marcel's involuntary memory returns his grandmother to him as the *outside of thought*: that is, not as someone who can be desired or appropriated or dialectically related to, but simply as someone who existed beside him, a mere other presence in the world. A relation of desire has, it would seem, been replaced by a juxtaposition. This change is of course noted with despair, and yet it could also be said that Marcel now experiences his grandmother's death as a retroactive—and spectral—rediversification of the world. Desire in Proust works to reduce the world to a reflection of the desiring subject; death, however, would seem to be the condition for an escape from the self-repetitions initiated by desire and a restoring to the world of those differences that promoted anxious desire in the first place. From this perspective, death recreates (in, so to speak, reverse affectivity: pain is substituted for excitement) Marcel's exhilarated shock, frequently recorded in the early volumes, at discovering his own absence from the world.

Death experienced within an involuntary memory thus helps to define involuntary memory as a kind of death. For if such memories revive the past as nothing more than the self that lived it ("le moi qui le vécut"), they also effect, belatedly and retroactively, a radical separation of the self from the world. If, for example, the madeleine resurrects a wholly internalized Combray, it also projects or throws forth from within that internalization a Combray of pure appearance, a Combray that persists phenomenally, from which all Marcel's past interests—from which Marcel himself—have been evacuated and to which a new relation must be invented. I want to approach the consequences for art of this contradiction by way of a long detour. Perhaps the most curious aspect of the passage from *Sodome et Gomorrhe* I have been discussing is the narrator's undecidable relation to it. There are two temporal perspectives in the passage (the moment of the memory at Balbec and the moment of writing) and three central terms (the painful *impression* itself, the *truth* to be extracted from that impression, and the role of *intelligence* in the extracting process). At the end of an extremely dense analysis of "cette contradiction si étrange de la survivance et du néant entrecroisés en moi," the narrator writes:

> I did not know whether I should one day distil a grain of truth from this painful and for the moment incomprehensible impression, but I knew that if I ever did . . . it could only be from such an impression and from none other, an impression at once so particular and so spontaneous, which had neither been traced by my intelligence nor attenuated by my pusillanimity, but which death itself, the sudden revelation of death, striking like a thunderbolt, had carved within me, along a supernatural and inhuman graph, in a double and mysterious furrow. (2:786–787; 2:759)

What can this mean? We might reasonably think that the few pages we have just read *are* the expression of any "truth" which may have been contained within that past impression. The narrator has been moving easily—as he does throughout the novel—from certain interpretations of his experience (or, as he would say, certain truths) that appear to date from the time of the involuntary memory to reflections on the incident as he now writes about it. He had apparently already understood and suffered from the contradictory nature of his grandmother's "resurrection," while certain other thoughts presented as general laws are perhaps disengaged at the moment of writing. Thus the narrator's remark that "the living reality" of the past "does not exist for us until it has been recreated by our thought," and the sentences in which, again using the present, he traces the relation between the "perturbations of memory *(troubles de la mémoire)*" and "the heart's intermittences *(les intermittences du coeur)*" bring a kind of interpretative closure *now* to Marcel's memory at Balbec (2:783–784; 2:756). But the status of these confidently formulated laws—obviously made with the aid of intelligence—is suddenly thrown into doubt by the claim that if he were one day to disengage some truth from his involuntary memory, it could only be from the "particular" and "spontaneous" impression itself, which had not, he adds, been traced by his intelligence. Furthermore, since it was in the past that he realized these preconditions of truth, this insight into that peculiar intersection of survival and nothingness—an insight also belonging to the past—cannot really be part of the desirable truth apparently still to come.

Will it ever come? And what is the relation to that truth of the text we have been reading? It is as if the narrator were making explicit here the ambiguous status of the entire Proustian text. I speak of an ambiguity that has led some of Proust's readers to raise the extremely peculiar question of whether or not the text we have is the one the narrator tells us, at the end of *Le Temps retrouvé,* that he finally set out to write. It is the Proustian narrator himself who sows the seeds of that doubt by promoting, throughout the work, precisely the kind of undecidability we have located in the passage from *Sodome et Gomorrhe.* And his hesitation about whether the work he is writing is the work he has chosen to write can be traced to the effects, on the process of writing, of a conception of art as a kind of remedial completion of life.

If the narrator encourages the reader's doubt about whether this is the work he speaks of writing at the end of *Le Temps retrouvé,* he leaves us in even greater doubt about the relation of this work to his life. On the one hand, "the function and the task of a writer," as the narrator will conclude in *Le Temps retrouvé,* "are those of a translator" (3:926; 3:890). Art would be "our real life, reality as we have felt or experienced it (notre vraie vie, la réalité telle que nous l'avons sentie)" (3:915; 3:881). Moved by what would appear to be the extreme purity of this referential aesthetic, the narrator even distrusts the element of *work* in art. In *A l'Ombre des jeunes filles en fleur* he recalls wondering if "the differences between one man's books and another's were not the result of their respective labours"—and if art would not thereby be mere artifice, or even deception ("s'il n'y a pas dans tout cela un peu de feinte")—"rather than the expression of a radical and essential difference between diverse personalities" (1:591; 1:549). And during the period of his love for Albertine in Paris, Marcel is "troubled" by Wagner's "habileté vulcanienne": "if art is no more than that"—that is, superior craftsmanship, "the result of industrious toil"—then "it is no more real than life" and there is no reason to regret his lack of literary talent (3:159; 3:161–162). Art, then, is "real" to the degree that it discovers and expresses a preexistent truth; it is "factitious" (the "réel-factice" opposition is Proust's) to the extent that it produces a "truth" of its own, a truth derived from the conditions and constraints of literary performance.

But how are we to understand a translation more real than its original? Marcel's literary education culminates in the discovery that the only life worth living is life "realized within the confines of a book *(réalisée dans un livre)*" (3:1088; 3:1032). Outside a book, that same life is both worthless and a source of suffering: hence the narrator's astonishing and relentless condemnation of his nonetheless meticulously recorded experience. If Marcel continuously reproaches himself for having friendships, for going into society, even for falling in love, it is, he suggests, because he should have been at home trying to get to the bottom of his impressions of friendship, society, and love. In the work of art, a certain type of representation of experience will operate both as an escape from the objects of representation and as a justification (retroactive, even posthumous) for having had any experiences at all. In Proust, art simultaneously erases, repeats, and redeems life. Literary repetition is an annihilating salvation.

It would be a simplification of this project to say of it, as Sartre has said of Flaubert, that for Proust art is a strategy of derealization. In *La Recherche* the imaginary is considered as the mode in which life is most authentically realized: art is a kind of epistemological and moral surreality, the interpretation of sensations, as the narrator writes in *Le Temps retrouvé,* as signs of laws and ideas. If the Proustian novel's relation to the Proustian narrator's experience is, however, necessarily and irremediably ambiguous, this is because Proust is continuously having to decide how to place phenomena within an essentializing version of them. The subject of the Proustian novel is the relation between truth and existence, and the ontological undecidability of all the events recorded in the novel reflects the problematic nature of that relation. In what mode do phenomena persist in the record of their essence? In a sense, *La Recherche* moves toward a relatively simple answer to that question: in the later volumes, the phenomenal is more and more absorbed in the universally valid formula, the general law. The adequate formulation of a truth would make the representation of phenomena superfluous. But Proust is clearly reluctant to divorce truth entirely from the experience that it ultimately invalidates. His narrator therefore seeks to "repeat" his experience in a way that will deprive it of any existential authority. The transcendence of phenomena depends on a certain discrediting of phenomena at the very moment of their representation.

As the major step in this maneuver, experience is divorced from a securely locatable subject of experience. Whose life is the narrative recording? The autobiographical "I" of *La Recherche* is not named until we are more than two thousand pages into the novel. Even then, only a first name is given in a dizzyingly hypothetical manner. The narrator is speaking of Albertine waking up in the bedroom of his Paris apartment: "Then she would find her tongue and say: 'My' or 'My darling' followed by my Christian name, which, if we give the narrator the same name as the author of this book, would be *(eût fait)* 'My Marcel' or 'My darling Marcel' " (3:69; 3:75). This extraordinary violation of the convention according to which a fictional narrator cannot possibly "know" the author of the novel in which he himself figures is nonetheless consistent with the destabilization of self initiated by the act of writing. *A la Recherche du temps perdu* is a nonattributable autobiographical novel. The experience it records may, it is suggested, belong to Marcel Proust, or it may belong to a fictional character named Marcel, or it may belong to a fictional character not named Marcel. Or, finally, it may belong to no one at all. In *Le Temps retrouvé* the narrator praises the modest heroism of the rich Larivière couple during World War I who, after their nephew's death at the front, come out of retirement to work fifteen hours a day, without wages, in his young widow's Parisian café. Theirs, we are told, is the only real name and the only real story in the entire work; everything else is fictive, everything else has been invented "in accordance with the requirements of my theme *(selon les besoins de ma démonstration)*" (3:876; 3:846). If this is the case, and if we are to take the narrator's literary program seriously, we would have a book of nearly unimaginable originality: a wholly invented translation. The translation of particular experience into general laws is conceivable and is not, properly speaking, an invention; much more difficult to conceive is an entirely fictive life that would nonetheless be the "real life," life as he felt or experienced it, of—whom? Is the narrator himself to be included among the "invented" elements of his work? If the narrator is *not* to be thought of as his own invention, how do we locate, and what is the status of, a figure whose real life is "remembered" entirely in fictive terms? How can the reality of the subject be distinguished from the wholly invented experience by which, after all, we know that subject?

One could say that the narrator momentarily steps outside the fictive relations he has invented for himself in order to pay tribute to the Larivière couple. One is, of course, even more tempted to appeal to biography in order to say that the tribute represents an unassimilated intrusion into the narrative of Proust himself. The passage is, however, less interesting as a strictly local puzzle or anomaly than as a crystallization of a more pervasive doubt in the novel. In *La Recherche,* translation into art means departicularization, and this is the case even when particular people and events are being represented. It is as if the narrator—or

Proust—had first of all abstracted his experience into general laws and then deduced another version of the particular from those laws, a kind of second-degree particularity of experience disengaged from existence. The narrator suggests something very much like this when he writes in *A l'Ombre des jeunes filles en fleur:* "Thus it is useless to observe customs, since one can deduce them from psychological laws" (1:552; 1:513). In *La Recherche* the situation is somewhat more complicated, since it is the already fictive narrator—and not Proust the author—who speaks of having entirely invented a past for the purposes of his "démonstration." Thus a fictive narrator's invented past would ultimately derive from that narrator's "real" life—which of course means from an equally fictive life. The latter would, however, be a fiction that has not been invented; having been, as it were, bypassed in the move from the more or less verifiable real life of the author Marcel Proust to the narrator's invention of *his* life, it would have the remarkable referential status of a necessary origin that has never been realized, either biographically or novelistically.

Gilles Deleuze has compared Proustian essences to Leibnizian "monads," each of which expresses the world from a distinctive point of view. The world thus expressed, Deleuze writes, "does not exist outside the subject expressing it, but it is expressed as the essence not of the subject but of Being, or of the region of Being which is revealed to the subject."[3] Thus the "morceau idéal" of Bergotte is at once the most individual and the least particular aspect of Bergotte. It is an individuality somehow detached from the point of view of experience, a repetition or translation of Bergotte that is simultaneously wholly different from Bergotte. In art, the particular is resurrected as the individual; or, to put this another way, art in Proust is, at least ideally, *truth liberated from phenomena.*

What is, however, most striking about this program in *La Recherche* is that it is indissociable from the kinds of questions I have been raising—questions about the narrator's identity, about the invented or remembered nature of his recorded past, about whether this is the book the theory of which is given at the end of *Le Temps retrouvé,* and—to return to the question raised by the "intermittences du coeur" passage from *Sodome et Gomorrhe*—about the degree to which the work we are reading is actually expressing those truths or essences that literature presumably disengages from experience. That is, Proust problematizes the very signs by which we might recognize the success of his narrator's literary enterprise. And in each case the problematizing takes the form of an uncertainty, traced within the text itself, about whether experience has been sufficiently departicularized to qualify as truth. It is, moreover, as if this uncertainty were being expressed in relation to the particular itself—which would mean that the move into truth or essences would not be necessarily, or even primarily, a generalizing move, but would require a *displaced repetition* of the particular.

We are meant to see the narrator in two quite different relations to each of the people and events he records: first, as Marcel knowing these people and living these events (in *La Recherche,* this essentially means in relations of desire to them) and, second, as the narrator now writing about the first relation. The second relation is the only justification for the first one. Furthermore, it is a justification that, strictly speaking, requires no content: it is the narrator's present *position* that principally operates the reversal of value. And this position can be defined as the intrinsically superior one of death. "All those men and women who had revealed some truth to me and who were now no more, appeared again before me, and it seemed as though they had lived a life which had profited only myself, as though they had died for me." The narrator continues: "A book is a huge cemetery in which, on the majority of the tombs, the names are erased and can no longer be read" (3:939–940; 3:902). The perspective of death permits the resurrection of others as redemptive truths. But, unlike the involuntary memory that resurrects Marcel's grandmother as a wholly other presence in the world—a presence that no longer contains Marcel and that he can no longer appropriate—the death evoked as a condition of art in *Le Temps retrouvé* is the retrospective absorption of others into the narrator's "monadic" point of view. *A la Recherche du temps perdu* proposes death as a metaphor for the artist's relation to the world in two contrasting ways. On the one hand, the death of others definitively ejects or expels Marcel from their being and thereby recreates the world as difference. On the other, their death both ends all resistance to Marcel's voracious desire to appropriate them *and* allows him to reconstruct the objects of his desires as invulnerable truths. Experience destroys; art restores.

In what way is experience—or, more precisely, desire—destructive? Rather than attempt to answer my question directly, I will reformulate it in other contexts—thereby evoking the concentric circles of *La Recherche* itself, in which each section is a mistaken yet illuminating replication and *approfondissement* of the preceding section. Proust's novel offers us the model for a circular, or nonnarrative, criticism. Although *La Recherche* proceeds narratively toward a conclusive vindication of Marcel's vocation as an artist in *Le Temps retrouvé,* this classical movement toward a resolution and revelation is undermined as it takes place. Because the entire work is written after its own climax, the reader is implicitly invited to find the theoretical formulations of the final pages superfluous: we should, ideally, be able to infer them from the work they inform from beginning to end. Suspense is promoted as a primary value of reading at the same time that the reader is encouraged *to read without suspense*—or, in other terms, to invent a motive for reading unsustained by a promise of epistemological gain. Everything is present from the start, and this is rendered thematically visible by the schematic treatment of all the major topics of *La Recherche* (memory, nature, love, social life, art) in *Combray*. The subsequent sections of the novel, instead of adding anything radically new to what the early pages have already given us, provide a kind of mnemonic hermeneutics on the themes of the first volume. *La Recherche* continues to repeat its own beginning with an increasingly bloated intelligibility. The rather simple chronological linearity of the novel is thus complicated by a movement of circular repetition—or, more exactly, by the simultaneously amplifying and replicative movement of concentric circles.

We may see in the tension between these two movements a structural analogue of Proust's conflicting views of the relation between phenomena and truth, or between experience and art. Is life always prior to the essences that art alone disengages? Or is art a certain type of repetition of the phenomenal itself, a repetition that, far from substituting truth for appearances, continuously re-presents appearances in order to test modes of interpretation freed from the constraints of anxious desire? If I now turn away from Proust in order, as it were, to repeat him psychoanalytically, this move can be taken as the procedural expression of my own interest in the possibility of a circular hermeneutics—that is, in the possibility of repetition as the occasion for revising the terms of our interest in the objects of our interpretations.

*   *   *

What is the place of sexuality in culture? Or, to put this question in Freudian terms, how are cultural activities "invested" with sexual interests? In one of her first papers—the 1923 essay entitled "Early Analysis"—Melanie Klein proposes what her later work compels us to recognize as some very non-Kleinian answers to these questions. The essay I refer to—based on three unpublished papers—is difficult and diffuse. The first half is an extremely dense theoretical discussion; the second half is a considerably more relaxed, and intellectually less interesting, case history. Klein begins with a therapeutically oriented discussion of the role of anxiety in the "neurotic inhibitions of talent."[4] The basis of such inhibitions is, as we might expect, "a strong primary pleasure which had been repressed on account of its sexual character" (EA, 77). The analyst reverses the inhibiting mechanism by helping the patient to release, recognize, and work through the anxiety that the mechanism has "bound" and thus to return to the original, anxiety-provoking pleasure. But now the pleasure can be enjoyed: "By successful removal of the inhibition, I do not simply mean that the inhibitions as such should be diminished or removed, but that the analysis should succeed in reinstating the primary pleasure of the activity" (EA, 78). This local conclusion on the paper's second page is extremely important, for it raises questions that will lead to the most original moments in the discussion. There is apparently a nonproblematic, nonneurotic, sexualizing of ego interests—of those "talents" referred to in the essay's first sentence. The patient's analysis ends not with a separation of libidinal tendencies from ego activities, but rather with a recognition of their compatibility. In other words, the nonsexual can be sexualized in an analytically irreducible way: therapy ends here, and there is nothing more to be interpreted.

How has this happened? After a couple of pages of following Freud on the question of the repression of affects and their transformation into anxiety, Klein comes back to the mechanism of inhibition as a potentially healthy mode of binding and discharging anxiety. Such apparently nonneurotic inhibitions imply, Klein writes, "that a certain quantity of anxiety had been taken up by an ego-tendency which already had a previous libidinal cathexis" (EA, 81). Thus the argument returns—in different terms—to the "primary" investment of ego activities with sexual pleasure. The so-called nonneurotic inhibition leans on an already established sexualizing of ego interests. Klein asserts that priority when, several pages later, she writes: "We may suppose that for a sublimation to be inhibited it must have actually come into existence as a sublimation" (EA, 90). The crucial notion of sublimation had entered the argument almost immediately after the sentence about anxiety's having been taken up by ego tendencies with "previous libidinal cathexis," and in this first appearance of the concept Klein equates "the capacity to sublimate" with "the capacity to employ superfluous libido [*before,* it is implied, either fixation or repression] in a cathexis of ego-tendencies" (EA, 81).[5]

A few pages later, in a paragraph of great originality that somewhat perversely manages to present itself as a summary of the theories of four other analysts (Hans Sperber, Sandor Ferenczi, Ernest Jones, and Freud), Klein discusses the origin of those libidinally invested ego tendencies that, by "taking up" the anxiety connected to sexual pleasures, help to produce inhibitions of "normal" rather than "neurotic" intensity. What she describes is a movement from identification to symbolism, and the description is particularly interesting in view of the very different ways in which identification is defined in her later work. Here identification would appear to be the exact opposite of object relationships; it is the activity of what might be called an appetitive narcissism. The first identifications in this process take place on the child's own body; referring to speculations made by Freud and Ferenczi, Klein speaks of equivalences that the child sees "in the upper part of its body for each affectively important detail of the lower part" (EA, 85). Identification thus works here as an extension of regions of pleasure: both the child's own body and the world of objects are tested for their capacity to repeat certain sensations, to generalize originally local sensations. Furthermore, in both identification and the displacement of libido to new objects and ego activities (a displacement that constitutes symbol formation), it is, for Klein, the identification itself that produces pleasure and not, as Jones argues, a prior "similitude of pleasurable tone or interest" that would be the precondition for comparisons and identifications (EA, 85). "Objects and activities," she writes, "not in themselves sources of pleasure, become so through this identification, a sexual pleasure being displaced onto them" (EA, 85).

Now when Klein gives examples of symbol formation, she actually seems to be describing symbolic *symptom* formation: that is, the choice of certain objects and ego activities because of their resemblance to the repressed memories and fantasies. In this view, the symbolizing process would be nothing more than a compulsive substitute for the frightening or forbidden original pleasures. It is here that the originality of Klein's argument risks being dissipated as sublimation once again begins to look like a specialized branch of symptomatology. This blurring of definitions has of course occurred frequently in the history of psychoanalytic theory. Freud himself left us no sustained analysis of sublimation, and his own discussions of literature and the visual arts tend to stress either the compensatory or the symptomatic nature of art. Not only do the mechanisms of sublimation often seem indistinguishable from those of repression and symptom formation in much psychoanalytic writing; the work of art is often "treated"—interpreted and, one might almost say, cured—as if it were little more than a socialized symptom. It is therefore all the more interesting to see Klein's attempt in "Early Analysis" to locate the specificity of a sublimating mechanism. Perhaps the most crucial factor in this effort is her assumption of a certain quantity of "superfluous" or "suspended" libido. She speaks, for example, of "the ability to hold libido in a state of suspension" as a "contributing factor" to the capacity to sublimate (EA, 87). It is as if the history of an individual's sexuality included a moment of significant uncertainty about the fate of sexual energy. Or, in other terms, it is as if sexual excitement exceeded the representations attached to it and therefore became greedily, even promiscuously, available to *other* scenes and *other* activities. And the displacement of libido onto other object and ego activities can be called symbol formation only if we specify that these objects and activities *act symbolically without symbolizing anything external to them.*

Only if we see her argument moving in this direction can we understand Klein's surprising remark that when "pleasurable situations, actually experienced or phantasied" are "given play in an ego-tendency . . .

the fixations are divested of their sexual character" (EA, 87–88). What can this mean except that the ego tendencies in question can no longer be considered "symbolic" in the sense in which Klein—like most analysts—usually understands that word? We would have a nonallusive or nonreferential symbol. In sublimation, ego activities become "symbols" in the sense that the most diverse cultural activities "symbolize" the libidinal energy with which they are invested. We would not have a symbol that merely participates in the nature of an extrinsic symbolized object or activity (as, to use one of Klein's own examples, "athletic movements of all kinds stand for penetrating into the mother" [EA, 86]). Rather, forms of culture would symbolize nothing more than that which is already contained within them: the sexual energy that thereby "acts as the stimulus and driving force of talent" (EA, 88). Thus the most varied ego interests would represent symbolically not specific sexual fantasies but the very process by which human interests and behavior are *sexually moved.* From this perspective, sublimation can no longer be described (as it usually has been) in terms of a drive whose aim has been changed or displaced, for the drive in question would be, precisely, an aimless one, a kind of floating signifier of sexual energy. Sublimation would describe the fate of sexual energies detached from sexual desires.

*   *   *

But the view of sublimation as coextensive with sexuality occupies only a marginal place in the development of Kleinian theory. "From the beginning of my psycho-analytic work," Klein wrote in 1948, "my interest was focused on anxiety and its causation, and this brought me nearer to the understanding of the relation between aggression and anxiety."[6] In effect, during more than forty years of analytic practice and speculation, Klein elaborated the most radical—at once the most compelling and the most implausible—theory regarding infantile anxiety and aggression in the history of psychoanalysis. I will assume a certain familiarity with the broad outlines of this theory. Klein divides the first year of human life into two periods, or "positions," the first dominated by anxiety over external and internal threats to the preservation of the ego (the "paranoid-schizoid position") and the second characterized principally by anxiety about dangers felt to threaten the loved parent as a result of the infant's fantasized aggressions (the "depressive position"). Also crucial are the notion of a defensive mechanism preceding repression, a mechanism that would involve the splitting of the introjected object into a good one and a bad one; the contention that Oedipal conflicts and the development of a superego take place much earlier than Freud thought; finally, the fundamental argument—on which everything else depends—about the importance of fantasy from almost the very beginning of life. If we accept the argument about fantasy, then we should also recognize that Klein's scenarios of infantile violence, for all their apparent extravagance, rigorously and brilliantly spell out the consequences for our object relations of those destructive desires that Freud had already associated with infantile sexuality. Klein traces the history of the infant's attempts to deal with the anxieties engendered by a sexuality that is *born as aggression*. This history begins at birth. A complex nonverbal syntax of fantasmatic introjections and projections constitutes the infantile ego's defenses against internal and external bad objects, against, perhaps most profoundly, its own impulses to destroy both itself and the objects it loves.

Sublimation becomes, in this view, the infant's most sophisticated defense against its own aggressions. The awesome nature of this defensive enterprise can be understood from the following description in the essay "The Early Development of Conscience in the Child":

> In attacking its mother's inside . . . the child is attacking a great number of objects, and is embarking on a course which is fraught with consequences. The womb first stands for the world; and the child originally approaches this world with desires to attack and destroy it, and is therefore prepared from the outset to view the real, external world as more or less hostile to itself, and peopled with objects ready to make attacks upon it. Its belief that in thus attacking its mother's body it has also attacked its father and its brothers and sisters, and, in a wider sense the whole world, is, in my experience, one of the underlying causes of its sense of guilt, and of the development of its social and moral feelings in general. For when the excessive severity of the super-ego has become somewhat lessened, its visitations upon the ego on account of those imaginary attacks induce feelings of guilt which arouse strong tendencies in the child to make good the imaginary damage it has done to its objects. And now the individual content and details of its destructive phantasies help to determine the development of its sublimations, which indirectly subserve its restitutive tendencies, or to produce even more direct desires to help other people.[7]

Sublimations have now become symbolic reparations, and in the light of the new concept Klein has begun to modify the entire process outlined in "Early Analysis." In a 1930 reference to that essay Klein, speaking once again of Ferenczi's and Jones's notions of identification and symbol formation, writes: "I can now add to what I said then . . . and state that, side by side with the libidinal interest, it is the anxiety arising in the phase that I have described [of "excessive sadism" toward the mother] which sets going the mechanism of identification." From this point on, the emphasis is on identification not as an attempted repetition of pleasure but as an attempted flight from anxiety. The child conceives a dread of the organs it wishes to destroy (Klein mentions "penis, vagina, breasts"), and "this anxiety contributes to make him equate the organs in question with other things; owing to this equation these in their turn become objects of anxiety, and so he is impelled constantly to make other and new equations, which form the basis of his interest in the new objects and of symbolism." In this way, Klein concludes, "not only does symbolism come to be the foundation of all phantasy and sublimation, but, more than that, it is the basis of the subject's relation to the outside world and to reality in general." Generalized anxiety has more or less replaced generalized libidinal interest. More precisely, symbolism deflects anxiety by bringing "into phantasy the sadistic relation to the mother's body."[8] This process will be described in somewhat more positive terms in subsequent formulations (Klein will assert that love for the first objects must be maintained in successful sublimations), but even then symbols remain "substitute objects." That is, whatever the distribution of anxiety and love may be in the move from the mother's body and the child's fantasized contacts with her body, to other objects and other activities, the latter have now become, in Kleinian theory, *restored versions* of the former.

In what sense can these new relations properly be called object relations? In the sublimating process outlined in "Early Analysis," libidinalized ego interests are not substitutes for some original (but now repressed) pleasure. In that version of sublimation, sexuality provides the energy of sublimating interests without defining their terms. We would have, as I have suggested, a nonallusive or nonreferential version of sexualized mental activities; as a result, the sexualization of those activities could be thought of as a heightening rather than as a blurring of their specificity. But from the perspective of Klein's later theory of sublimation, the ego's "new" object relations are, by definition, new relations to old fantasy objects. Originally the ego is involved in a relation to a real other body (the mother's) but, curiously enough, as the ego develops, its relations become more spectral or fantasmatic. The objects and interests that symbolically represent the subject's early relation to the world of objects are restitutive repetitions of those early relations, which means that they fantasmatically recreate what was already a fantasmatic remodeling of the world. These new sublimations are, as it were, at two removes from any real objects; they are fantasy reparations of fantasy destructions.

We can see the basis for a return to Proust in this psychoanalytic echo of the Proustian notion of art as a redemptive replication of damaged or worthless experience: in both cases, sublimations integrate, unify, and restore. But this restorative activity would make no sense if it were not being performed on earlier or original experience. The very function of art in Proust would be threatened if it introduced us to a world of authentic difference: in an aesthetic of reparation, the artist's life—a life at once "translated" and made "more real"—is the only legitimate subject of art. Klein herself points to the solipsistic nature of this operation when, in "A Contribution to the Psycho-Genesis of Manic-Depressive States," she traces "the desire for perfection" to "the depressive anxiety of disintegration, which is thus of great importance in all sublimations." She speaks of patients who have "a beautiful picture of the mother, but one which was felt to be a *picture* of her only, not her real self. The real object was felt to be unattractive—really an injured, incurable and therefore dreaded person."[9] What is restored therefore never existed; the "perfect" object is nothing more than a function of the attacked object. And this is by no means true only of disturbed or neurotic patients. Insofar as the process of idealization "is derived from the need to be protected from persecuting objects, it is a method of defense against anxiety."[10] Excessive idealization denotes that persecution is the main driving force,"[11] but the logic of Kleinian theory would, I think, allow us to rephrase this as: "Some degree of persecution is always the motivating force of any degree of idealization." If the sublimated object is by definition an idealized object—both a mental construct and a "better" (repaired and made whole) version of an originally dangerous, injured, and fragmented object—we can also say that sublimation is disguised as transcendence.[12] Intellectually valuable pursuits and aesthetically pleasing objects are, in this view, disguised repetitions of an infantile defense against infantile aggressions.

My aim is neither to deny nor to defend the validity of this theory of sublimation. It may in fact be the case, as Jean Laplanche has suggested, that sublimation has two quite different modes of operation: one corresponding to what Klein described in "Early Analysis" as the investment of ego interests with a kind of floating or suspended sexual energy, and the other corresponding to the appropriation of the entire cultural field either as "substitute objects" for the desired and feared objects or as a repository of more or less socially useful activities in which the aims of sexuality can be symbolically deflected.[13] Significantly, a theoretical shift or hesitation analogous to Klein's can also be located in Freud. It could be shown, for example, that while proposing in the first chapter of his essay on Leonardo da Vinci a view of sublimation very much like the one outlined in "Early Analysis," Freud nonetheless goes on to treat Leonardo's work as psychologically compensatory and symptomatic. Indeed, far from pursuing a concept of sublimation as an appropriation and elaboration of sexual impulses, Freud will come to consider sublimation as one of the desexualizing activities of the ego—an activity that, furthermore, makes the ego particularly vulnerable to the death instinct. This shift, I think, must be understood in connection with the development of a theory of the ego as itself constituted by a partially desexualizing process of identification with lost or abandoned love objects. From the point of view of the tripartite systemic view of the mind elaborated in *The Ego and the Id* (1923), sublimation would be a relation to objects that is structurally determined by the already established relations among those internalized and lost objects which make up an ego and a superego.[14]

In Freud, and particularly in Klein, the kinds of spectral repetitions on which art in Proust seems to depend are presented as a goal of normative development. What I have wished to suggest is that such theories of the restitutive or redemptive power of cultural forms and activities are themselves symptomatic versions of the very process they purport to explain. Both this process and its theoretical legitimations give us extraordinarily diminished views of both our sexuality and our cultural imagination. The forms of culture become transparent and—at least from an interpretive point of view—dismissible: they are, ultimately, regressive attempts to make up for failed experience. And the fragmenting and destructive aspects of sexuality gain the ambiguous dignity of haunting the invisible depths of all human activity. Sexuality is consecrated as violence by virtue of the very definition of culture as an unceasing effort to make life whole, to repair a world attacked by desire. A fundamentally meaningless culture thus ennobles gravely damaged experience. Or, to put this in other terms, art redeems the catastrophe of history.[15] To play this role, art must preserve what might be called a moral monumentality—a requirement that explains, I believe, much of the mistrust in the modern period of precisely those modern works that have more or less violently rejected any such edifying and petrifying functions. Claims for the high morality of art may conceal a deep horror of life. And yet nothing perhaps is more frivolous than that horror, since it carries within it the conviction that, because of the achievements of culture, the disasters of history somehow do not matter. Everything can be made up, can be made over again, and the absolute singularity of human experience—the source of both its tragedy and its beauty—is thus dissipated in the trivializing nobility of a redemption through art.

*   *   *

What *are*—to draw a final interpretive circle—the dangers of desire in Proust? Let us first of all acknowledge the outlines of a novel of *happy* desire in *La Recherche,* of a desire that exuberantly dismembers its objects. There is a Baudelairean mobility of desire in Proust, an extravagant excess of desirous fantasy over a presumed original object of desire. Like Baudelaire, the Proustian narrator shows desire cutting persons into bits and pieces, happily transforming them into partial objects. Perhaps no volume is more abundant than *A l'Ombres des jeunes filles en fleur* in what might be called the appetitive metonymies of desire, the simultaneous reduction and enrichment of Albertine and her friends through those extrahuman associations by which, for example, they are metamorphosed into stems of roses profiled against the sea. If Marcel's desires here are, as he claims, never for persons ("The most exclusive love for a person is always a love for something else" [1:891; 1:833]), it is because those desires are too impatient for any such psychologically constitutive and reflective activity. Indeed, the constitution of persons is linked to the emergence of a novel of *un*happy desire, a novel that depends, we might say, on Marcel's misreading of the otherness inherent in desire. Desire becomes identical to anxiety as soon as Marcel begins to understand the disappearance of the object not as a function of the energy of his desire but rather as the consequence of an evil intention on the part of the other. Thus desire's mobility is interpreted paranoiacally: the other has a secret, and that secret is itself a desire excluding Marcel. Significantly, it is now that the other is reconstituted as a personality—as a psychological individual who can make Marcel suffer. Thus what would appear to be a humanizing of the other—the transformation of Albertine from a "moment" or unit in the metonymic chain of desires into a young girl with a particular history and particular desires—is actually a tactic of intended mastery over the other. Only as a person can Albertine perhaps be penetrated and made to suffer; the desexualization of desire and the invention of character are, in Proust, the preconditions for a ruthless if futile effort to absorb the other.

The most radical manifestation of this effort is of course Marcel's imprisonment of Albertine in his Paris apartment. The motive for the imprisonment, recorded in the remarkable final pages of *Sodome et Gomorrhe*, is the discovery that Albertine is a friend of Mlle. Vinteuil and of her female lover. We return once again to an involuntary memory, this time to the most painful one of all: Albertine's revelation catapults Marcel back to the lesbian scene between those two young women he had witnessed years before through the window of Vinteuil's home at Montjouvain. Once he feels convinced of Albertine's lesbianism, the only truthful way to portray her relation to him would be "to place Albertine, not at a certain distance from me, but inside me" (2:1154; 2:1116). What is this internalized yet impenetrable otherness?

To repeat the psychological law I just quoted: "The most exclusive love for a person is always the love of something else." If the narrator occasionally encourages us to understand this as a formulation of desire's mobility (to desire Albertine is to desire a certain type of seascape), it can also be taken to summarize the novel's more frequent demonstrations of desire's fixity. A certain resemblance among the women we love, the narrator writes, can be traced to "the fixity of our own temperament"; the different loved ones are nothing more than a product of that temperament, "an image, an inverted projection, a negative of our sensibility" (1:955; 1:894). Is it possible, then, to see one's own temperament or sensibility apart from these alien images of desire? The narrator's discovery of repetition in desire (of similarities among the women he pursues) leads him to a question about himself analogous to the one we have seen him ask about others. Jealousy of the other is the paranoid interpretation of desire's mobility. But, toward the end of *La Prisonnière,* the narrator writes: "As there is no knowledge, one might almost say that there is no jealousy, save of oneself" (3:392–393; 3:386), which suggests that the withheld secret Marcel anxiously pursues in others may be the projected secret, the fantasy formula, of his own desires.

The most accurate sexual metaphor for a hopeless pursuit of one's own desire is undoubtedly the heterosexual's jealousy of homosexuality *in the other sex.* I spoke of Albertine's sudden displacement from outside Marcel to inside Marcel as the internalization of an impenetrable otherness. I should now refine this formula: first of all, it is her inwardness that Marcel has internalized. The Albertine now making him suffer within himself is not the body that made an excited Marcel move from her to the sea but, instead, the desiring Albertine, the girl who could give Marcel the key to her desires by letting him hear "the strange sound of her pleasure *(le son inconnu de sa jouissance)*" (2:1154; 2:1117). This internalized interiority of otherness is, for Marcel, the experienced otherness of his own interiority. Albertine's lesbianism represents a nearly inconceivable yet inescapable identity of sameness and otherness in Marcel's desires; lesbianism is a relation of sameness that Marcel is condemned to see as an irreducibly unknowable otherness. He shares Albertine's love for women, but not her point of view: from what perspective of anticipated pleasures does she seek out bodies in which she will find reminders of her own? Thus in the final pages of *Sodome et Gomorrhe* the banal thematization of homosexuality in the essay that opens the volume—a thematization at once sentimental and reductive—is brushed aside (as is the secondary and, in a sense, merely anecdotal question of "sexual preference") by an extraordinary reflection on what might be called the necessity of homosexuality in a universal heterosexual relation of all human subjects to their own desires.

The last pages of *Sodome et Gomorrhe* depict several agitated displacements. Marcel is thrown back to the scene at Montjouvain and to the anguish of the *drame du coucher* at Combray; Albertine moves from somewhere outside Marcel to somewhere within him; and, in an echo of the passage we began by considering, Marcel's mother, as she enters his hotel room at dawn, resembles *her* mother so strongly that Marcel momentarily wonders if his grandmother has been "resurrected." These displacements and metamorphoses bring us back to what has always been a central question in *La Recherche:* how does one thing evoke another? Or, more fundamentally, what are the modes of mobility in consciousness? The Proustian protagonist is always asking questions about what lies behind phenomena. There is a more or less happy version of this movement at Combray, in Marcel's anticipation that the spectacles of nature will "open up" and reveal "the secret of truth and of beauty" behind them. But the final pages of *Sodome et Gomorrhe* introduce us to the anguish of transcendence: "Behind Albertine," the narrator writes, "I no longer saw the blue mountains of the sea, but the room at Montjouvain where she was falling into the arms of Mlle Vinteuil with that laugh in which she gave utterance, as it were, to the strange sound of her pleasure" (2:1154; 2:1117).

The narrator conceives of both the happy and the unhappy examples of this movement as leading to a kind of truth: to the essences behind natural phenomena, to the presumed reality of Albertine's desires. But *Sodome et Gomorrhe* suggests that the truth behind appearances may be nothing more than a degraded version of appearances, a kind of shadowy simulacrum. The spectralizing effect on reality of this movement into truth—of this essentializing or antiphenomenal movement—is obliquely indicated by the narrator's description, on the last page of *Sodome et Gomorrhe,* of the dawn as a kind of abstract or unreal sunset. Looking out of his window at the end of the sleepless night following Albertine's revelation, Marcel finds, in the new day, reminders of evening: both in the sight of the woods that he and Albertine, after a late afternoon nap, would often leave at sunset, and in the spectacle of boats that Marcel had frequently seen bathed in the oblique light of sunset as they returned to harbor in the evening and that are now illuminated by the slanting rays of the rising sun. Thus dawn evokes dusk, but dusk perceived as "an imaginary scene, chilling and deserted, a pure evocation of a sunset which did not rest, as at evening, upon the sequence of the hours of the day which I was accustomed to see precede it, detached, interpolated, more insubstantial even than the horrible image of Montjouvain which it did not succeed in cancelling, covering, concealing—a poetical, vain image of memory and dreams" (2:1168; 2:1130). In the sickening inconsistency of this false sameness, we are far from the presumed Proustian ecstasy of metaphorical equivalents. Here that trembling of surfaces—often the sign of a revelatory intrusion of essences and of temporal depths into the world of perceived phenomena—is repeated as a kind of contamination of nature itself by Marcel's willful and anguished pursuit of the truth of desire, of desire reduced to its essential formula. The perception of a certain type of light common to dawn and dusk is experienced as the nausea of inhabiting the desert of metaphorical essences, and it provokes in Marcel a nostalgia for the "impurities" of temporal sequences and contexts.

I propose that we consider this scene as an unintended emblem of an aesthetic of art as truth divorced from phenomena, a truth seen here as merely an evocative sameness, an exact yet alien repetition of phenomena. In the myth of art as both a translation of life and as more real or more essential than life, the imaginary adheres to the real not in order to impart an existential authority or legitimacy to art, but instead to reproduce the real without any such authority, to demonstrate the superiority of the image to the model. And yet, precisely because of this adherence, the "substitute objects" of art continuously remind us of the objects they are meant to annihilate or transcend; what purports to be an essentializing repetition turns out to be the symbolic reminder, the symbolic symptom, of phenomena at once erased and indelible.

And yet, as in Klein, we have seen hints in Proust of a quite different view of the sublimating activity of art. I have spoken of the involuntary memory that resurrects Marcel's grandmother as possibly, and paradoxically, inaugurating a presence at last freed from Marcel's appropriation of that presence, and I have referred to the appetitive metonymies of desire in *A l'Ombre des jeunes filles en fleur*. If consciousness in Proust seeks most frequently to go *behind* objects, there is also a move—wholly different in its consequences—*to the side of* objects. In the passage we have been considering from *Sodome et Gomorrhe,* the encouragement to make the latter move comes from an unexpected source. In order to distract Marcel from his suffering, and to keep him from losing "the benefit of a spectacle which [his] grandmother used to regret that [he] never watched," his mother points to the window (2:1167; 2:1129). But while she thus encourages a lateral mobility away from her and from the hotel room and toward the sea, the beach, the sunrise, Marcel sees *behind* the sea, the beach, and the sunrise the spectacle of Albertine at Montjouvain with Mlle. Vinteuil. However little Marcel appears to attend to it, we may nonetheless consider the mother's gesture as an instructive reminder of the power of appearances to defeat what may be imagined to lie "behind" them. Or, to put this in terms I have already used, we could say that Marcel's mother seeks to distract him from his hallucinated transcendence of phenomena and thereby to point, ultimately, to *the possibility of pursuing not an art of truth divorced from experience, but of phenomena liberated from the obsession with truth.*

Still the substance of the very passage in which this possibility is raised appears to preclude it. Not only does Marcel see Montjouvain behind the spectacle of sea and sun; more fundamentally, the rising sun becomes a lurid metaphor for Marcel's future inability *not* to see behind such spectacles, for the reduction of the world to a monotonous and ineluctable reflection of his suffering:

> And thinking of all the indifferent landscapes which were about to be lit up and which, only yesterday, would have filled me simply with the desire to visit them, I could not repress a sob when, with a gesture of oblation mechanically performed and symbolizing, in my eyes, the bloody sacrifice which I was about to have to make of all joy, every morning, until the end of my life, a solemn renewal, celebrated as each day dawned, of my daily grief and of the blood from my wound, the golden egg of the sun, as though propelled by the rupture of equilibrium brought about at the moment of coagulation by a change of density, barbed with tongues of flame as in a painting, burst through the curtain behind which one had sensed it quivering for a moment, ready to appear on the scene and to spring forward, and whose mysterious frozen purple it annihilated in a flood of light *(creva d'un bond le rideau derrière lequel on le sentait depuis un moment frémissant et prêt à entrer en scène et à s'élancer, et dont il effaça sous des flots de lumière la pourpre mystérieuse et figée).* (2:1166; 2:1128)

"The bloody sacrifice of all joy" that Marcel sees symbolized in the spectacle of the sunlight bursting into his room is the sacrifice of the spectacle itself. It is the sacrifice of the pleasure he had earlier known of anticipating scenes from which he is absent, landscapes beneficently resistant to his need to find himself in them. These waves of light symbolize their own pathetic availability to the symbolic imagination.

But the narrator's account of that past moment partially defeats its symbolic content: its literary reformulation helps to *desymbolize* it. The sentence I have quoted reinstates lost appearances. Far from being erased in the burst of sunlight, "la pourpre mystérieuse et figée" of the curtain is—verbally—highlighted. Placed at the end of this long sentence in which the skeletal structure has itself been nearly buried by all the modifying phrases and clauses, the curtain negates its own disappearance and *appears*—climactically and triumphantly (if also mistakenly)—as the strongest presence of the remembered scene. Syntactic resources operating independently of the impulse to symbolize "save" the purple curtain both from being erased by the sun's golden light *and* from having that luminous erasure interpreted as a mere symbol of Marcel's pain. Like the resurrections of involuntary memory, the return to the past in literature means a certain loss of Marcel as an actor in that past and results in an unprecedented visibility of past appearances. The death of the past is also a liberation from the constraints of anxious desire, constraints that threatened to erase the phenomenal diversity of the world from the field of Marcel's troubled vision.

Thus the move to art in *La Recherche* is not only an annihilating and redemptive replication of experience; it also makes possible a kind of posthumous responsiveness to surfaces, a redefining enactment of Marcel's interest in the world. From this perspective, art would be our "real life" not in the sense of an essentializing version of experience, but rather as a first or original (but originally missed) contact with phenomena. *The reappearance of the world* in Marcel's book is perhaps anticipated by his mother's pointing to a spectacle that her son will take in only when he gives it back to the world, this time as literature. In a final, Kleinian version of that maternal lesson—a version faithful to Proust's unsophisticated and salutary insistence (already formulated by the grandmother in *Combray*) that consciousness *profit* from art (that the only just criticism is a moral criticism)—let us say that the occasions of our interest in reality far exceed the range of our symbolic use of the real to rewrite a history of anxious desire. Furthermore, for Marcel—but perhaps not only for Marcel—to desymbolize reality may be the precondition for reeroticizing reality. On the basis of this rapid reading of Proust and the Klein of "Early Analysis," I will—especially in the sections on Baudelaire and Bataille—be seeking to define the terms of an erotic art independent of the anxieties inherent in desire. No longer a corrective replay of anxious fantasy, such an art may even reinstate a curiously disinterested mode of desire for objects, a mode of excitement that, far from investing objects with symbolic significance, would enhance their specificity and thereby fortify their resistance to the violence of symbolic intent.

CHAPTER 2

Erotic Assumptions:
Narcissism and Sublimation in Freud

Homosexuals do not have anal characters. This is the rigorously logical conclusion of the genealogy of character that Freud proposes in his 1908 essay "Character and Anal Eroticism." Freud himself, it is true, presents the conclusion somewhat more tentatively: if, he writes, there is "any basis in fact" for the relation he has just sketched between certain character traits and anal eroticism, then "one may expect to find no very marked degree of 'anal character' in people who have retained the anal zone's erotogenic character in adult life, as happens, for instance, with certain homosexuals. Unless I am much mistaken, the evidence of experience tallies quite well on the whole with this inference."[1] The strength of anal character traits is directly proportionate to the weakness or even the absence of anal pleasures in an individual's sexual life. Children whose rebellious or idiosyncratic reactions to toilet training point to an exceptionally strong "erotogenicity of the anal zone"—an erotogenicity, Freud suggests, perhaps genetically determined—lose that zone as a privileged area of pleasure as they grow up. But they develop "character traits of orderliness, parsimony and obstinacy," which "are to be regarded as the first and most constant results of the sublimation of anal erotism" (170–71).

"Character and Anal Erotism" was one of Freud's most scandalous performances. Today we are more likely to think of its thesis as a prime example of Freudian reductionism than as a shocking and epoch-making discovery in the history of psychoanalysis. And yet the somewhat coarse intellectual argument of the essay reformulates one of psychoanalysis' most original and disturbing questions: does the nonsexual exist? And if it does (as Freud consistently maintained), where exactly does it begin? Recognizably sexual pleasure is, after all, only the tip of the sexual iceberg: psychoanalysis has taught us to read dreams, jokes, the accidents of ordinary language, character traits, games, and works of art as disguised expressions of a variety of sexual excitements. The anal sensitivity of Freud's homosexual obviates the need for an anal character; the latter (the triad of orderliness, parsimony, and obstinacy) is at once a deflection of certain bodily pleasures away from the body and the legitimizing guarantee of their permanence. Like all sexual pleasures, anality is not circumscribed by the zone that gives it its name; for psychoanalysis, sexuality is a specific type of psychic infection.

Freudianism is perhaps the most radical of modern efforts to break (and to account for) our civilization's fascination with the mind-body dualism and to map what might be called the characterological and cultural migrations of bodily intensities. How does sexuality repeat itself? The mapping of this spread of the sexual is unproblematic so long as sexuality reproduces itself symptomatically. The Freudian cartographer needs certain specialized talents—those of an expert in symptomatological hermeneutics—but once he has acquired those talents, he can easily enough read back from the nonsexual to the sexual. This is exactly what Freud does in "Character and Anal Eroticism," where orderliness, parsimony, and obstinacy are traced back to such anal pleasures in childhood as fecal incontinence, bowel retention, and "doing all sorts of unseemly things with the feces that had been passed" (9:170). Anal character traits "give exactly the impression of a reaction-formation against an interest in what is unclean and disturbing and should not be part of the body" (9:172). A forbidden pleasure is now negatively represented—at once denied and partially satisfied—in a character trait: the interest in feces becomes an obsession with cleanliness. We would have what is essentially a neurotic structure: a repressed impulse and an element of conscious behavior that is both a defense against and an expression of this impulse. Anal character traits can thus be thought of as constituting a kind of character neurosis, as a massive structural reaction against the subject's being stuck or blocked at the anal stage of sexual development. The libidinal energy that invests orderliness, parsimony and obstinacy is anally fixated energy.

Fixated, and yet also free-floating. Because the explicit emphasis of "Character and Anal Eroticism" is centripetal (all the traits and activities described by Freud go back toward the anus), we may miss the essay's centrifugal pull. For Freud is at least implicitly arguing that even a sexual drive as fixated as anal eroticism is comparatively indifferent to the objects and activities by which it can be satisfied. More succinctly, the anus can become irrelevant to anal eroticism. It is as if—and we recognize an echo here of a central assumption in the *Three Essays on the Theory of Sexuality*—in sexuality almost anything will do the job. A sexual drive as specific as anal eroticism will make do with a compulsively renewed emptying of ashtrays or a bibliographical compilation. It will somehow coerce those activities into producing sensations not unlike those that

characterize the pleasures of fecal retention and expulsion—into producing what might be called abstract sensations, the pleasures of retention
and expulsion unattached to a retaining or expelling organ. The anal
character would, in short, express something like the essence—we might
even say the Platonic Idea—of anal eroticism.

It is perhaps only at this level of abstraction that the anal character
escapes being an oxymoron. In any case, the plasticity of the anal erotic
drive—its nearly promiscuous availability to a variety of character traits
and activities—suggests that the notion of fixated sexual energy is, at the
very least, highly problematic. The mobility of the anal drive puts into
question its identification *as* an anal drive. Or, to put this another way:
the sexualization of a character trait ruins definitional stability not only
with respect to the character trait (orderliness can no longer be defined
merely as the love of order), but also with respect to the drive presumed
to be its source. Freud is of course far from saying in "Character and
Anal Eroticism" that the sexualizing process is inherently a threat to
readability. Indeed the essay is famous—and was originally thought to
be infamous—for proposing just the opposite: we are told to read parsimony, for example, as a repetition of the pleasure of fecal retention. And
yet Freud also hesitates to equate character formation (even anal character
formation) with symptom formation, thereby suggesting that such traits
are less accountable to specific sexual drives than his own argument in
this essay appears to suggest.

Referring to his earlier discussion, in *Three Essays on the Theory of
Sexuality*, of the body's "erotogenic zones" ("the genitals, mouth, anus,
urethra"), Freud writes: "the amounts of excitation coming in from these
parts of the body do not all undergo the same vicissitudes, nor is the fate
of all of them the same at every period of life. Generally speaking, only
a part of them is made use of in sexual life; another part is deflected from
sexual aims and directed toward others—a process which deserves the
name of 'sublimation'" (9:171). Throughout his work Freud will frequently return to this definition of the sublimating process as a change in
instinctual aims. Character and culture, it would appear, are fueled by
"unserviceable" sexuality; they are constitutively a *pis aller*, outlets for
impulses that must be set aside but cannot be erased in normal sexual
development. Quantities of pregenital libido whose aims would threaten
the hegemony of the genital have to be exchanged for something else,
and, from the point of view of libidinal economy, it doesn't make much
difference if that something else is the character trait of parsimony or the
activity of reading books.

Thus it would seem that a culturally high aim consists in the representation of a sexually low aim. This view of sublimation as a miserly
hoarding and recycling of oral and anal energies may strike us as an un-

intended textbook example of anal theorizing. And yet, in an extremely interesting way, Freud suggests that what is hoarded is also lost or squandered. If the excitement derived from the erotogenic zones can invest character traits *without undergoing repression*, the anal character of formerly anal excitement may be dissipated or spent.[2] Freud writes that contributions are "made by numerous constituents and component instincts" to something like a pool of sexual drives, drives that change their original aims without being compelled to do so by the barriers of repression (9:170). While the impossibility of fulfilling a certain aim can of course lead to repression, before repression takes place there may be, as it were, an escape, a leakage of that blocked sexual energy into other, unrelated aims.

The question remains unanswered of how much these new or sublimating aims are "informed" by—or to what extent they can be interpreted in terms of—the sexual impulses whose aims have been inhibited. We are not after all dealing here with what Melanie Klein theorized in her early work as suspended or superfluous libido, that is, with sexual energy in excess of any particular sexual drive. But neither are we dealing with the fixated energy of repressed sexual drives, drives desperately seeking to disguise themselves in ego activities that will at least partially satisfy them. Like the early Klein, Freud seems interested in defining a sexualizing ego activity minimally determined—if at all—by sexual drives from the subject's past. To account for this activity, a concept different from that of symptom or reaction formation is clearly needed, and indeed the notion of sublimation *might* lend itself to the description of a nonspecific type of sexual activity—that is, sexual activity no longer attached to particular acts. Freud's parsimonious theory of character formation—a theory that can be interpretively reduced to the very complexes it offers as explanatory models—is undermined by its ambiguous inclusion of sublimation among the processes by which character is formed. That is, in the notion of repression-free sublimation, the theory is itself sublimated into a concept that both exemplifies and accounts for a differential (and nonsymptomatic) repetition of sexual or intellectual energies.

In sublimation, then, criteria of content could no longer be used to help us to recognize the sexualization of higher ego activities. I will return to this peculiar idea of a sexuality independent of sex; for the moment, I want to draw attention to Freud's hesitation, in "Character and Anal Eroticism," about whether sublimation should be distinguished from reaction formation. Immediately after the sentence in which he defines the deflection from sexual aims as a sublimating process, Freud describes reaction formations "such as shame, disgust and morality" that "rise like dams to oppose the later activity" of sexual drives; anal eroticism, having thus become "unserviceable for sexual aims," is sublimated into orderliness, parsimony and obstinacy (9:171). Here sublimation seems to be merely the final step in the process of reaction formation, although the disguised symptomatic expression of a dammed-up (should I also say "repressed"?) anal eroticism would appear to be quite different from a *nonsymbolic* repetition of excitement once connected with sexual drives. Indeed the last sentence of Freud's essay explicitly formalizes the difference between the two processes: "the permanent character-traits are *either* unchanged prolongations of the original instincts, *or* sublimations of those instincts, *or* reaction-formations against them" (9:175).

*   *   *

Should character traits be called neurotic symptoms, reaction formations, or sublimations? And to what extent are these processes independent of one another? Most important, what is at stake in Freud's shifting position on these questions? It is as if his hesitation on the question of how character traits are formed were expressing a more general uncertainty about the necessity of a concept of sublimation. Are the clinical concepts of psychoanalysis adequate to account for such extraclinical phenomena as human character and art? A well-known mystery in the history of psychoanalysis is whether Freud's unpublished papers on metapsychology included a discussion of sublimation. He wrote five metapsychological papers in the spring of 1915 (all are in volume 14 of the Standard Edition); seven more were apparently written during the summer of the same year, but since they were never published it seems likely that he destroyed them. The subjects of five of these lost papers are mentioned in Freud's letters of the period; it has been assumed, on the basis of references in other papers, that the subject of one of the other two papers was sublimation. Did Freud really destroy that paper? If so, why?

It is tempting to imagine the various forms of unacceptability that discussion may have taken. Let us assume, first of all, that from a metapsychological point of view, Freud showed in the paper that a wholly independent theory of sublimation was unnecessary. Works of art are produced by the same psychic mechanisms as neurotic symptoms and dreams. An essay on the sublimating process would therefore do for culture what *The Interpretation of Dreams* had done for dreams; Freud's *Kunstdeutung* might have been an exercise in psychoanalytic narratology. Or—to try a second rewriting of that possibly unwritten piece—Freud may have elaborated a process almost wholly distinct from repression with symptom or reaction formations. The ego's cultural interests would owe nothing to the child's sexual interests. This kind of essay on sublimation would necessarily define the limits of psychoanalytic competence, and this in one of two different ways. We would have either a description of those desexualizing mechanisms by which a new mind-body dualism would be reinstated at certain levels of cultural achievement, or we would have an account of certain modes of sexualized behavior that owe nothing to repressed sexual desires. The immense interest of the second of these accounts would be to destroy the myth of an essential discontinuity between culture and bodily intensities, at the same time that, having demonstrated what I have called the nonspecific eroticizing of cultural interests, Freud would also be drawing the interpretive line of all psychoanalytic demonstrations. He would have described the process by which psychoanalytically unanalyzable interests are produced.

Everything I have just said in my reconstruction of two different essays on sublimation is in fact said, or at least suggested, by Freud himself—but not in an essay on sublimation. We have already seen some of these arguments sketchily proposed in "Character and Anal Eroticism," and we will find a further elaboration of them—as well as reactions to them—in Freud's 1914 piece on narcissism. But the point is that no one work explicitly confronts the contradictions between these various positions. What are the strategic advantages of this failure to resolve the relation of the sexual to the presumably nonsexual? We can imagine a kind of superior prudence working to eliminate the first of our two essays from the Freudian corpus. Nothing has been worse for the public image of psychoanalysis than its reductionist stance with regard to the sacred cows of culture. Thus in a move that anticipates the pious denegations of generations of later psychoanalytic critics, Freud assures us that Leonardo was not neurotic while analyzing his work as a case of monumentally arrested development, a case requiring analytic interpretation. But such inconsistencies are better—for the "image" of psychoanalysis—than a theory that would erase them and declare that art obeys exactly the same mechanisms as the neurotic symptom. Indeed, almost all psychoanalytic criticism since Freud has been an effort to disguise an argument for the regressive nature of art.[3] Our second essay may, however, be even more unacceptable than the first. For now the danger is that psychoanalysis will conceptualize itself into a narrow area of specialization. By theorizing the cultural as either the nonsexual or as a psychoanalytically noninterpretable version of the sexual, Freud would have defined his new discipline as merely another branch of medical science. Psychoanalysis is reserved for the pathogenic in human behavior; the rest remains untouched. Thus Freud would have destroyed what was to become for him a more and more exciting and necessary prospect: the prospect of psychoanalysis as a cultural rather than a simply medical or therapeutic hermeneutics.

What interests me most, though, is a much stranger possibility. I want to argue for another kind of danger—another type of unacceptability—in our hypothetical second essay on sublimation. Consider the possibility that sublimated sexuality might put into question both the notion of neurotic sexuality and the definition of the sexual supporting that notion. The essay that would have argued for what I have too rapidly called a psychoanalytically noninterpretable version of the sexual, instead of limiting the interpretive scope of psychoanalysis, might have universalized its competence in an inadmissable way. What is most unacceptable in psychoanalysis is—as has always been popularly assumed—its definition of the sexual, but now we must think of that definition as unacceptable to Freud himself. The failure to publish (perhaps even to write) a paper on sublimation could then be thought of as the rejection of an unwanted extension of power. Sublimation is not a liminal or unnecessary psychoanalytic concept; rather it is the concept that, by legitimizing psychoanalysis' claim to being a philosophy of culture, can either reinforce or threaten its strained complicity in the culture of redemption—in a notion of art as making over or repairing failed experience. The theory of sublimation that defines art symptomatically must itself be seen as a symptom of psychoanalysis' uneasy relation to its own radical views on sexuality and culture—more specifically, to a view of art as nonreparatively or nonredemptively eroticized. I will therefore be doing a symptomatological analysis of Freud's moves away from a nonsymptomatological theory of sublimation. What, in short, had to be repressed in his views of culture as a type of sexualized production?

*   *   *

I will address this question by discussing an essay to which it may at first seem irrelevant. Freud's reluctance to pursue the idea of a nonspecific eroticizing of cultural activities should be understood in relation to an even more crucial repudiation of his early theory of sexual pleasure. And this repudiation takes place—obliquely yet irreversibly—by way of his speculations on narcissism and the constitution of the ego. Freud begins his 1914 essay "On Narcissism: An Introduction" by arguing for a type of narcissism that "would not be a perversion, but the libidinal complement to the egoism of the instinct of self-preservation, a measure of which may justifiably be attributed to every living creature." Thus there would be "an original libidinal cathexis of the ego," or "a primary and normal narcissism" (14:73–75). In one sense, this new concept—usually considered a landmark in the history of psychoanalysis—goes back to something quite old in Freud's thought. Sexuality, he had argued in the *Three Essays* of 1905, begins by being autoerotic. It may take place from the very beginning within an object relation (the infant's relation to the mother's breast), but Freud suggests that the specifically sexual nature of that relation implies an indifference to the object. In the origins of sexuality, the breast is irrelevant to the pleasure caused by the sensation of warm milk flowing through the lips and into the digestive tract. We must, as Freud admonishes us, learn to loosen the bond that exists in our thoughts between instinct and object (7:148).

Very early in his essay on narcissism, Freud himself asks the question to which these remarks point: "what is the relation of the narcissism of which we are now speaking to auto-eroticism, which we have described as an early state of the libido?" The answer has to do with the difference between a part and the whole: "we are bound to suppose that a unity comparable to the ego cannot exist in the individual from the start; the ego has to be developed. The auto-erotic instincts, however, are there from the very first; so there must be something added to auto-erotism—a new psychical action—in order to bring about narcissism" (14:76–77). This *seems* to suggest that the ego and the sexual instincts develop on separate tracks. We would first of all have autoeroticism without the psychic unity created by an ego; then some other operation would take place in the subject which would constitute an ego that can be loved. There is, however, a certain ambiguity in Freud's phrasing. Having asserted that "the ego has to be developed" (in order for narcissism to exist), he elaborates this idea by suggesting that "a psychical action" must be added to autoeroticism: This is by no means the same thing as saying that an ego (constituted by a developmental process not elaborated here) is the precondition for narcissism. The last sentence of this short passage raises the possibility that *the ego itself comes into being as the result of a certain development of autoeroticism.*[4]

We should return here momentarily to Freud's association of sexual pleasure in the *Three Essays* with a pleasurable-unpleasurable tension, a pleasure significantly different from that of tension release, which Freud of course associates with genital sexuality. The most anguishing problem for Freud in the *Three Essays*—a problem I speak of at some length in *The Freudian Body*—is to account for a type of desire that, unlike the desire principally identified with genitality, does not seek its own extinction in "satisfaction." Not only that; the pleasurable-unpleasurable tension of sexuality—the pain of a self-shattering excitement—aims at being maintained, replicated, and even increased. The human subject is originally *shattered into* sexuality; in the *Three Essays* Freud simultaneously moves toward and retreats from a definition of sexual excitement as a kind of masochistically enjoyed disturbance of psychic equilibrium. At least in the mode in which it is constituted, sexuality may be a tautology for masochism.

The concept of narcissism can be thought of as an extension of that definition. It is as if the inherently solipsistic nature of sexuality—and its correlative indifference to object and to organ specificity—allowed for a development of autoeroticism in which the source of pleasure and, consequently, the object of desire became the very experience of *ébranlement* or self-shattering. The need to repeat that experience can be thought of as an originary sublimation, as the first deflection of the sexual instinct from an object-fixated activity to another, "higher" aim. "Higher" here, however, would have no connotation whatsoever of reparation or restitution; instead it signifies a primitive but immensely significant move from fragmented objects to totalities, a move taking place at this stage as a form of self-reflexiveness. It is as if a certain split occurred in consciousness, a split that paradoxically is also the first experience of self-integration. In this self-reflexive move, a pleasurably shattered consciousness becomes aware of itself as the object of its desire. To repeat the activity of an eroticized consciousness becomes a new sexual aim, one that replaces the aim of repeating certain specific activities (such as sucking the mother's breast or holding back feces).

This originary sublimation can also be thought of as the initiating model of all sexual desire in that it aims—purely, even abstractly—to repeat the reverberating, pleasurably painful tensions themselves, apart from the acts that may at first have produced them. It is perhaps only by grounding a theory of sublimation in speculations such as these that we can guarantee the distinction between the sublimating process and the processes of symptom and reaction formation. For the energy of the originary sublimation would be, by definition, a nonfixated energy. The object of desire would be that which is objectless in the *jouissance* of any object relation. Subsequently, of course, sublimated energy will attach itself to specific ego interests and activities, but the paradigm of all such sublimations is the project of distilling sexual excitement from all its contingent occasions. A sublimation is only secondarily (and not even necessarily) an ennobling, or a making sublime; it is, most profoundly, a burning away of the occasion, or at least *the dream of purely burning*. Far from being a transcendence of the sexual, sublimations are thus grounded in unalloyed sexuality. The concept should therefore be used to describe not merely the fate of nonfixated sexual energy, but also those movements in certain cultural activities—in, perhaps above all, art—which partially dissolve the materiality of the activity, which blur its forms and its identity and allow us fleetingly to experience a pure excitement.

Sublimated energy is inherently nonreferential. It is nonreferential not merely because it has escaped repression and can therefore attach itself to new aims and new objects with a minimal compulsion to find substitutes for old aims and old objects, but also because it was originally motivated by a pleasure with no reference. The originating model of all sublimation is consciousness pursuing its own sexualizing potentialities. It does not have to free itself from specific aims and objects because it is as if[5] it had become fascinated with the prospect of initiating sexuality through self-reflection. It is, I would suggest, precisely that fascination which has been "added to auto-eroticism . . . in order to bring about narcissism." The "new psychical action" creating what Freud calls primary narcissism is the sublimation of auto-eroticism. And, as we should now be able to see, that first narcissistic love is inescapably masochistic. Wholly devoid, however, of such moral components as the guilt with which a later, secondary masochism will be burdened (and corrupted), the primary masochistic desire would seek merely to repeat the ecstatic suffering of a pure ébranlement. *The first psychic totality would thus be constituted by a desire to shatter totality.* The ego, at its origin, would be nothing more than a kind of passionate inference necessitated by the anticipated pleasure of its own dismantling. In psychoanalysis, the first ego is an erotic ego; it is constituted by an erotic assumption.[6]

*   *   *

What are the signs, in adult life, of this "original libidinal cathexis of the ego"? Since, Freud argues, "certain special difficulties seem . . . to lie in the way of a direct study of narcissism," the subject will have to be approached indirectly, with the help of pathological disturbances, organic disease, and "the erotic life of the sexes" (14:82). Freud's evidence for the existence and importance of primary narcissism becomes more and more general, and the central interest of the essay is the connection he will establish between narcissism and the creation of a normal self. In part 3 Freud turns to "the psychology of repression" in order to discover what happens to the ego-libido of normal adults. "We have learnt that libidinal instinctual impulses undergo the vicissitude of pathogenic repression if they come into conflict with the subject's cultural and ethical ideas . . . Repression, we have said, proceeds from the ego; we might say with greater precision that it proceeds from the self-respect of the ego" (14:93). Something quite new is beginning to emerge here: the idea of an attachment of the ego to its own moral worth. And it is as if Freud then interpreted that idea structurally. An attachment implies two terms, and by the end of the paragraph from which I have been quoting, the ego's self-respect and the subject's cultural and ethical ideas have become the actual ego's relation to an ideal against which it is measured and judged. The groundwork, as we can see, is being laid for *The Ego and the Id*.

How is such a relation narcissistic? In Freud's earlier discussions of repression, the emphasis was on the conflict between libidinal impulses and the cultural and ethical ideas opposing them. He now infers from that conflict *another* libidinal relation, this time between the ego and those very ideas, or ideals, opposing libidinal satisfaction:

> The ideal ego is now the target of the self-love which was enjoyed in child-hood by the actual ego. The subject's narcissism makes its appearance displaced on to this new ideal ego, which, like the infantile ego, finds itself possessed of every perfection that is of value. As always where the libido is concerned, man has here again shown himself incapable of giving up a satisfaction he had once enjoyed. He is not willing to forgo the narcissistic perfection of his childhood; and when, as he grows up, he is disturbed by the admonitions of others and by the awakening of his own critical judgment, so that he can no longer retain that perfection, he seeks to recover it in the new form of an ego ideal. What he projects before him as his ideal is the substitute for the lost narcissism of his childhood in which he was his own ideal. (14:94)

The recovery of narcissism described here is in fact a radical transformation of it. The primary narcissism Freud described earlier is retroactively moralized. Did the infantile ego really "find itself possessed of every perfection that is of value," or was that ego, as I have speculated, created by a kind of appetitive reflexiveness? The infant's narcissism is "the libidinal complement to the egoism of the instinct of self-preservation"; or, from another perspective, it is autoeroticism "promoted" to the status of a psychic unity, a process in which autoeroticism plays the role of a sexualizing principle of individuation. This is quite different from that ethical self-appreciation with which infantile narcissism is identified in part 3 of "On Narcissism," an identification that allows Freud to mask the incongruity of equating the ego's relation to an ideal version of itself with a revival of primary narcissism.

Furthermore, the "ideal ego" does not really even belong to the subject who loves it; this "substitute for the lost narcissism of his childhood" is imposed from without, is in fact the enemy of the subject's pleasures. "For what prompted the subject to form an ego ideal, on whose behalf his conscience acts as watchman, arose from the critical influence of his parents (conveyed to him by the medium of the voice), to whom was added, as time went on, those who trained and taught him and the innumerable and indefinable host of all the other people in his environment—his fellowmen—and public opinion" (14:96). Shortly before this passage, Freud introduced the idea of a censoring agency in the following way: "It would not surprise us if we were to find a special psychical agency which performs the task of seeing that narcissistic satisfaction from the ego ideal is ensured and which, with this end in view, constantly watches the actual ego and measures it by that ideal" (14:95). In other words, narcissistic satisfaction has become a duty; it has to be obtained from a "superior" alien self. What has often been noted as the blurring of psychic boundaries between the ego ideal and what Freud would later call the superego is easily understandable. The theory of the superego is the phenomenology of the ego ideal: it describes the experience of the ideal as a guilty consciousness of inner distances.

This parodistic revival of primary narcissism—in which the ego is ordered to find pleasure in loving an ideal to which it is guiltily inferior—is also a distorted repetition of primary masochism. I referred earlier to my suggestion that sexuality is born as masochism. This type of masochism has nothing to do with self-punishment; to speak of it as constituting the sexual is an attempt to describe the peculiarly human adaptive mechanism by which the infant pursues the repeated shattering of its psychic stability as a source of pleasure. But the essay on narcissism points to a wholly different form of masochism, in which the ego's self-condemnation is experienced as pleasure. In seeing to it that "narcissistic satisfaction from the ego ideal is ensured," the "special agency" of which Freud speaks perpetrates the narcissism of moral masochism.

In a sense, of course, the notion of the ego ideal affirms the importance of the object in human sexuality, whereas primary narcissism *could* be thought of as inherently subversive of our relations with the world. Freud's discovery of the importance of narcissism reconfirms his much earlier discovery of a gap between human sexuality and the human relations presumably served by sexual desire. In his discussion of "the erotic life of the sexes" in "On Narcissism," Freud exposes the narcissistic desire in various types of object love. "People whose libidinal development has suffered some disturbance," he writes, "such as perverts and homosexuals . . . have taken as a model not their mother but their own selves." Most women, according to Freud, love narcissistically. And object love in heterosexual men is partially motivated by a nostalgia for the narcissism they have presumably given up. Strongly narcissistic women (similar in this to children, great criminals in literature, "cats and the large beasts of prey") "have the greatest fascination for men . . . as if we envied them for maintaining a blissful state of mind—an unassailable libidinal position which we ourselves have since abandoned" (14:89). Thus in the very best of cases (which, in Freudian terms, would mean cases of post-Oedipal genital heterosexuality), *the sexual always involves a turning away from the other.* The move from autoeroticism to primary narcissism reinforces the autotelic nature of human sexuality by giving a structural stability to our solipsistic jouissance.

And yet it can also be argued that primary narcissism as Freud sketchily defines it at the beginning of his essay on narcissism initiates and later helps to maintain the relations of our sexual life. Primary narcissism allows the infantile ego to be masochistically shattered without being destroyed. It is perhaps the infant's best erotic defense against the eroticizing bombardments of his environment. Narcissism replays the shattering stimulations of that environment in the paradoxical form of a *structuralizing self-shattering*. Far from having anything to do with the infantile ego's perception of itself as "possessed of every perfection that is of value," primary narcissism is that ego's (nonethical) appreciation of its capacity to be sexually shattered. It allows the subject to enter into relations with the world that are not sadomasochistic. In contrast to this passionate form of adaptivity, the most mysteriously dysfunctional aspect of human development may be the ego's repudiation of its own erotic worth and its willed subjection to an antierotic ideal. Freud writes that the ego's departure from primary narcissism "is brought about by means of the displacement of libido on to an ego ideal imposed from without"—to which he adds, astonishingly: "and satisfaction is brought about from fulfilling this ideal" (14:100). The "vigorous attempt to recover" primary narcissism is thus defined, in the final pages of Freud's essay, as exactly identical to the departure from it. According to this definition, the satisfactions of primary narcissism would be dependent on—and defined by—the very process that erases them. The narcissistic love for the ego ideal is a delibidinalized narcissism.

What does all this have to do with sublimation? In two extremely interesting paragraphs in part 3 of the essay on narcissism, Freud insists on the importance of distinguishing between "the formation of an ego ideal" and "the sublimation of instinct." It is precisely the demands of the ego ideal that work against sublimation. The ego ideal drives sexual impulses into repression: "the formation of an ideal . . . is the most powerful factor favoring repression." As a result, those impulses remain unsublimated—in their primitive form—in the unconscious. Sublimation, on the other hand, "is a way out, a way by which [the ego's] demands can be met *without* involving repression" (14:94–95). What we should also see, however, is the possibility of sublimation's being contaminated by idealization. Freud makes his emphatic distinction between the two processes within a discussion that has already laid the ground for a blurring of their conceptual boundaries. It could, after all, be said that his description of how we exchange our primary narcissism for "homage to a high ideal" is strikingly similar to descriptive accounts of sublimation elsewhere in his work. In that exchange, instinctual narcissism has replaced a sexual aim (satisfaction from "an original libidinal cathexis of the ego") with a nonsexual aim (satisfaction from fulfilling the requirements of an ideal ego). More exactly, the relation between the ego and the ideal ego outlined in the essay on narcissism can be thought of as taking place in two stages. An object "is aggrandized and exalted in the subject's mind" (this would be idealization), and the subject's narcissism changes its original aim and is satisfied if the ego fulfills the requirements of that exalted internalized object (this would be sublimation). What should be underlined is that the second process cannot help being affected by the first. The ideal ego's fundamental requirement is that the ego be de-sexualized in order to be worthy of it. If that ideal is to become, as Freud writes, "the target of the self-love which was enjoyed in childhood by the actual ego," the nature of self-love itself must be changed. Or, in other words, the change in aim is inseparable from a change in the very essence of narcissistic desire. In the ego's relation to the ideal version of itself, narcissism is itself idealized, sublimated into something more sublime. The ego's relation to the ideal ego is the ground on which all subsequent idealizing and desexualizing sublimations will be built.

*   *   *

How will psychoanalysis speak of the ego? This, I believe, is the major question raised by Freud's essay on narcissism, and the way in which that question is answered has important consequences for a theory of sublimation. At times sublimation in Freud's works appears to be grounded, as I have suggested, in the erotic ego of primary narcissism, and at other times its model is the ego's masochistic relation to its ideal. In discussing the tension between these two views of narcissism, I have not meant to suggest that one is more valid as a description of psychic reality than the other. "On Narcissism" can be read as a description of the vicissitudes of early ego formation. Freud seems first of all to be arguing for the emergence of the ego as a consequence of sexual excitement; at its origin, the stabilizing structure of the ego would have been desired into being. He then gives an account of the intersubjective perils that the ego cannot help confronting. Its strategy in dealing with parental criticism and its surrogates is to internalize—and to identify with—the source of that criticism. This identification entails an internal split, and a more or less unworthy ego represses its unlawful desires in order to close the gap between itself and its ideal, as well as to stifle the criticism of the censor on whose approval narcissistic love now depends. The anomaly in Freud's discussion is the link he establishes between these two moments in the ego's history. That is, the formation of the ideal ego is seen as an attempt to recover the satisfaction of primary narcissism, whereas the constitution of the ideal depends on a repressive desexualization of the ego created by primary narcissism.

"On Narcissism" somewhat confusingly theorizes Freud's hesitation between a concept of sublimation as the investing of ego interests with unrepressed sexual energy and a wholly different view in which the boundaries between sublimation and symptom or reaction formation are blurred. In the first of those views, Freud proposes that sublimations are always narcissistically invested. They are extensions of self-love; more precisely, they are interests and activities that contain an expansive narcissism. Far from being a transcendence of self-interest, sublimations are the elaborated forms of self-enjoyment. Just as autoeroticism is repeated and structured in the narcissistic self, so primary narcissism is recovered and objectified in our sublimating activities. The pleasure of play, work, art, and philosophical or scientific investigations would, then, have to be defined in terms of a turning away from the objects we love and back to the objectless jouissance in which, as Freud suggests, we were perhaps born into sexuality.

This is not to say that the activities just mentioned do not include object relations. In psychoanalytic terms, the question is rather whether such relations can account for the specificity of the pleasure that motivates and sustains our interest in various types of cultural symbolization. That turning away from the object so crucial to Freud's definition of sexual excitement is sexuality's most intimate and most secret movement, a movement that psychoanalysis itself has attempted to repress in its frequently frenzied attention to the ways in which we adapt to the world of objects. Sexual pleasure would be just as autotelic in object libido as in narcissistic libido, although in an *un*sublimated relation of desire to objects the object itself remains indispensable, must be possessed if the jouissance in which it ultimately disappears is to be reached. If, as Freud suggests, sublimations originate in narcissistic libido, then sublimations necessarily imply a disinterested relation to objects. The common notion of sublimated aims as higher aims corroborates this view, although it does so by idealizing the disinterestedness. What I am suggesting is that the transformation of aims with respect to objects— from, say, sexual desire to friendship or altruism—depends not on a suppression or transcendence of the sexual, but rather on a shift in the object itself. The self has solipsistically become its own source and object of pleasure.

To consider sublimation in this way is, finally, to reinforce Freud's contention that we sublimate unrepressed sexual energies. The repression of a desire, far from liberating it from its object, condemns that desire to the permanent if disguised pursuit of the object. In sublimation, the object of desire (the libidinal object) is nothing other than the consciousness that is pursuing a nonsexual aim. This is, we might say, psychoanalytic realism rather than psychoanalytic idealism. The most notable achievements of culture and morality do indeed involve an abstraction from the sexual. And this means a certain civilizing indifference to our cultural achievements and our ethical ideals, an indifference without which tolerance becomes problematic and the fanaticism of the ideal returns. In the extraordinary human accomplishment that Freud tentatively sought to explain under the name of sublimation, the sexual authentically produces the nonsexual, where interests and activities are narcissistic distillations.

An inevitable consequence of such a concept of sublimation is the renunciation of what has generally been recognized as the psychoanalytic criticism of art. The more successfully the artist sublimates, the fewer traces there will be of fixated (interpretable) sexual energy in his work. Nor can the nonspecific sexualization of ego interests be confirmed by a presumed dominance of primary characteristics in the artist's "thinking." The principal model from which Freud derived those characteristics—the model of dreams—is much too primitive and private a mental phenomenon (which may of course take very intricate and puzzling forms) to be useful in our attempt to describe the eroticizing of ego interests in artistic production. The consciousness of reality is sexualized in a work of art in ways that the melodramatic syntactic disturbances of the primary processes cannot account for. The way, then, is open for a criticism of art that would be thoroughly psychoanalytic in its recognition of art as the record of a special mode of eroticized consciousness, and yet just as decidedly nonpsychoanalytic in its conviction that psychoanalysis itself has done little to provide us with the terms in which to describe that ébranlement. The vocabulary of psychoanalysis is, in large part, designed to domesticate its own discoveries; only by maintaining a kind of ascetic reserve with regard to that vocabulary can we maintain a psychoanalytic perspective on culture.

At least for cultural studies, our theory of sublimation might thus be inclined to neglect the discipline in which it is grounded. If Freud has determined more than anyone else the ways in which I read art, his theories have been less important to me than the experience of having followed the modes of theoretical failure and even collapse in his work, the processes by which arguments are at once elaborated and disformulated. The Freudian text's frequent sacrifice of its own theoretical coherence should lead us to a restatement of Freudian theory as an inference from the troubled experience of reading Freudian theory. Freud's work is an exemplary version of these disruptions of human discourse, which it of course also attempts to account for systematically—disruptions that psychoanalysis has rightly recognized as crucial to what we call the aesthetic but that it has identified somewhat naively. The theoretical inferences I referred to a moment ago should not, I believe, solidify into theoretical positions but should operate as theoretical *dispositions* in front of the work of art—and among these dispositions I would include a readiness to locate repetitions masked as progressions, a turning away from the object (the inference from the essay on narcissism is obvious here), and a simultaneous confidence in and rejection of narrative orders. In my own work, I hope to show how pervasively such dispositions can operate in criticism even when the usual signs of a so-called psychoanalytic approach are absent from the critical work. Finally, and in partial defiance of what I have just been saying, I will momentarily solidify all these dispositions into more recognizable psychoanalytic language and say that in art the secret identity between narcissism and masochism is performed as the subversive eroticizing of representational projects.

But, as we have seen, Freud's essay on narcissism points to wholly different cultural analyses. The theory of sublimation suggested in the final sections of the essay is itself a repressive, idealizing sublimation of that other view of sublimation, as ego interests invested with unrepressed sexual energies. The history of Freud's thought—and, to a large extent, of psychoanalysis itself—is the history of the repression of the psychoanalytic definition of the sexual. It has apparently been more acceptable to treat the achievements of culture as ambiguously successful reparative repetitions of developmental disturbances than to think of those achievements as sustained by the uncommunicable and uninterpretable intensities of a masochistic jouissance. Fearful of what might be called an intrinsic indifference to others in human sexuality, Freud managed to reinterpret his theory of primary narcissism as he formulated it so that narcissistic pleasure itself would appear as a derivative of object relations. I have argued, both here and in *The Freudian Body*, that Freud's most original speculative move was to deconstruct the sexual as a category of intersubjectivity, and to propose a definition of sexual excitement as both a turning away from others and a dying to the self. The appeal of that dying—the desire to be shattered out of coherence—is perhaps what psychoanalysis has sought most urgently to repress. But the compulsion to eliminate from life the incomparable pleasure of dying has led to the infinitely more dangerous idealizing of that pleasure as moral masochism. The inadequately repressed and inadequately satisfied desire to renew the ébranlement of the sexual thus repeats itself by turning against itself: self-shattering is turned into rageful aggressiveness, and the excited dismantling of identity is degraded into the longing for a merely biological death.

Finally—and to return to my point of departure—Freud himself, in the speculation of "Character and Anal Eroticism," perhaps located the moment of our greatest susceptibility to such transformations. It is as if we were most vulnerable to the temptation to deny the sexual at precisely that moment in our development when sexual pleasure is experienced as a denial or a retention. In what Freud describes as the anal character, we may have the unique configuration of a perfect identity between unrestrained sexuality and its brutal repression. Anality is the mode of sexuality that most closely literalizes the affinities of the sexual with death. In anality, the ébranlement of sexual excitement is promoted—in a certain sense, sublimated—to a fantasy of massive destruction. The anal character trait is anal sexuality negativized, a negativizing that—as in the case of individual and social compulsions for order—can present itself as a reparation, indeed almost as an atonement for a defiling explosiveness. But the potentially murderous atonements of order can repeat—literally, historically—the fantasmatic devastations they punish. Animated by the furies of anality, the culture of redemption is the culture of death.

CHAPTER 3

Boundaries of Time and Being:
Benjamin, Baudelaire, Nietzsche

Is it possible not to be modern? More exactly, can we ever *experience* a time other than our own? I emphasize the word "experience" both to indicate a relation more profound, or more authentic, than a knowledge of how people lived in the past and to suggest how difficult it is to say what we mean by such a relation. To call the inescapable conditions of our experience our "modernity" is perhaps to accept the challenge of defining *other* conditions of experience, conditions significantly different from our own and predating the modern. Such a compulsion is never ideologically neutral. The type of historical reflection about the times we live in, expressed by efforts to define discontinuities between the present and the past, is perhaps always motivated by a need for historical celebration or historical mourning. Modernism was rich in this type of reflection, and it included paeans to the presumably new consciousness of the times and elegiac expressions of regret for the invaluable and irrecoverable modes of consciousness presumably enjoyed in former times. And each of these moods can of course nourish the other: an apocalyptic sense of loss gives an unprecedented glamor to the notion of modernity; it summons the modern writer to nothing less than the reinvention of the terms and conditions of human experience. Thus if *Ulysses* demonstrates the unavailability of one of our culture's ancient stories as a mythical paradigm for modern experience, and if it does this by showing how easily that story can be insignificantly repeated in modern experience, *Finnegans Wake* can, and must, destroy the very language that still carries those comically recurrent myths in *Ulysses* in order to start again, unburdened by what, before *Finnegans Wake*, we could neither use nor forget.

Even in writers far more reluctant than Joyce to admit that anything new can replace the lost values and explanatory models of the past (I'm thinking especially of Eliot), the modern nonetheless retains an incomparable aura: that of being spiritually stranded, uniquely special in its radical break with traditional values and modes of consciousness. And to say this is to return to the logical problem I raised at the start: if an exacerbated consciousness of the modern is necessarily characterized by the sense of being cut off from the premodern, how can we understand the terms in relation to which, more exactly against which, the modern itself is to be defined? This very problem is perhaps a creation of the modernistic modernity to which I have just referred. If the concept of modernity always implies the sense of a break with the past, of living at moments when certain important thresholds are crossed (thresholds of political or economic modes of organization, of demographic movements and the distribution of social pressures and loci of power, of cultural hierarchies—including the place of religion in a culture's resources for making its experience intelligible and for guiding ethical choices), it does not necessarily imply that modern times are chiefly characterized by an inability to do something that past epochs were able to do: to make connections and, more precisely, to connect with their own traditions. Now, however, the modern is understood not merely as a break with the past but as an inability to understand the past. The modernity of the twentieth century includes the loss of what other modernities did not necessarily give up when they defined their own distinctiveness: an understanding of the tradition to which that modernity added something new. The break with the past now is marked by a mournful sense of the break itself as unique. *We* are modern because our modernity makes absolute the notion of discontinuity implicit in all discourses on modernity, reformulates discontinuity as a loss of the aptitude for continuities. To speak of the past therefore becomes nearly inconceivable once it is no longer merely a question of describing other customs, other systems of justice, other sets of beliefs, but rather the lost capacity of consciousness to place itself in relation to history. Modern consciousness, in short, is irremediably cut off from other ways in which human beings have understood their modernity, their comparatively limited break with their own past. This is the apocalyptic nature of our modernity, which in this century has frequently been spoken of as if it were a mutation of consciousness rather than the latest in a series of regular turns, accretions, and ruptures within an organically whole tradition. How, then, can we speak of that from which we have mutated? Is the mournful consciousness that describes this evolutionary drama the vestigial remnant of an extinct mode of being?

Benjamin

The strains—and the straining—to which this mode of thought is subject are exceptionally visible in the work of Walter Benjamin. Benjamin cannot, it is true, be reduced to a single or consistent set of attitudes toward the modern. His later work is less theologically oriented than his early writing, and, especially in what may be his most famous essay, "The Work of Art in the Age of Mechanical Reproduction," he seems to be primarily interested in the revolutionary potential of modern art, acknowledging that in a period like our own, of inauthentic art, films can nonetheless "promote revolutionary criticism of social conditions, even of the distribution of property." (The "tremendous shattering of tradition" that results in the loss of art's "aura" can, that is, also become a more beneficently destructive critique of the established injustices in the property relations of a capitalist society. Furthermore, the same masses that were bound to respond in a reactionary manner to Picasso and surrealism could respond progressively to a Chaplin movie.)[1] But these, I will argue, are nuances within Benjamin's overwhelmingly negative judgment of the modern. If, for example, he was fascinated by what modernity had brought to Paris, Moscow, and London, he also felt that life in these cities had become a constant reminder of personal and cultural loss. The facile nature of his pronouncements of loss can be staggering. Thus, in his essay "On Some Motifs in Baudelaire," he offers particularly unilluminating versions of an idea that was already a cliché of philosophy and cultural criticism at the beginning of the century: "the standardized, denatured life of the civilized masses" is the opposite of true experience (156). And in an essay on Nikolai Leskov entitled "The Storyteller": "experience has fallen in value. And it looks as if it is continuing to fall into bottomlessness. Every glance at a newspaper demonstrates that it has reached a new low, that our picture, not only of the external world but of the moral world as well, overnight has undergone changes which were never thought possible" (83–84).

What do these statements really mean? Benjamin's most tantalizing distinctions serve to disguise the difficulty of satisfactorily answering that question. His thought is full of pairs—with one term referring to something inauthentic but familiar, the other to something authentic but lost. The best known of these pairs is *Erlebnis* and *Erfahrung,* both of which are translated into English by "experience."[2] Benjamin uses *Erlebnis* to characterize Bergsonian *durée,* from which death and tradition have been excluded: "It is the quintessence of a passing moment that struts about in the borrowed garb of experience" ("On Some Motifs in Baudelaire," 45). In the modern city, *Erfahrung* has become nearly impossible, for citydwellers live in a state of shock in which they defensively inhibit impressions from being fully integrated into their history. "The greater the share of the shock factor in particular impressions, the more constantly consciousness has to be alert as a screen against stimuli; the more efficiently it does so, the less do these impressions enter experience *(Er-*

fahrung), tending to remain in the sphere of a certain hour in one's life *(Erlebnis)*" (163). What are those impressions presumably outside experience? Contextually, Benjamin's meaning is clear enough: *Erlebnis* is a "passing moment" isolated from the past. "The man who loses his capacity for experiencing feels as though he is dropped from the calendar." The superiority of Baudelaire to Bergson is that, while the latter tries to pass off *Erlebnis* as *Erfahrung* in his concept of durée, the former's representation of *spleen* exposes "the passing moment in all its nakedness," stripped of any associations with history (184–185).

Can there be such a thing as a "naked" passing moment? In making his argument for the importance of shock experience in modern life (and in modern poetry), Benjamin appeals to Freud's discussion of traumatic dreams in *Beyond the Pleasure Principle*. It is typical of Benjamin's procedure to move quickly among various references, to blend extreme mobility and apparent density in a way that discourages us from trying to figure out if what is moving so precipitously ahead is a coherent argument or a kind of nervously journalistic and jerkily brilliant mind. Presumably what Benjamin means by the "shock factor in particular impressions" is clarified by Freud's idea of shocks as the effect of "the excessive energies at work in the external world," energies that risk "breaking through the [mind's] protective shield against stimuli." The dreams that reproduce the catastrophic shock are, Freud writes, efforts "to master the stimulus retroactively, by developing the anxiety whose omission was the cause of the traumatic neurosis" (161). Such dreams thus express the failure of consciousness to have originally developed strategies (above all, anxiety) to help it parry or register the shock. From Benjamin's point of view, the function of consciousness as a protection against stimuli is interesting mainly in connection with something else Freud says about consciousness in this same section of *Beyond the Pleasure Principle*: "becoming conscious and leaving behind a memory trace are processes incompatible with each other within one and the same system." Thus, in the mental system that shields us against traumatic shocks, impressions die without leaving behind memory traces. "The attribution of 'permanent traces as the basis of memory' to processes of stimulation is reserved for 'other systems,' which must be thought of as different from consciousness" (160–61).

The reference to Freud is meant to provide a "more substantial definition" of the Proustian distinction between *mémoire volontaire* and *mémoire involontaire* and, in Benjamin's own terms, between *Erlebnis* and *Erfahrung*. But Freud's hypothesis about consciousness as incompatible with permanent memory traces describes certain functional differentiations within the mental apparatus and is not offered to account for the loss of an ability to "have" experience. Potentially traumatic shocks do, in a way, threaten that ability, and it may also be true, as Benjamin suggests, that shock defense can work by "assigning to an incident a precise point in time in consciousness" and by disintegrating impressions (as Theodor Reik suggested) in order to facilitate that exact temporal assignment. Nor is it wholly implausible to argue that "the share of the shock factor in particular impressions" may be greater in modern urban crowds than in older rural settings, although it is precisely Benjamin's strong historicizing of consciousness' role in parrying shocks that distorts the Freudian view of the mind's economy. Benjamin's constant implication is that the consciousness which, in "a peak achievement of the intellect," turns a threatening incident into a mere "moment that has been lived *(Erlebnis),"* is a kind of historical curse, a fallen way of dealing with experience. In the essays I am discussing, the fall is associated with modernity, and after only a page-and-a-half summary of Freud's ideas, Benjamin switches his reference to Valéry who, we are told, "seems to have had something similar in mind. The coincidence is worth noting, for Valéry was among those interested in the special functioning of psychic mechanisms under present-day conditions" (160–167).

This hurried excursion through Freud and Valéry (preceded by a few pages on Proust, all in an essay on motifs in Baudelaire) ends with a paragraph on the hyperreflective nature of modern poetry. In an age in which "the shock experience has become the norm" poetry will have "a large measure of consciousness"; "a plan" will be "at work in its composition." This, Benjamin points out, is indeed the case with such important modern figures as Baudelaire, Poe, and Valéry. But are Poe's and Valéry's theories of composition typically modern? Are there no historical precedents for the kind of self-reflexive, calculated poetry that Benjamin sees as characteristic of an age of shock experiences? More fundamentally, can we imagine a poetry in which a plan is *not* at work, which does *not* have "a large measure of consciousness?" It turns out, as we learn at the end of this brief section, that Benjamin is thinking mainly of historical consciousness. Quoting a quite ordinary remark by Valéry to the effect that Baudelaire's "reason of state" was "to become a great poet, yet neither Lamartine nor Hugo nor Musset," Benjamin takes this to mean Baudelaire's "emancipation from experiences" (162). That is, Baudelaire *intended* his work to be historical (didn't the Pléiade poets of the French Renaissance have the same intention?), which, to fill in the blanks here, is perhaps the inevitable consequence of living in a shock-saturated environment where consciousness must play a disproportionately large role and where poetry becomes too cerebral, cut off from that integrated experience *(Erfahrung),* that poetry of enduring memories, of a present organically integrated to the past, which is always the governing and unexamined ideal principle behind the entire argument.

We have of course come a long way from Freud. The Freudian argument is, as I have suggested, not invulnerable to a certain historical translation of the play it describes between stimuli, consciousness, and memory, but Freud was interested in the mechanisms by which the mind deals with the constant threat of being overpowered by "the excessive energies at work"—always and everywhere—"in the external world." The interest of Freud's argument lies in his effort to account for the very survival of the species. How, he asks, does a living organism manage to continue to exist, even to exercise a certain mastery over its environment, in a world where the odds of stimuli exchange are overwhelmingly against it? This is a far more profound, and generous, question about human life than Benjamin's at once tendentious and nihilistic reformulation. We soon enough discover in reading Benjamin that "the modern" is merely a metaphor for the historical—for the experiential—itself. "Merely"—and yet this places an immense burden on the notion of modernity. In his essay on Leskov, Benjamin delivers another of his vatic pronouncements: "The art of storytelling is reaching its end because the epic side of truth, wisdom, is dying out." What I find most interesting is Benjamin's apparent qualification of this assertion:

> This, however, is a process that has been going on for a long time. And nothing would be more fatuous than to want to see in it merely a "symptom of decay," let alone a "modern" symptom. It is, rather, a concomitant symptom of the secular productive forces of history, a concomitant that has quite gradually removed narrative from the realm of living speech and at the same time is making it possible to see a new beauty in what is vanishing. (87)

The final phrase is a concession that, here and elsewhere, costs Benjamin nothing. Indeed, to allow for a certain "beauty" in the modern serves the larger purpose of indicting history itself. The stakes are much larger than the presumed effects of urban crowds on the modern consciousness, and the very historicizing of Freud's ideas can also be thought of as disguising the way in which Benjamin, like Freud (but with a very different purpose), is making an ahistorical argument about mental structures and functions. The real traumatic shock is nothing less than "the secular productive forces of history" or, to abbreviate that, secular history.

But Freud is not positing some *other* way of having impressions enter experience. He is describing an economy constitutive of human mental life, an economy of survival, and it can hardly be said, given his complex theory of the relation between perception and the unconscious, that he gave any special value to those "powerful" and "enduring" memory fragments traceable to incidents that "never entered consciousness" ("Baudelaire," 160). That is, unlike Benjamin, Freud does not promote the unreflective to the status of a lost paradisiac capacity for experience, a move that, in Benjamin, leaves us with reflective consciousness as a kind of *pis aller,* "a peak achievement" of an intellect whose highest achievement is actually its awareness of its own hegemony as a fall from the grace of *Erfahrung.* If Freud's description of the mind appears ahistorical, it is largely because he could imagine *nothing but history* as a theater for life, whereas for Benjamin history is the theater in which we cease to live authentically.

*   *   *

The theological conclusions to which we are now rapidly moving will hardly come as a surprise to readers of Benjamin. I have deliberately delayed any direct consideration of them in order to suggest how they guide his argument at every turn. That is, I have not mentioned the profound religious orientation of his thought in order to emphasize its necessity; his thought makes no sense without it. The great popularity that Benjamin has enjoyed among literary intellectuals might lead us, wrongly, to assume that we can bracket his religious yearnings as we admire and profit from his observations on Proust, Kafka, Baudelaire, and Goethe. But those observations always lead back to Benjamin's postlapsarian dirge, even when the particular object of analysis seems unrelated to the theological thesis. He was a brilliant man, and his writing has many insightful flashes, which we might just as accurately call flashy insights. His essays are full of fragmented thought, and though it is fashionable to admire the rigor with which he practiced a literary form consonant with his idea of the fragmentariness of modern consciousness, it is less frequently noted that his central thesis *about* fragmentariness presupposes his own capacity for a sustained transcendence of that condition and for the most extraordinary totalizing assertions about, most notably, the prehistorical and historical consciousness.

Very little of what he said makes any sense—and this is especially true of his elaboration of such distinctions as *Erlebnis* and *Erfahrung*—unless we place it within the logical assumptions behind all his thought: assumptions of lost wholeness, of fallen being. Benjamin was at once incoherent and wholly consistent. Richard Wolin is right to argue for this consistency, to maintain that "a relentless desire for redemption . . . represents the inner drive behind the entirety of Benjamin's theoretical *oeuvre.*"[3] In the light of this fidelity, Benjamin's fascinated attention to the details of modern life[4] has something profoundly morbid about it. Such attention is not merely a function of the epistemological article of faith—elaborated in the prologue to his *Trauerspiel* study—according to which "truth-content is only to be grasped through immersion in the most minute details" of the object of one's thought.[5] Adorno, even while arguing that "the only philosophy which can be responsibly practiced in face of despair is the attempt to contemplate all things as they would present themselves from the standpoint of redemption" (or "in the messianic light"), also noted the "utterly impossible" nature of any such philosophy because "it presupposes a standpoint removed, even though by a hair's breadth, from the scope of existence, whereas we well know that any possible knowledge must not only be first wrested from what is, if it shall hold good, but is also marked, for this very reason, by the same distortion and indigence it seeks to escape."[6]

We must go one step further, for it is not merely a question of the philosopher being *in* (and therefore being marked by) the world whose "distortion and indigence" he exposes. That distortion and that indigence are in his thought before his thought even applies itself to the world. They are themselves *decisions of that thought* about the world and not objective characteristics of an environment that can only infect anyone who, as it were, happens to be in such an environment. The disease of modernity (more profoundly, of history) that Benjamin analyzes is first of all (and perhaps last of all) the disease of his perception of modernity. The redemptive need in Benjamin's critique of the modern condemns that critique to a kind of mystified morbidity; it always *has* to be a question of "truth" breaking in upon, or being made to emerge from, degraded phenomena—degraded by virtue of their very phenomenality. It is tempting to see Benjamin's great popularity today as a sign of our complicity in such mystifications. It is perhaps, more pointedly, a sign of the extraordinary hold on our thought of the culture of redemption. For in Benjamin we find the traits most deeply characteristic of this culture: the scrupulous registering of experience in order to annihilate it, and the magical and nihilistic belief that immersion in the most minute details of a material content will not only reduce that content but simultaneously unveil its hidden redemptive double.

The pairs of thought in Benjamin's work operate as conceptual reminders of this process of annihilation and resurrection. There is not only *Erlebnis* and *Erfahrung*. The man of the crowd is opposed to the flaneur. Baudelaire, according to Benjamin, mistakenly equates the two—perhaps because "Baudelaire's Paris preserved some features that dated back to the happy old days." In the man of the crowd, "composure has given way to manic behavior. Hence, he exemplifies, rather, what was to become of the *flâneur* once he was deprived of the milieu to which he belonged" ("Baudelaire," 172). There are even desires—such as the gambler's "desire to win and make money"—which are not wishes *(Wünsche)* "in the strict sense of the word." A wish belongs to the category of authentic experience; indeed, "a wish fulfilled is the crowning of experience." (The distinction is explained by a further distinction: "It is experience that accompanies one to the far reaches of time, that fills and divides time." This "good" time is spatial: the crowning experience of a wish fulfilled is properly symbolized by the shooting star, "which plunges into the infinite distance of space," whereas "the ivory ball [on the gambling table] which rolls into the *next* compartment, the *next* card which lies on top are the very antithesis of a falling star" [178–79].) We also have the difference between information and stories. In a culture suffering from "the increasing atrophy of experience," it becomes almost impossible to tell stories; instead we have information isolated from experience, isolated because information "does not enter 'tradition.'" For Benjamin, Proust's work "conveys an idea of the efforts it took to restore the figure of the storyteller to the present generation" (159).

What is the strategic purpose of these distinctions in Benjamin's thought? If the privileged term in each of the pairs I have mentioned is the lost term, this is because the redemptive double of modern (or, once again, historical) experience is an authentic origin. Benjamin does not have to mean this in a literal sense: the authentic origin, like Rousseau's state of nature, is an ontological priority rather than a fact of history, and this of course adds greatly to its power. It is not something we can merely regret; it is a mode of being toward which we can aspire, which can be "restored" (or perhaps even realized for the first time). The conceptual visibility of this ontological preference depends on its *presentation* in historical metaphors, its translation into a temporal priority. In a sense, this "redeems" all the factitious oppositions between past and present in Benjamin, for he really acknowledges no responsibility to historical truth in spite of his announced "immersion in the most minute details of subject-matter." Not only is history devalued as a referent; the historical method itself is nothing more than the principal tactic within a strategy designed to rescue truth from history. Thus the incoherence of an historical argument can be thought of as irrelevant to its truth content—and this is characteristic of religious history.

From this perspective, Benjamin can get away with almost anything, from the misreading of a single poem to the most sweeping statements about modern man's being "cheated out of his experience" ("Baudelaire," 180). Thus he reads Baudelaire's sonnet "Correspondances" as if it were saying the same thing as "La Vie antérieure." The latter poem might be read as an evocation of lost correspondences, but it is difficult to see how the former thematically belongs to a "cycle of poems . . . devoted to something irretrievably lost." Benjamin says almost nothing about either poem for that matter—his essays never include sustained discussions of the literary works they refer to—but, as far as I can make out, he reads "Correspondances" as describing "data of remembrance—not historical data, but data of prehistory," which we have lost. Yet

Baudelaire does not say that nature was once a "living temple" of veiled symbols, but that it is that temple (and that, consequently, its "confuses paroles" can still be heard). Furthermore, nothing in the poem describes correspondences as those "data of remembrance" connecting us to "prehistory," which establish an "encounter with an earlier life" (181–182). Rather, the poem outlines two types of correspondences: in the first stanza, between those "forêts de symboles" that constitute nature and whatever (possibly transcendent) reality they symbolize, and in the rest of the poem, correspondences among the various orders of sensory perception ("Les parfums, les couleurs et les sons se répondent").[7] No matter—Benjamin's tendentiousness often takes the form of an insistent blindness, and if all of human history is ultimately expendable, there is no reason to expect a particular poem to escape the teleological bias of his thought. What is important is to detect how or where fallen art can be redeemed, and in order to do this Benjamin invents the terms in which art presumably mourns what it has lost.

*   *   *

Benjamin's remarks on Baudelaire's "Correspondances" formulate irretrievable loss in aesthetic terms. When the experience of correspondence presents itself as the beautiful, "the ritual value of art appears" ("Baudelaire," 182). Now the known ritualistic origins of certain forms of art (the origin, for example, of Western tragedy in the religiously significant reenactments of familiar myths) are not in themselves an argument for the superiority of ritual in art. What exactly have we lost in losing the ritual value of art? We can look to "The Work of Art in the Age of Mechanical Reproduction" for an answer to this question. "The whole sphere of authenticity is outside technical—and, of course, not only technical—reproducibility." Why? Because authenticity depends on "the presence of the original," and the quality of the actual work of art's presence is always depreciated as a result of "the situations into which the product of mechanical reproduction can be brought." For example, "technical reproduction can put the copy of the original into situations which would be out of reach for the original itself. Above all, it enables the original to meet the beholder halfway, be it in the form of a photograph or a phonograph record." The argument, as we might expect, is not excessively clear, since by "the original" Benjamin seems to mean both an original work of art and, say, the landscape an artist paints. Photographic reproduction of works of art *and* of scenes of nature can "depreciate" the originals by the very skill with which they "bring out those aspects of the original that are unattainable to the naked eye yet accessible to the lens, which is adjustable and chooses its angle at will." As Benjamin says: "This [effect of depreciation] holds not only for the work of art but also, for instance, for a landscape which passes in review before the spectator in a movie" ("The Work of Art," 220–221). We may wonder why paintings in an earlier age of manual reproduction did not depreciate the aspects of nature they depicted. A Renaissance rendering of a Tuscan landscape certainly had the effect of putting the original "into situations which would be out of reach for the original itself" (even if those situations were limited to a patron's house or, later, a public museum). No matter—Benjamin is less concerned with damaged originals than with the preponderance, now, of art forms in which *no one copy* has more worth than any other copy. There is no original against which the value of each copy can be measured; indeed, there is *nothing but copies*. This is of course true of film, in which all copies produced with the same technical expertise are of equal aesthetic value; as long as there are excellent copies around, we do not need the original roll of film to appreciate Chaplin's genius. This also applies to musical recordings produced inside a recording studio, where—unlike the recording of a live performance—there is no full or finished performance that actually took place prior to, or apart from, its existence on records, on thousands of copies each one of which is as original as all the others.[8]

To have an original would be to have something unique; it is the only version of a work of art that is not a copy of the work. The original is unique in that it is only itself; it is incompatible with the very notions of copies or versions. Uniqueness in Benjamin does not have the romantic or avant-gardist connotations of something incomparable, of psychological or aesthetic originality, of a work without models, a work, in short, for which the tradition cannot account. On the contrary: "the uniqueness of a work of art is inseparable from its being embedded in the fabric of tradition." Or, to put this in terms of authenticity: "The authenticity of a thing is the essence of all that is transmissible from its beginning, ranging from its substantive duration to its testimony to the history which it has experienced." Historical testimony is jeopardized when the original or unique work of art can no longer be located, disappears. Interestingly enough, then, the value of the original is inseparable from its immersion in a history that may in fact make its uniqueness problematic. If, for example, the tradition is itself "alive and extremely changeable," an art object will have different meanings at different moments. "An ancient statue of Venus, for example, stood in a different traditional context with the Greeks, who made it an object of veneration, than with the clerics of the Middle Ages, who viewed it as an ominous idol" ("The Work of Art," 223, 221). To what extent is the statue independent of these different meanings? On the one hand, the object's authenticity is inseparable from its transmissibility, from its variability as a locus of sense within a history of responses to it. On the other hand, the history of variable sense is itself authenticated by the permanent presence within it of an unchanging, unique object: the original, nonreproducible work of art. We begin to see that the value of an original may be that *we can never know it as an original*. We know the statue of Venus only as a history of contingent interpretations, at once absolutely essential to them and infinitely removed from them.

In other words, we know the object itself—in its unchanging uniqueness as a nonreproducible original—as a phenomenon of distance. What we see of the original is its aura, which is precisely what separates us from it.[9] Aura is "the unique phenomenon of a distance, however close it may be." In "The Work of Art in the Age of Mechanical Reproduction," Benjamin proposes this as a definition of the aura of natural objects (he speaks of the aura of a mountain range when it is looked at by someone "resting on a summer afternoon" [222]), although in a note to the essay he specifies that this formula for the aura "represents nothing but the formulation of the cult value of the work of art in categories of space and time perception" (243). In art, then, "the unique phenomenon of a distance" has to do with "cult value." This is crucial, although it should also be mentioned that in still another context Benjamin, speaking of Proust's *mémoire involontaire,* identifies aura as "the associations which . . . tend to cluster around the object of a perception," thus suggesting that the aura is what makes objects familiar to us ("Baudelaire," 186). But this would be a superficial reading (one perhaps strategically encouraged by Benjamin himself) of how the aura affects our perception of art objects and, more specifically, of the effect of "associations" on that perception. Transposed to the history of art, the associations gathered around objects in our personal experience (each person's history is in large part the history of the objects in his or her life) can be compared to those "different traditional contexts" through which the ancient statue of Venus has moved in the Western tradition. Yet Benjamin's emphasis on the sense of distance as central to the effect of the aura makes it clear that even the most familiarizing associations leave the object itself intact in its intrinsic unknowability. Indeed, as he explicitly says, the primary effect of the aura—I am tempted to say its primary function—is to make the original, the unique work of art *unapproachable:*

> Distance is the opposite of closeness. The essentially distant object is the unapproachable one. Unapproachability is indeed a major quality of the cult image. True to its nature, it remains "distant, however close it may be." The closeness which one may gain from its subject matter does not impair the distance which it retains in its appearance. ("The Work of Art," 243)

The loss of the original in art is merely the modern sign of a much greater loss, one that predates modernity: the loss of the cult or of ritual as the expression of "the contextual integration of art in tradition." Indeed, "the unique value of the 'authentic' work of art has its basis in ritual, the location of its original use value" (223–224). In other words, the authenticity of art has little to do with qualities intrinsic to the object; it is a function of the originally "ceremonial character" of artistic performance ("Baudelaire," 188). Or, more exactly, since that which creates the inestimable value of an original is unknowable or unapproachable, we can recognize and certify that value only in terms of "use value." For Benjamin, the sacredness of the original can be established only by an aesthetic of reception. What he saw as the fascist aestheticizing of the political (which, he wrote, could only culminate in war) cannot be authentically opposed by the communist politicizing of art. Both alternatives are possible because of a cataclysmic shift in the context of art's reception from ritual to politics. Ideally, the fascist and communist uses of art would *both* be reversed in order to reinstate the cultic value of art, its reintegration into ritual.

*   *   *

In a sense, then, our most urgent task is to make the work of art unapproachable again. If Benjamin looks closely at particular works (which in fact he does not; that is merely his announced intention), it is in order to seek out those places where the work leaps back or away from us, where a distancing aura might intervene between art and its audience. Art can be redeemed only by being remystified. That we are dealing with a mystification—and, as I will argue in a moment, with an inescapably political mystification—is clear from Benjamin's essays on "The Task of the Translator" and "On Language as Such and on the Language of Man." "Naming," he writes in the latter piece, "is that by which nothing beyond it is communicated and *in* which language itself communicates itself absolutely." *"In naming the mental being of man communicates itself to God."*[10] Benjamin defines the Fall as a fall from naming, as the name stepping outside of itself and lapsing into a degraded status in which language becomes knowledge of things as well as of good and evil. "God made things knowable in their names. Man, however, names them according to knowledge." Knowledge is the postlapsarian curse that condemns us to a mediated relation to things (whereas in God the "name because it is inwardly identical with the creative word, [is] the pure medium of knowledge"). All art manifests this fall, for it never rests "on the ultimate essence of language-mind, but on language-mind confined to things, even if in consummate beauty."[11]

So it is not a question of opposing the modern to the premodern, but rather of positing a prehistorical—more precisely here, a prelapsarian—state of language. Ritualized art is already a fall from the creative word.

This does not make Benjamin's implicit nostalgia for ritual any less significant. For what might be called a materialist reading of his work requires that we give emphasis not to the speculations on Genesis in the essay on language, but rather to the historical derivatives or consequences of the distinction in that piece between "language as such" (the inward identity of the name with the creative word of God) and "the language of man." The ontology of language outlined in the essay on language can be thought of as the abstract superstructure—or, in psychoanalytic terms, as the *repressive* sublimation—which at once obscures and illuminates the political implications of Benjamin's mourning over the loss of art's original "use value" in ritual. It theologically legitimizes the devaluation of knowledge (by knowledge we need mean nothing more than our represented relations to the world) which is also present, more nakedly, in Benjamin's fastidious critique of the need of contemporary masses to "get close" to art objects. The cult value of art helped to prevent art from falling into the debased condition of knowable, approachable objects. Once we move from Adamite perfection to postlapsarian history, however, unapproachability cannot help having political implications. To say that "the earliest art works originated in the service of a ritual" is also to describe a type of "introduction of aesthetics into political life" ("The Work of Art," 223, 241). The communal cohesiveness apparently served by such rituals has a special appeal for a period, like ours, in which a strong sense of belonging to a community, especially at the national level, has become extremely problematic, given the suffering and the destruction that loyalty to a nation has been made to vindicate. But in tending to idealize more or less primitive versions of collective life, we can easily forget, or at least neglect, the fact that ceremonies celebrating a community's founding myths and shared values always have the function of perpetuating traditional structures of power. Using a Foucaultian distinction, we can say that it is not necessary to believe naively that the aestheticizing of politics in religious rituals was ever—at a particular moment in history and by particular individuals—intended to serve certain structures of power in order to recognize such an effect as their strategic function. The cultic use value of art that Benjamin claims we have lost is actually an archaic version of the fascist use of art as he dramatically defines it in "The Work of Art in the Age of Mechanical Reproduction": the aestheticizing of politics.[12]

Ritual mystifies art for political purposes. It is the perfect antithesis not only, as Benjamin himself saw, to such mass art forms as film, but to a profound modern sense of art as a mysteriously errant phenomenon, as likely "to be" anywhere (without that "being" having anything essential about it)—a sense of art as at once familiar and defamiliarizing, as simultaneously delineating and erasing boundaries, as, finally, *uniquely without authority*. Ritual obscures or frankly suppresses this aspect of art; it is the consummate institutionalizing of art, the solemn assigning to art of an authoritative social "place." And that is what art has, most profoundly, lost: "what is really jeopardized when the historical testimony is affected is the authority of the object" ("The Work of Art," 221). As we have seen, such authority depends on the object's unapproachability, on its being a sacred object rather that the object of our "knowledge," of our representations. A collective participation in ritual does not bring the sacred object nearer. Indeed, the communal value of ritualized ceremony depends on an implicit willingness to be mystified, to share a sense of awe, that is, of being close to others in a collectively experienced distance from an object of veneration. The authenticity of Benjamin's original is identical to its power of mystification.

If, however, Benjamin sees all history as a fall from Adamite being, he can afford to sound almost remarkably progressive. Precisely because the regressive tendencies in Benjamin's thought transcend historical regressiveness, he never behaves like an aesthetic or political reactionary. Thus the modern period can even appear to be celebrated for its having emancipated the work of art from "its parasitical dependence on ritual" ("The Work of Art," 224). The kind of time Benjamin is interested in is not time at all, and therefore the past is irrelevant to it. He knew, as Proust knew (for very different purposes), that our only chance for experiencing the timeless (or something we feel tempted to call the timeless) lies in a special type of receptivity to the present. So Benjamin promotes "the notion of a present which is not a transition, but in which time stands still and has come to a stop." Only in that immobilized present can we perhaps "blast open the continuum of history." Such statements express not only Benjamin's critique of a cause-and-effect reading of historical time but, more positively, set the conceptual and experiential precondition for what he called a *Jetzzeit,* a "time of the now" that can be "shot through with chips of Messianic time" ("Theses on the Philosophy of History," 262–263). Such chips corrode the present more than any historical past or future could ever hope to do. For the Messiah, as Benjamin writes in the "Theologico-Political Fragment," "consummates all history, in the sense that he alone redeems, completes, creates its relation to the messianic." That consummation is also a consuming; Messianic time *burns away* history in a redemptive conflagration. Nature itself is messianic "by reason of its eternal and total passing away. To strive after such passing . . . is the task of world politics, whose method must be called nihilism."[13] Without messianic time, history is always nature, unredeemed existence. The modern city and modern technology make even more visible, somewhat paradoxically, the bare, denuded aspect of nonmessianic being. Benjamin defines Baudelairean spleen as exposing "the passing moment in all its nakedness. To his honor, the melancholy man sees the earth revert to a mere state of nature. No breath of prehistory surrounds it: there is no aura" ("Baudelaire," 185).

In Benjamin's aesthetic, the critic seeks to make even more visible, to exacerbate, the artist's representation of mortified life; his reading is governed by a kind of negative semiology according to which Baudelairean spleen, for example, or the images of decay and death in German baroque tragedy, can actually be taken as "hieroglyphs of redeemed life," as images waiting to be blasted out of history by a movement of transcendence to which they negatively point.[14] Ruins, Benjamin writes in the *Trauerspiel* study, "the highly significant fragment, the remnant is, in fact, the finest material in baroque creation. For it is common practice in the literature of the baroque to pile up fragments ceaselessly, without any strict idea of a goal, and, in the unremitting expectation of a miracle, to take the repetition of stereotypes for a process of intensification." But the "miracle" is of course a miracle of reading, and all this inflated language is designed to celebrate the power of criticism—more specifically, of philosophical criticism—over art. "Criticism means the mortification of the works," the *promotion* of beauty to knowledge. "The object of philosophical criticism is to show that the function of artistic form is as follows: to make historical content, such as provides the basis of every important work of art, into a philosophical truth."[15] We should not underestimate the seductive appeal of this Benjaminian arrogance. The redemptive authority of art, it is suggested, can be exercised only by criticism. Art is blind to the redemptive possibilities inherent in its representations of fallen being. The culture of redemption ultimately depends on a supplemental voice, the authoritative core of the critical, philosophical, or psychoanalytic interpreter, of the one *who knows*. In Benjamin, the claim of much of our contemporary criticism to a masterful authority (masterful in spite of, in reality as a result of, its presumably privileged demystifications of textual authority) is vindicated as an eschatological necessity. Philosophical criticism turns out to be nothing less than the goal of art and of history. Benjamin has become the most prestigious precursor of this attempted appropriation of literature by philosophy— the latter's "insights" into the former's "blindness"—which is the more or less secret goal of much of what we call deconstructive criticism.

Messianic time is, in any case, intermittent, and it is discontinuous with historical time. Within history there is the memory, or the fantasy, of a time when the work of art, "embedded in the fabric of tradition," had not yet lost its uniqueness, its authenticity. In a note to "The Work of Art in the Age of Mechanical Reproduction," Benjamin writes that to the extent that the cult of value of painting is secularized, "the uniqueness of the phenomena which hold sway in the cult image is more and more displaced by the empirical uniqueness of the creator or of his creative achievement." Authenticity "always transcends," but is nonetheless somewhat threatened by, "mere genuineness. This is particularly apparent in the collector who always retains some traces of the fetishist and who, by owning the work of art, shares in its ritual power" (244). In cultures of the past, the art object was a sacred object whose uniqueness was inseparable from its unapproachability. *In a secular culture the sanctuary of art is the private collection.* The logical consequence of Benjamin's fantasies about authentic originals is the granting of an almost priestly function to the capitalist connoisseur, the rich collector. In a talk about book collecting, he said: "To renew the old world—that is the collector's deepest desire when he is driven to acquire new things, and that is why a collector of older books is closer to the wellsprings of collecting than the acquirer of luxury editions." In a private collection, the book or the painting is once again "embedded in a tradition," but the tradition—the historical continuity—is now provided by a private genealogy. "Actually, inheritance is the soundest way of acquiring a collection. For a collector's attitude toward his possessions stems from an owner's feeling of responsibility toward his property. Thus it is, in the highest sense, the attitude of an heir, and the most distinguished trait of a collection will always be its transmissibility." In his critique of modernity, Benjamin—unintentionally but ineluctably—exempts a kind of aristocracy of taste within the bourgeoisie, an aristocracy which implicitly reformulates transmissible values as inherited money. "For a collector—and I mean a real collector, a collector as he ought to be—ownership is the most intimate relationship that one can have to objects" ("Unpacking My Library: A Talk about Book Collecting," 61, 66, 67). Therein lie the beginnings of a startling vindication of private property. This is certainly not where Benjamin thought he was going but, until the Messiah comes, there may be nowhere else to go.

Baudelaire

Baudelaire begins his essay on Constantin Guys—"Le Peintre de la vie moderne"—with an attempt "to establish a rational and historical theory of beauty, in contrast to the academic theory of an unique and absolute beauty." The beautiful "is always and inevitably of a double composition"; it is composed of

> an eternal, and of a relative, circumstantial element, which will be, if you like, whether severally or all at once, the age, its fashions, its morals, its emotions. Without this second element, which might be described as the

amusing, enticing, appetizing icing on the divine cake, the first element would be beyond our powers of digestion or appreciation, neither adapted nor suitable to human nature.[16]

Benjamin, who quotes the central part of this definition in "The Paris of the Second Empire in Baudelaire," comments: "One cannot say that this is a profound analysis."[17] One can hardly disagree with this judgment, although there may be more interesting things to note about the passage than its patent lack of profundity. More interesting, possibly even more damning, is that Baudelaire's duality nearly collapses under the excessive weight of one of its terms. Not only is the "quantity" of the eternal element "excessively difficult to determine"; in religious art, "the ingredient of eternal beauty reveals itself only with the permission and under the discipline of the religion to which the artist belongs." Finally, in periods that "in our vanity we characterize as civilized . . . the eternal part of beauty will be veiled and expressed if not by fashions, at least by the particular temperament of the artist" (3; 685). What we see in art is "the relative, circumstantial element"; the "eternal element" would appear to be more of a theoretical assumption—or perhaps a theoretical necessity—than a determinable aspect of works of art themselves.

Furthermore this passage, like so much of Baudelaire's critical writing, is characterized by a certain preciosity of rhetoric that places us at some distance from its ideas. "*C'est ici une belle occasion, en vérité*, pour établir une théorie rationnelle et historique du beau"; "*Je défie* qu'on découvre un échantillon quelconque de beauté"; "*Je choisis, si l'on veut*, les deux échelons extrêmes de l'histoire"; "*Considérez, si cela vous plaît*, la partie éternellement subsistante comme l'âme de l'art."[18] The abstract argument with its religious ground is, as it were, caressed and somewhat softened by the introductory phrases I have italicized. The argument risks becoming elegantly dilettantish under the light but repeated pressure of a coaxing voice calling attention to the moves of its arguments. It draws attention to itself, even while obscuring its exact relation to the ideas being proposed. This disjunction between the speaker and his ideas is more difficult to account for than the more familiar inconsistencies, throughout Baudelaire's work, within the ideas themselves: between, for example, demonic and idealistic notions of art, or between scornful and flatteringly respectful views of the bourgeoisie's role as an audience for high art and an arbiter of cultural values. The first section of "Le Peintre de la vie moderne" gives us something far more elusive: a mode of presentation that, instead of highlighting the crude opposition it anxiously—at once deferentially and defiantly—introduces, turns our attention to a nervous, fussy, essentially *reserved* narrative persona. Finally, nothing suggests that this reserve has anything to do with intellectual doubt. It is a more abstract reserve: the possible withholding of assent by virtue of nothing more than a slightly exaggerated consciousness of merely having the ideas about to be put forward. Could there be a "self" definable primarily as the consciousness of its own intellectual or moral character, as nothing more than an apprehensive mode of being?

By asking this question I do not mean to suggest that Baudelaire is indifferent to the opposition he makes between the eternal and the relative elements in art. Indeed, it is as if he had to emphasize that opposition—with its shaky structure and logical contradictions—in order to reach a far more original view of his own activity as a modern writer. Let us look more closely at the presumed double nature of the beautiful. If the quantity of the eternal element of the beautiful is "excessively difficult to determine," it is not quite invisible. In hieratic art, the eternal part manifests itself "under the discipline of the religion to which the artist belongs," and in modern art it is at once "veiled and expressed if not by fashion, at least by the particular temperament of the artist." In other words, the eternal is visible *within* those very elements that Baudelaire has just defined as belonging to the relative or the circumstantial: the period, the fashions of that period, and perhaps even within the passions of an author's "particular temperament." A similar conclusion is reached when Baudelaire returns to the duality of art in section 4 of "Le peintre de la vie moderne." In traveling through "le grand désert d'hommes" of urban crowds, Guys is seeking something more than "the fugitive pleasure of circumstance." What he is looking for is "modernity" ("for I know of no better word to express the idea I have in mind"), which, curiously enough, Baudelaire distinguishes from the occasion. Or rather, modernity—like the eternal element of the beautiful—is not immediately visible in the modern scene: Guys must "extract from fashion whatever element it may contain of poetry within history," he must "distill the eternal from the transitory." Modernity is "the ephemeral, the fugitive, the contingent" in art, but to express it is to express what is eternal in the ephemeral or the transitory (12–13; 694–695).

It is tempting to see nothing more here than the danger of applying too much analytic pressure to such passages. But the apparent confusion in the essay seems to me worth noting as a sign of the difficulty Baudelaire has in imagining how art can ever be *anything but* "relative" or modern. Modernity does have a specificity, but in one sense it is not historical. Modernity is not (as it is for Benjamin) the privilege of the modern age, which means that Baudelaire—all the signs of nostalgic remembrance notwithstanding—did not think of his own time as having effected a radical break with the past through revolutionary changes in the very structure of human experience. "Every old master has had his own modernity"; it is what all artists—at all times—seek in their relation to their own time. What is special to the nineteenth century is perhaps only its material environment, an environment necessarily different, for example, from that of antiquity. Thus in discussing a visual artist Baudelaire gives special attention to certain developments in fashion, in the history of dress and furniture: "The draperies of Rubens or Veronese will in no way teach you how to depict *moire antique, satin à la reine* or any other fabric of modern manufacture, which we see supported and hung over crinoline or starched muslin petticoat. In texture and weave these are quite different from the fabrics of ancient Venice or those worn at the court of Catherine" (13; 695).

There is nothing trivial about this; such things constitute the artist's materials, and his modernity is a function of his relation to that material. Not only that: each artist's prospect of becoming a classic (of being considered worthy of attention by future generations) depends not at all on obscuring the signs of the historically contingent in his work, on his attempting to save his work from its immersion in the present, but rather on the most scrupulous rendering of all the material supplied by the present. "In short, for any 'modernity' to be worthy of one day taking its place as 'antiquity,' it is necessary for the mysterious beauty which human life accidentally puts into it to be distilled from it." And: "almost all our originality comes from the seal which Time imprints on our sensations" (13–14; 695–696).[19] Baudelaire is fascinated by the materials historically available to him, but he is not making an argument for their superiority to the materials of any other period. In speaking of those painters who represent scenes from modern life, he writes: "The pleasure which we derive from the representation of the present is due not only to the beauty with which it can be invested, but also to its essential quality of being present" (1; 684). The present is, in other words, both an all-important and an empty category; its value is not in what it contains, but in its presentness. Thus Benjamin's historical discriminations, to the extent that they are intended as historical judgments, are irrelevant to Baudelaire. What interests Baudelaire is the presentness of *any* period in history, and this both gives an extraordinarily rich historical content to discussions of presentness in art and erases from the concept of modernity the Benjaminian connotations of rupture and loss.

Return now to the difficult notion of an equivalence, or perhaps an overlapping, of the transitory and the eternal. It is not a question of simply transposing the materials of modern life into literature or painting; there is, we remember, the mysterious assertion that Guys's absorption in contemporary fashion is an effort to disengage the eternal from the transitory modes of life in which it is lodged. The notion of the eternal has not been discarded but displaced, and in a sense it has even more value now than when it stood on its own as one of the two terms of Baudelaire's duality. There is nothing but the transitory or relative, but the transitory turns out to have no value in itself. Not only is the presentness of *any* historical present more significant for an artist than the intrinsic worth of the historical materials he must use; the value of presentness itself is that it can be made to yield something wholly different from it. And yet Baudelaire never suggests that what he calls the eternal will finally emerge from the transitory as an independent element, that it can—like pure gold from impure ore—be extracted and isolated from the circumstantial. The artist can represent nothing but the transitory, but his representation is without value unless we can see the transitory taking a certain distance from itself, supplementing itself, perhaps even negating itself.

After explaining his pleasure in looking at a series of engravings from the late eighteenth century and the pleasure of finding "the moral and aesthetic feeling" of the time inscribed in the costumes worn by the figures in the engravings, Baudelaire writes: "The idea of beauty which man creates for himself imprints itself on his whole attire, crumples or stiffens his dress, rounds off or squares his gesture, and in the long run even ends by subtly penetrating the very features of his face. Man ends by looking like his ideal self" (2; 684). *The beautiful is the effect of our discovering the nonrepresented in the represented.* It is, I think, important to see that the artist does not simply discover that the eternal—or the ideal—already exists in the transitory. If that were the case, there would be no tension at all between the two; the artist would simply perceive how perfectly the relative incarnates the eternal, how *adequate* the former is to the latter. In the passage just quoted, Baudelaire speaks of seeing in engravings from the Revolution "the idea" that people then had of the beautiful, and we can translate this to mean their *ideal* of the beautiful. He does not say that man is what he would like to be; rather, he comes to resemble *(finit par ressembler)* what he would like to be. The relation of the ideal to the particular is analogous to that of the eternal to the transitory. The ideal and the eternal are the veiled presence of what the particular or the transitory lacks; they are the form the circumstantial takes in aspiring to be different from itself.

In portraiture, that difference is the space between incomplete and completed individuality. The completing activity, Baudelaire argues in the section "De l'Idéal et du modèle" in the *Salon de 1846,* saves the artist from the errors of both particularization and generalization. A portrait in painting or sculpture should be neither an "exact imitation" nor an "absolute ideal"; "I prefer the *Antinous* to the *Apollo Belvedere* or the *Gladiator,* because the *Antinous* is the ideal of the charming Antinous himself." There is "nothing absolute . . . nothing complete, thus everything has to be completed, and every ideal recaptured." Completion is, then, the idealization of an individual, not the direct rendering of the model but the artist's memory of the world "reconstructed or restored by brush or chisel to the dazzling truth of its native harmony." "Truth" here is a question of correspondences: a certain type of skin requires a certain type of hair, as "such and such a hand demands such and such a foot." The portrait is "an individual put right by an individual *(l'individu redressé par l'individu),*" and this "correction" consists in a *relational re-creation* of the model's body. If "art is a kind of mnemotechny of the beautiful," this is because in memory the artist creates the terms for correspondences, which means that he sees each part of his model's body in relation to other parts.[20] An individual body is completed or idealized (the two are synonymous here) to the extent that it is dematerialized by relations entirely internal to its own structure.

To complete or idealize therefore has nothing to do with that plenitude of presence characteristic of the universal type, the absolute ideal; it seems rather to be a question of "remembering" the model as composed of features each one of which is constantly "aspiring" toward, corresponding with, other features related to it by volume or texture. Art idealizes the model by forgetting the finality of the model's individual traits; without substituting a universal type for an individual, the artist can nonetheless be said to be subverting the notion of individuality by suggesting that an individual, or an individual trait, always tends to be in the space between its own material presence and those other material presences which it both remembers and toward which it projects correspondences. What Baudelaire calls the "broken line" of our "poor *self*" is therefore not straightened to conform to a universal topology of human lines in, for example, the sculpted memory of Antinous.[21] But even the resistant materiality of the Antinous bust suffers—or profits—from a loss of density because it idealizes Antinous's body. And that idealization is the formal eagerness of each of its parts to correspond to other parts. *Aesthetic idealization is the mobilizing of design.*

$$*\qquad\qquad*\qquad\qquad*$$

The Baudelairean aesthetic theorizes a relation to otherness that "Le Peintre de la vie moderne" also discusses as a physical experience of the artist himself. The essay is perhaps best known for its description of the "perfect flaneur"—assimilated here to Constantin Guys as artist—as

> the lover of universal life [who] enters into the crowd as though it were an immense reservoir of electrical energy. Or we might liken him to a mirror as vast as the crowd itself; or to a kaleidoscope gifted with consciousness, responding to each one of its movements and reproducing the multiplicity of life and the flickering grace of all the elements of life. He is an "I" with

an insatiable appetite for the "non-I," at every instant rendering and ex-plaining it in pictures more living than life itself, which is always unstable and fugitive. (9–10; 691–692)

A conscious kaleidoscope: the self's immersion in the nonself strips it down to a pure consciousness of that immersion. The "lover of universal life" enters the crowd not—as Balzac might have said—in order to im-print himself on others, but in order to be carried along by the crowd's "grâce mouvante," to know what Baudelaire calls in the lines preceding this passage the "immense joy [of setting] up house in the heart of the multitude, amid the ebb and flow of movement, in the midst of the fu-gitive and the infinite *(l'immense jouissance que d'élire domicile dans le nombre, dans l'ondoyant, dans le mouvement, dans le fugitif et l'infini)*." The self no longer has its own place; it is "away from home *(hors de soi)*" and yet it feels "everywhere at home"; it is "at the centre of the world" and yet "hidden from the world" (9–10; 691–692). The Baudelairean self is actively aware of its own passivity, even of its own erasure.

What might have been a relatively weak reformulation of a doctrine of empathy becomes a daring identification of aesthetic perception with erotic and divine excess. According to the following fragment from *Mon Coeur mis à nu,* love is inherently prostitution:

> What is love?
> The need to go outside oneself.
> Man is an adoring animal.
> To adore is to sacrifice oneself and to prostitute oneself,
> Thus all love is prostitution.

Adoration can only be understood in terms superficially foreign to it: the lover can be completed *as* a lover only by realizing the ideal of prostitu-tion—of prostitution not as it may or may not be lived by prostitutes, but rather of prostitution purely defined as an unconditional availability to others. Ideally, the prostitute's self is completely circumscribed by the other's desires: the prostituted self would be the wholly adequate re-sponse to the other's demand for love. And such a formulation naturally aspires toward still another completing reformulation: the ideal love to which a particular prostituted love corresponds is God's love for his crea-tures. "The most prostituted being is the Supreme Being *(l'être par excel-lence),* God Himself, since for every individual he is the friend above all others, since he is the common, inexhaustible reservoir of love." [22] From this perspective, God is indefinable not as the consequence of an incom-mensurability of being, but rather for the strictly naturalistic reason that there is nothing to be defined in absolute openness, in an unqualified readiness to take others in.

The prostitute-lover-artist-God series attests to the *power of recurrence* in the universe, or to what might be called an economy of replicative orders. Furthermore, for each term in the series, love is an absolutizing of correspondences between the *moi* and the *non-moi*. And this implies a transgressive extension of the very notion of correspondences, which is no longer limited to either formal analogies or substantive resemblances and which has been stretched to include an identity of being. The prostituted "I" of the artist, the lover, or God corresponds to others not on the basis of similarities or of complementarity but in self-erasure, in *fusion* with others. The difficulty of linguistically describing this fusion is reflected in Baudelaire's hesitation about whether it should be described as "the need to go outside oneself" and an entering into others ("the lover of universal life" penetrates the crowd), or as a taking in of others (God is "the common, inexhaustible reservoir of love," and, in "Le Peintre de la vie moderne," the child—prefiguring the artist—absorbs and is possessed by "the picture of external life" [8; 690]). For Baudelaire, such terminological distinctions are insignificant, for the entering into others is no more an imposition of the subject's will than a passive opening up to others. The Baudelairean artist—as well as the Baudelairean lover and the Baudelairean God—are androgynous not because they share so-called masculine and feminine features, but rather because the very notion of combining features is superseded by a sense of the comparative irrelevance of how movement toward self-erasure is directed (does the subject enter others, or do others enter the subject?).[23] "The most prostituted being" is God, "l'être par excellence"—a formula we can turn around and present as: "l'être par excellence" is the most prostituted being, that is, the ideality of all being (even God's?) is outside all particular being. In aspiring to a state of completeness, creatures (and perhaps even the Creator) reach toward the ultimate difference-from-themselves that is self-effacement. Being manifests its "memory" of perfection by aspiring to nothingness.

Less abstractly, however, Baudelaire is also acutely aware of the risks involved in having an "'I' with an insatiable appetite for the 'non-I.'" In *The Ego and the Id* Freud writes: "The ego is first and foremost a bodily ego; it is not merely a surface entity, but is itself the projection of a surface." In commenting on this passage in *The Freudian Body* I wrote: "the ego is not only, in Freud's mental topography, that part of the mental apparatus most directly influenced by the body's contact with the world, it is also a mental projection of bodily surfaces . . . It fantasmatically repeats the body's contacts with the world in something, perhaps, like metaperceptual structures. The ego is not a surface; it is *a psychic imitation* of surfaces."[24] Baudelaire now suggests to me another way of putting this: the ego is the psychic agency in closest conformity to the body's place in the world. The ego does not simply reflect and monitor our relations with the external world; nor is its function limited to that of submitting mental processes to "reality testing." The ego also imitates a body's boundaries; it is the mental replication of the human organism's limited mastery of the world. The ego's representations of the world conform to, and thereby implicitly recognize, these limitations; the psychic specificity of its *bounded* nature consists in its representational control of stimuli, its capacity to protect itself against stimuli that cannot be placed within a representational structure.

The Baudelairean flaneur-artist's self aims at nothing less than a transgression of the very boundaries of ego representation. And since, of necessity, the *moi* becomes the *non-moi* without ever really leaving itself, the self-prostitution inherent in the Baudelairean artist's contacts with the world is a potentially dangerous overloading of representational circuits. This overloading characterizes the child's absorption of the forms and colors of its environment, an absorption that Baudelaire explicitly connects to the artist's "inspiration." The child, who has weak nerves, risks being overwhelmed by its appetite for otherness. One of Baudelaire's painter-friends remembers the "mixture of amazement and delight *(une stupeur mêlée de délices)*" with which, as a child, he would contemplate his father's muscles, "the gradual transitions of pink and yellow in his skin, and the bluish network of his veins." "The picture of external life was already filling him with awe and taking hold of his brain. He was already being obsessed and possessed by form." Filled with awe, obsessed, possessed: the external sign of this is, in Baudelaire's striking phrase, "the fixed and animally ecstatic gaze of a child confronted with something new, whatever it be, whether a face or a landscape, gilding, colours, shimmering stuffs, or the magic of physical beauty assisted by the cosmetic art." If genius is only "*childhood recovered* at will—a childhood now equipped for self-expression with manhood's capacities and a power of analysis which enables it to order the mass of raw material which it has involuntarily accumulated," it is also true that the abundance of materials to be organized once the self opens up insatiably to the nonself can gravely congest a purely recipient self: "I am prepared to go even further and assert that inspiration has something in common with a convulsion, and that every sublime thought is accompanied by a more or less violent nervous shock which has its repercussion in the very core of the brain" (8; 690–691). Inspiration—the precondition of artistic composition—is a state of painful jouissance.

Baudelaire's description is strikingly similar to Freud's account, in the *Three Essays on the Theory of Sexuality,* of the genesis of sexuality: "It is easy to establish . . . that all comparatively intense affective processes, including even terrifying ones [spill over into] sexuality *(auf Sexualerregung übergreifen)*."[25] What Freud analyzes in the *Three Essays* as the pleasurable-unpleasurable tension of sexual excitement would occur when the body's "normal" range of controllable (structurable, represent-able) stimulation is exceeded, and when the organization of the self is momentarily disturbed by sensations or affective processes somehow be-yond those compatible with psychic organization.[26] As we have seen, Baudelaire himself describes artistic inspiration in exactly the same terms he uses for his definition of love. The self possessed by the external world, or prostituted to others, is shattered into sexuality by what I have called its unconditional availability to otherness. The artist and the child take in the world "with a mixture of amazement and delight," and the perfect flaneur, like the lover, knows the *immense jouissance* of sacrificing the *moi* to the *non-moi*. The Baudelairean aesthetic is inseparable from Baudelairean erotics, and in both jouissance is identical to the masochistic pleasure of self-shattering.[27]

Can it be said that this erotically charged inspirational state is also—to return to my discussion of Freud in Chapter 2—a revival of primary narcissism? The inspired artist's convulsive state and the lover's self-sacrifice and self-prostitution may of course seem incompatible with narcissistic pleasure: far from enjoying the pleasure of self-love, the Baudelairean artist and lover have emptied themselves of a self that might be loved, and their jouissance may be identical to the masochistic ecstasy of a desired failure to resist being overwhelmed by otherness. The con-tradiction may, however, only be apparent. "L'être par excellence," we remember, is also the most prostituted being—as if the ultimate self-completion of particular beings were equivalent to self-effacement. This apparent contradiction might be thought of as a highly sublimated refor-mulation of the suggested identity, in Freud's 1914 essay on narcissism, of self-shattering and self-constitution. According to the reading of Freud proposed earlier, primary narcissism would be the experience of pleasurably shattered consciousness, which has become aware of itself as the object of its desire. An ego is perhaps created by such desire—that is, by the desire to repeat the activity of an eroticized consciousness (instead of merely repeating such specific activities as sucking the mother's breast). In primary narcissism, the infant moves from fragmented objects to totalities, although the ego constituted by that move is "loved" *for its aptitude to be shattered*. A totalizing move (which is also an erotic move) is therefore indistinguishable from the desire to repeat the jouissance of self-fragmentation. The ego of primary narcissism is the psychic assumption necessary for the repetition of the pleasure of autoeroticism, a pleasure now pursued apart from the objects that originally caused it. Baudelairean inspiration is a sublimation of primary narcissism (which is itself an originary sublimation in that it is the first deflection of the sexual instinct from an object-fixated activity to another, "higher" aim). In primary narcissism, however, the new aim remains sexual; it is to repeat the reverberating, pleasurably painful tensions of sexuality. The wholly sexual nature of the originary sublimations is the necessary ground for our view of later sublimations as the investing of ego interests and activities with unrepressed sexual energies. The new *aims* of these later sublimations are nonetheless nonsexual. The pursuit of these aims is narcissistically invested in that there is a libidinal object in sublimation, but it is nothing other than the consciousness pursuing a nonsexual aim.

These Freudian reflections should help us to formulate more explicitly the connection between the Baudelairean notions of artistic inspiration and of the aspiration of particular beings to completed or idealized being. "Il faut tout compléter" is not a sexual aim. Baudelaire appears to locate the tendency to complete, to idealize, or to eternalize in both the artist and his material. The eternal is *in* the relative; creation aspires to perfection, the phenomenal aspires to the noumenal, and that aspiration is what the Baudelairean artist represents in his depictions of modern life. In artistic inspiration, the prostituted self's unreserved openness to the nonself repeats the move toward self-completion (a move, for Baudelaire, inherent in all created being) as the jouissance of being penetrated and possessed by otherness. Constantin Guys does not merely "disengage" impassively the poetic from the historical, the eternal from the transitory; in actively collaborating with the idealizing impulse latent in all the spectacles of modern life, he is also ecstatically "completing himself" by his self-shattering fusions with those spectacles. *The Baudelairean phenomenology of artistic inspiration is an ascetic erotics.* The precompositional work of Guys "setting up house in the heart of the multitude" has the self-sacrificial aim of absorbing, of being shaken and congested by, otherness, and if being can be perfected only by being generalized, which for the lover and the artist means an obliteration of the differences between self and nonself, then absolute narcissistic satisfaction must coincide with an explosion of the self's boundaries. The implicit equivalence in Freud between primary narcissism and the simultaneous constitution and shattering of ego boundaries is, in wholly different terms, anticipated in Baudelaire as the jouissance of a self carried away (both ecstatically transported and removed from itself) by its own prostitution.

What is the place of objects in that jouissance? We should remember that as he travels through "le grand désert d'hommes" looking for subjects for his work, Constantin Guys "has an aim loftier than that of a mere *flâneur,* an aim more general, something other than the fugitive pleasure of circumstance." The *non-moi* by which he allows himself to be penetrated is not exactly identical to the visible aspects of things; he must disengage from their presence the poetic and the eternal. Similarly, a portrait is "a model complicated by an artist," an "idealized model," which is to say the individual "reconstructed and restored by brush or chisel to the dazzling truth of its native harmony." It is not accurate observation of the real that is hindered by too much particularizing and too much generalizing, but rather, Baudelaire significantly says, "memory," or that inner repertory of forms from which, for example, an ancient artist sculpted the ideal Antinous.[28] In a sense, then, the artist's, the lover's, and God's unconditional availability to otherness, their sacrificial prostitution of the self, is an openness to a *non-moi* that they already possess. The correspondences through which objects complete themselves by connecting to related forms are always represented correspondences, correspondences perceived—or, perhaps more accurately, remembered—by a human subject. The overloading of the representational circuit that Baudelaire equates with inspiration is a *reactivation of images* and not, as we at first thought, the invasion of consciousness by external spectacles.

The insatiable appetite of the self for the nonself does indeed destroy an equilibrium, but it is not exactly the equilibrium between the self and the world; it is rather, in Freudian terms, the balance between ego structures and the innumerable (dormant, suppressed, or repressed) representations that are generally not allowed to break through the ego's boundaries. The external stimuli that gravely, and erotically, "shake" us are those that reactivate—faster than they can be mastered—memory traces of other stimuli. The nonself in which a particular self seeks ecstatically to be obliterated is the internally inscribed history of the self's relations with the world. Very strangely, then, the penetration of the artist by "the picture of external life" is also a turning away from all such real scenes; it is a going out of oneself, indeed an uncontrollable breakdown of the very boundaries of selfhood, which is also an exceptional self-expansion, a kind of celebration of the self-as-world, in short a narcissistic jouissance.[29]

*　　　*　　　*

The individual does, however, get lost in that which completes him, even if, as in the case of the poet-lover, it is his own memory. Memory, after all, is filled with images of the nonself; and if we are right to say that poets and lovers turn away from the world of objects in their jouissance, it is also true that they rediscover the nonself *within* the self. It is in themselves that their insatiable appetite for otherness is satisfied; in art and love, the self is penetrated by the alien nature of its own contents, by a world it now remembers having contained. What Freud called the ego can perhaps be thought of as the *individuating containment* of the world. It is—to move to another sense of "contain"—the result of a containing strategy, the creation of inner boundaries, of an inner form, which reduces all that we contain to the psychologically shaped and distinctive space of a particular subjectivity. It is that subjectivity—or, in ordinary usage, that self—which is menaced by the narcissistic self-expansions of love and of art.

To put this in more specifically Baudelairean terms, we could say that *individuation is threatened by correspondences.* The notion of correspondences is a theory of identity: it implies that identities are always relational. Certain perfumes are inadequately defined—imprisoned, unjustly contained—by their own odor; they have, they *are,* the cool freshness of a child's skin and the greenness of prairies. Each sense must go out of itself—in a move of synaesthetic desire—in order to be itself. Swedenborg, Baudelaire writes in an essay on Victor Hugo, "had already taught us that *the sky is a very tall man;* that everything, form, movement, numbers, colors, perfumes, in the spiritual world as in the natural world, is significant, reciprocal, converse, *corresponding.*" "Everything is hieroglyphic"; the poet is "a translator, a decipherer" who draws his images from "the inexhaustible resources of *universal analogy.*"[30] There are moments—such as the first stanza of "Correspondances"—when Baudelaire appears to conceive of correspondences in vertical or, more exactly, symbolic terms. All creation would be an immense book in which God's intentions can be read. In such a system of correspondences, mobility is primarily transcendental. Material objects relate symbolically to spiritual realities; they signify other orders of being. But in many of his theoretical statements, and certainly in most of his poetic practice, Baudelaire suggests something quite different: the horizontal correspondences of a finite universe in which all objects are continuously moving toward and away from one another. They do not simply signify realities that transcend them; rather, they never cease manifesting different types of affinities. Phenomena do not "mean" the other phenomena with which they enter into relation; it is as if each term of an analogy, for example, positioned itself more satisfactorily in the universe—completed itself—by thus contributing to the universe's always shifting designs.

"Universal analogy" perhaps implies a finite universe—or, at the very least, finitude as the accepted limit for our sense-making imagination. Once we "think" the infinite, we posit the possibility of terms that may have no analogy whatsoever to our known terms. Symbolism is a way of constituting a relation with the infinite, a relation that depends, however, on the notion of material reality as the creation of a spiritual reality at once incommensurable with its own creation and yet partially revealed within it. The finite symbol contains the mnemonic trace of its infinite origin. The Baudelairean notion of correspondences can be thought of as a response to the loss of vertical symbolism, of a supernatural dimension in sense-making projects (to which Baudelaire also tenaciously clings). If that loss deprives the world as we know it of transcendental dimensions, it also sets phenomena free for relations now wholly unconstrained by any permanent designs. There is no divine plan to which all relations must ultimately conform; design is always provisional and mobile. Thus loss is an immense analogical gain; the most remote objects and phenomena may eventually be experienced as having at least momentary affinities.

Most dramatically, this involves both an enrichment and a breakdown of the very notion of the human. Benjamin is, I think, referring to this breakdown when he writes that Baudelaire "always avoided revealing himself to the reader." He then cites "the most competent observers" of what he sees as a strategically evasive gesture on Baudelaire's part.

> Gide noticed a very calculated disharmony between the image and the object. Rivière has emphasized how Baudelaire proceeds from the remote word, how he reaches it to tread softly as he cautiously brings it closer to the object. Lemaître speaks of forms which are constituted so as to check an eruption of passion, and Laforgue emphasizes Baudelaire's similes which, as it were, give the lie to the lyrical person and get into the text as disturbing intruders. Laforgue quotes "The night thickened like a partition" ("La nuit s'épaississait ainsi qu'une cloison"), and adds: "A wealth of other examples could be found."

In a note Benjamin gives the following good examples of these "disturbing" intruders:

> Nous volons au passage un plaisir clandestin
> Que nous pressons bien fort comme une vieille orange.
> (We hastily steal a clandestine pleasure
> Which we squeeze very hard like an old orange.)

> Ta gorge triomphante est une belle armoire.
> (Your triumphant bosom is a fine wardrobe.)

> Comme un sanglot coupé par un sang écumeux
> Le chant du coq au loin déchirait l'air brumeux.
> (The distant cock-crow rent the hazy air like a sob stifled by
>   frothy blood.)

> La tête, avec l'amas de sa crinière sombre
>   Et de ses bijoux précieux,
> Sur la table de nuit, comme une renoncule,
>   Repose.
> (The head with the mass of its dark mane and its precious jewels
>   rests on the night table like a ranunculus.)

Baudelaire "is on the lookout for banal incidents in order to approximate them to poetic events," a "linguistic gesture" that Benjamin finds "truly significant only in the allegorist": Baudelaire "took up a profusion of allegories and altered their nature fundamentally by virtue of the linguistic environment in which he placed them." This gave to his writing a quality of "brusque coincidence" that, Benjamin notes, Claudel formulated as the combination of "the style of Racine with the style of a journalist of the Second Empire." Baudelaire "reconnoitred, besieged, and occupied" subjects by this rhetorical putsch in which allegory is juxtaposed with "the most banal word."[31] From our perspective, it is perhaps the psychological simplifications and clarifications of allegory itself that are "besieged" in this putsch. The subject, no longer constrained by a theory of human nature ultimately sanctioned by a Christian metaphysics, is set loose in its newly discovered finite universe and, perhaps most startlingly, discovers its possible affinities with the inanimate.

This is the lesson of the "Spleen" poem beginning *J'ai plus de souvenirs que si j'avais mille ans* (in which Benjamin mainly sees Baudelaire's "empathy with inorganic things," with "matter that has been eliminated from the circulation process"),[32] which includes the following bizarre identifications: the poet is "un gros meuble à tiroirs encombré de bilans, / De vers, de billets doux, de procès, de romances," as well as "un cimetière abhorré de la lune" and "un vieux boudoir plein de roses fanées." It is not merely from economic processes of circulation that the splenetic poet has been removed but, more radically, from the circuit of animate creatures:

> —Desormais tu n'es plus, ô matière vivante!
> Qu'un granit entouré d'une vague épouvante,
> Assoupi dans le fond d'un Saharah brumeux;
> Un vieux sphinx ignoré du monde insoucieux,
> Oublié sur la carte, et dont l'humeur farouche
> Ne chante qu'aux rayons du soleil qui se couche.
>
> Hereafter, mortal clay, you are no more
> than a rock encircled by a nameless dread,
> [dozing deep within the foggy Sahara],
> —an ancient sphinx omitted from the map,
> forgotten by the world, and whose fierce moods
> sing only to the rays of setting suns.[33]

J'ai plus de souvenirs que si j'avais mille ans expresses a mock horror at these new identificatory possibilities. And there is good reason for the poet's ambiguity. First there is not only the new richness of being created by the mobility of horizontal correspondences; there is also something like a new guarantee of order in this ceaselessly mobile world. In the finite universe of horizontal correspondences, there are no unrelated terms. The repertory of forms in this universe is immense but limited; finitude is at least the promise of an inescapable order, the order of total relationality.[34] If, however, we can feel certain that, in and with time, nothing will escape this order, the mobile relations of a finite universe can never be totalized. If relations are continuously being recomposed because they are continuously being broken, they never really add up to anything. Not only does this eliminate the possibility of any deep structural order stabilizing particular relational modes; it also means that identity can never be formulated as anything more than a history of successive relational moves. The individual is a passing or contingent event, an event in which each term's self-completion—its identification with another term—ruins the possibility of an individuating identification.

There are signs in Baudelaire of an attempt to stop, or to deny, all this movement. Thus the nightmare of *J'ai plus de souvenirs que si j'avais mille ans* may be a preliminary strategic move. The poem's relational terms are immobilized but not yet eliminated. It is as if the analogical circuits had broken down, and far from enjoying the lightness of being induced by the *bercements* of desire, the poet is merely burdened by inert alien being. And there would appear to be no individuating distance at all from a series of images that fully constitutes the subject. The poet is not *like* a piece of furniture or a cemetery, he *is* each of those objects; instead of the metaphorical correspondences of "La Chevelure," "L'Invitation au voyage," and "Le Beau Navire," we have a succession of total identifications. We are not moving among related representations (with each term less important than the movement it initiates); rather, in the *Spleen* poem we have a succession of identities that simply pile up. Now the poet is one thing, now another; the first identification hasn't been lost and hasn't propelled him to the second—it has merely been deposited. What I have been describing as the intrinsic insatiability of the *moi* for the *non-moi* has now taken the form of subjectivity as a junkyard or, as one of the poet's own identifications indicates, as the cemetery where the world comes to die.

In what sense are the grim identifications of the splenetic poet a strategic move? What are the profits of immobility? *J'ai plus de souvenirs que si j'avais mille ans* is only one moment in a general pattern of resistance in Baudelaire's perception of subjectivity as mobile correspondences. To have had that perception means to have experienced a certain indistinctness in the boundaries between external reality and the internal world of the subject. It implies the recognition that the very language of "inside" and "outside" obscures the nature of our presence in the world. For on the one hand every human subject is *only* outside in the sense that he or she is nothing but a certain volume in the spaces of the real; and on the other, the world in which we are lost is imprisoned within those representations by which we recognize ourselves. The Baudelairean notion of prostitution—and the related suggestions about a natural tendency toward self-completion and ideality in the particular and the contingent—acknowledge the irreducible ambiguity of this presence and this relation. But Baudelaire is also interested in salvaging a more traditional view of the distinction between subjects and objects, a distinction that gives a kind of plausibility to the idea of individuality—even though the wholly distinct, wholly bounded individual self may be nothing more than an inert collection of transposed and decathected objects.

Thus, for example, the *Journaux intimes* both advance and repudiate the idea of love and art as prostitution. Baudelaire's misogyny is founded on that repudiation, on relegating to woman the "abominable" need to give herself over to her body, to her desires, to others; she is, in short—and the Christian bias of the judgment is of course clear—*merely* natural. "To screw is to aspire to enter into another person, and the artist never goes outside himself." If the artist prostitutes himself, it is, somewhat mysteriously, "in a particular way," for "glory is to remain *one (la gloire c'est rester un)*," and "the man of genius wants to be *one,* thus solitary." "Woman," Baudelaire writes in *Mon Coeur mis à nu,* "is the opposite of the dandy,"[35] but in "Le Peintre de la vie moderne" the dandy is the opposite of the artist, which of course brings abominably natural woman very close to the artist. "The dandy aspires to insensitivity, and it is in this that Monsieur G., dominated as he is by an insatiable passion—for seeing and feeling—parts company decisively with dandyism" (9; 691). If the artist is "an 'I' with an insatiable appetite for the 'non-I,'" the dandy is ruled by "the burning need to create for oneself a personal originality, bounded only by the limits of the proprieties. [Dandyism] is a kind of cult of the self" (27; 710). In order to be "sublime without interruption," the dandy "must live and sleep in front of a mirror."[36]

Dandyism is the bizarre modern form of individualism. No longer sanctioned by the social authority of an aristocracy, the individual—this, at any rate, appears to be the experience of the Baudelairean lover and artist—discovers himself to be a purely psychological myth. The dandy brilliantly refuses to defend that myth. He makes no claims whatsoever for his own interiority, but he forces others to infer, more exactly to create, his uniqueness. And they can't help inferring it *because* there is no sign of it. Dandyism is above all "the joy of astonishing others and the proud satisfaction of never being astonished." The dandy's beauty "consists above all in an air of coldness which comes from an unshakable determination not to be moved; you might call it a latent fire which hints at itself, and which could, but chooses not to burst into flame" (28–29; 710, 712). There is, in short, nothing to be seen in the dandy except the determination not to let anything be seen. In a sense, no one is more prostituted to others than the dandy; his aristocratic individuality depends entirely on how others will interpret his heroically scrupulous erasure of any signs whatsoever of individuality, an erasure that may depend literally on the truly heroic, truly impossible feat of monitoring the movements of one's sleeping body in a mirror. If in their self-prostitution the lover and the artist find themselves dispersed in the images of otherness within them, the dandy—more radically dependent on others—exists only in the astonished fabulations of those he seduces into inventing him.

More interesting than the phenomenon of the dandy, however, is the attention Baudelaire gives to it. The description of dandyism is out of place in "Le Peintre de la vie moderne." It is true that the dandy is one of Constantin Guys's pictorial subjects, but Baudelaire's digressive tribute to the dandy can only operate as a kind of theoretical reserve, perhaps even of theoretical negation in the context of his discussion of Guys's talent and of artistic inspiration in general. The dandy checks that discussion; he opposes to the convulsed, penetrated aesthetic consciousness an image of an ideally closed consciousness, unfathomably different from an external world by which it never allows itself to be possessed. Similarly, *J'ai plus de souvenirs que si j'avais mille ans* opposes its affectless immobility to the indeterminate desiring selves of "La Chevelure," "L'Invitation au voyage," and "Le Parfum" and "Le Cadre" (poems 2 and 3 of "Un Fantôme"). The image of the dandy suggests the fantasized gain in this killing of affect: the gain of an inviolable, unmoved, unique self. But the *Spleen* poem may unintentionally reveal the interiority of dandyism, the unexpected but wholly logical equivalence between the unmoved and bounded self, and a subjectivity oppressively burdened with all that alien debris of being with which it originally designed itself. *J'ai plus de souvenirs que si j'avais mille ans* should perhaps be thought of as the dandy's secret soliloquy.

*   *   *

Far from being an individuating move, the killing of affect produces a reified subject, an "I" exactly identical to the arrested and congealed otherness that gives it its "character." And yet individuation cannot be dismissed as a mere ideological illusion. Our reading of Beudelaire, at any rate, suggests that individuation is a phenomenological certainty, though one that *cannot be represented.* The subject's representations are always representations of otherness. Even more: representation itself may always be an alienating activity. The poet can "speak himself" only by re-presenting the world; but, as the hyphen is meant to indicate here, his images are never presentations of the world but are mnemonic perspectives on, or interprétations of, the world. Is there a mode of subjectivity behind or before these alienated representations, some immediate testimony to the subject's uniqueness?

There is, first of all, the "I" responsible for the artist's craft, the "I" without which inspiration would never become composition. Constantin Guys, it will be recalled, enters the crowd as if he were plunging into "an immense reservoir of electrical energy." Inspiration always "has something in common with a convulsion, and . . . every sublime thought is accompanied by a more or less violent nervous shock which has its repercussion in the very core of the brain." But if this self-shattering is intrinsic to artistic perceptions, it may in fact be inimical to artistic composition. In the poem "Les Sept Vieillards," the poet, unlike the passionate Guys, starts out as the detached spectator of a scene of replicated identity. On a Parisian street he sees seven versions of the same miserably poor and wicked-looking old man. This poem from *Les Tableaux parisiens* can be thought of as allegorizing the indeterminacy of the boundaries between subjects and objects as a procession of exactly identical individuals, each one of whom is both subject and object for all the others. But the poet is shaken out of himself as a result of this spectacle; the final stanzas phenomenologically replay—from the perspective of the poet's shattered consciousness—the allegorical scene. His reason is like a ship crazily tossed about on a sea that has no shore, no boundaries. This of course means that "Les Sept Vieillards" dramatizes the loss of the poet's ability to write a fiction such as "Les Sept Vieillards." Having returned home, the poet can no longer compose himself, can no longer compose. Guys's compositions may be equally threatened by the inspiration that precedes them, and Baudelaire describes the painter's return home as an embattled repetition of his ecstatically convulsed fusion with the crowd. While others sleep, Guys

> is bending over his table, darting on to a sheet of paper the same glance that a moment ago he was directing towards external things, skirmishing with his pencil, his pen, his brush, splashing his glass of water up to the ceiling, wiping his pen on his shirt, in a ferment of violent activity, as though afraid that the image might escape him, cantankerous though alone, elbowing himself on. (12; 693)

The "lover of universal life" has become a duelist. Guys must fight with the paper he draws on if composition is not to be an exact repetition of inspiration. It is of course interesting that the former is nonetheless in a mimetic relation to the latter: Guy looks at his paper as he had looked at the crowd. All the earlier interpenetrations of the *moi* and *non-moi* are repeated: Guy is "cantankerous though alone, elbowing himself on," and if, as Baudelaire continues, "the external world is reborn upon his paper," it is both as it was in itself and yet different from itself: "natural and more than natural, beautiful and more than beautiful, strange and endowed with an impulsive life like the soul of its creator." But now

Guys's congested, shaken consciousness resists; more exactly, from being passively convulsed it has become nervously active. Guys is not drawing from memory; to draw is to reenact the encounter with what is to be drawn. What is represented in the drawing is not scenes from city life, but rather the drama of the artist's and the city's interpenetrations. In a sense, then, to draw is to be inspired again; indeed, it is the state of inspiration that is drawn. The materials of Guys' art—his pen, his brush, his paper—do not merely transmit and receive images; the images themselves are the product of his struggle with those materials. But now the encounter is, precisely, a struggle, a struggle that must end in an ordering of images: "All the raw materials with which the memory has loaded itself are put in order, ranged and harmonized, and undergo that forced idealization which is the result of a childlike perceptiveness—that is to say, a perceptiveness acute and magical by reason of its innocence!" (12; 693–694).

In this inaccurate replication of inspiration that is composition, nothing has been lost. The "childlike perceptiveness" resulting in a "forced idealization" is, as we have already been told, a perception of the *moi*'s correspondence and fusion with the *non-moi*. But within such mobilities and indeterminacies of being, lines have now been drawn. They are not lines separating the subject from the object; rather, within those images where Guys himself never appears as a figure, there are differences, orders, intervals, boundaries that *are* the presence of the *moi* in the *non-moi*. The duelist's jabs impose design on the fusion of being, and in a certain sense they reinstate individuality in the real. But the individuality of Guys's art—perhaps *l'individuel* of all art—is distinct from subjectivity; it is produced by *the appearance of appearances,* by an arresting of correspondences that results in visible forms. Correspondences, because they are thus immobilized and inevitably violated in art, are visible only in art. Art represents the relationality that undoes the privileges and remedies the lost solitariness of psychological individuality, and it offers to our perception and understanding an individuality indifferent to the human subject.

If those traced fusions produce the effect of beauty, then beauty is always sterile, for it is an attribute of metaphysical rather than of physical being. For Baudelaire, the miracle of makeup is that it operates a transfer of ontological register. Eye shadow, he writes in the section on "L'Eloge du maquillage" in "Le Peintre de la vie moderne," by giving to a woman's eye "a more decisive appearance of a window open upon the infinite," removes woman from her abominable natural function of procreation (34; 717). Her individuality is no longer bounded or framed by the biology of a particular body; she is now at once lost in and enriched by an appearance suggesting that it can be "completed" or truly identi-

fied only beyond itself. Baudelaire's first title for *Les Fleurs du mal*—
a title he held on to from 1845 to 1847—was *Les Lesbiennes*. He was
perhaps less interested in the moral melodrama of *femmes damnées* than in
lesbianism as a sexual allegory of ontological replications. On the island
of Lesbos, everything was doubled: no sigh ever remained without an
echo ("jamais un soupir ne resta sans écho"), and:

> Lesbos, terre des nuits chaudes et langoureuses,
> Qui font qu'à leurs miroirs, stérile volupté!
> Les filles aux yeux creux, de leurs corps amoureuses,
> Caressent les fruits mûrs de leur nubilité.
>
> Lesbos, where on suffocating nights
> before their mirrors, girls with hollow eyes
> caress their ripened limbs in sterile joy
> and taste the fruit of their nubility.[37]

But that "sterile joy" is the precondition of a profundity of being. Saphic
narcissism is only secondarily a moral or a psychological phenomenon;
if Baudelaire loves these "poor sisters," as he writes in the "Femmes
damnées" poem beginning *Comme un bétail pensif sur le sable couchées,* as
much as he pities them, it is because they are contemptuous of the real:

> O vierges, ô démons, ô monstres, ô martyres,
> De la réalité grands esprits contempteurs,
> Chercheuses d'infini . . .
>
> Virgins, demons, monsters, martyrs, all
> great spirits scornful of reality,
> saints and satyrs in search of the infinite . . .[38]

In desiring themselves outside themselves, lesbians transform sex from a
biological need to a metaphysical pursuit. Their presumed narcissism, far
from being a defect in their desire, is what frees their love from repro-
ductive servitude, from that multiplication of subjects that we falsely
interpret as the multiplication of *l'individuel.* Lesbianism naturalizes the
metaphysical, and its pathos for Baudelaire may lie in its inescapably
sacrificial destiny. Unable to *produce* anything except an anamolous empirical rendering of an indeterminacy of being, Baudelaire's lesbians experience their sterility as a curse rather than as the sign of unique
privilege: that of being nonreproducible subjects, subjects in search of a
"corresponding" sameness-in-difference that alone can complete them.

So too Baudelaire never sees his relation to his own work as a paternal
one. We can, however, easily imagine an aesthetic modeled on paternity, and Balzac immediately comes to mind as a writer whose work
is guided by such an aesthetic. The structure of Balzac's novels is fundamentally generative: the classical Balzacian exposition teems with the

action and the characters that follow it, whom we can easily recognize as its progeny. The generative nature of this structure is repeated in the Balzacian narrator's relation to his narrative: all the players in *La Comédie humaine* have a family resemblance, and Balzac's characteristically controlling narrative voice—his omniscience, judgments, digressions—makes unmistakably clear who has sired the entire family, from what all-seeing, fertile, and law giving father everyone and everything derives. Nothing is more different from Baudelaire's dispersion in his work, the unfaithful self-repetitions in which we recognize both correspondences to and inconsistencies with other moments in the text. Baudelaire creatively repeats the mobility that is the subject of so much of his writing by trying himself out differently throughout his work. There is the mobility of the erotic poems of *Les Fleurs du mal,* as well as the procession of identities in *J'ai plus de souvenirs que si j'avais mille ans* and "Les Sept Vieillards," and the puzzling, even anguishing shifts of affect between the narrator and the figure he describes in pieces from *Le Spleen de Paris.* More generally, several of the prose poems can be taken as allegorical representations of the notion of correspondences, as their immobilization in uncanny—although in fact, not quite exact—symmetries of being.

Baudelaire exercises no paternal authority over his work; he is, we might say, not even responsible for his own presence in his work. I began this discussion of Baudelaire by drawing attention to a preciosity of rhetoric that places us at a certain distance from the ideas about the relation between the eternal and the transitory in "Le Peintre de la vie moderne." The phrases introducing these ideas create a nervous, reserved persona. We can now better understand a reserve that in no way detracts from the seriousness of the ideas but does tend to deprive them of an unambiguous authorial support, of authorial authority. The tonal distance of this passage—like so many others—might almost lead us to suspect that Baudelaire is elegantly summarizing someone else's ideas, except that it is precisely this impression that makes of Baudelaire's criticism *art.* His presence in "Le Peintre de la vie moderne" is as much a question of relational mobilities as it is in "La Chevelure"—except that in the essay the relations are among concepts and between a narrative voice and those concepts, and in the poem they are among desiring fantasies as well as between the poet's teasing, willful recitation of those fantasies and an apparently compliant lover. In both cases—and this may be even more striking in the critical essays—the aesthetic effect depends on an absence, the absence of a subject as the authoritative source or origin of fantasies and ideas.

Yet an individual is perhaps discernible in this very absence of an authoritative subject. And now I mean *l'individu* and not *l'individuel.* I am no longer speaking of the arresting of correspondences that results in the visible forms, the traced fusions, of art, but rather of the individuality of the psychological subject. Within a pattern of resistance in Baudelaire to his perception of subjectivity as mobile correspondences, the dandy would be his most sophisticated fantasy of inviolable selfhood, a fantasy that includes the killing of affect and the total dependence of the presumably autonomous dandy on the creative admiration of others. The individual subject authenticates itself much more convincingly in the Baudelairean narrator's ironic voice. And that voice is of course heard most frequently in the prose poems, where the narrator's tonal distance from the anecdotes he relates is much more pronounced—much more intentionally an important part of the interest of those anecdotes—than the roughly similar distance of the narrative voice in "Le Peintre de la vie moderne." The latter is a function of relational mobilities—can it be said that the concepts of this essay really belong to the dismissively dilletantish voice that presents them?—but this ironic distancing can also be heard as a personal intrusion. It is, paradoxically, only in this disappearing act that the narrator, as an individual subject, utters himself.

In writing *Le Spleen de Paris,* Baudelaire was fully conscious of the importance of cultivating that voice. "Which of us," he wrote in the dedicatory note to Arsène Houssaye, "has not, on days when he felt most ambitious, dreamt of the miracle of a poetic prose, one that would be musical without rhythm and without rhyme, supple and abrupt enough to adapt itself to the lyrical movements of the soul, the rise and fall of reverie, and the sudden starts of conscience?" "Lyrical movements of the soul" and "the rise and fall of reverie" are not the best terms to describe the allegories of brutality and perversion in *Le Spleen de Paris,* but it is still significant that Baudelaire himself locates the principal interest of his prose poems not in their subject—"the frequenting of enormous cities" merely gave birth to this "obsessive ideal"—but in their demonstration of how the poet's existential truth might be substituted for the externally imposed conventions of rhythm and rhyme.[39] The pedagogical dryness of Baudelairean allegory is, as it were, relieved by the musical prose that is allegory's medium. To call that prose self-conscious would not appear to be saying much for it were it not for the fact that the allegorical message so frequently problematizes the very possibility of self-consciousness. Some of Baudelaire's most impressive achievements in *Le Spleen de Paris*—"Le Vieux Saltimbanque," "Une Mort héroïque," "Assommons les pauvres!"—represent the self as both subject and object, as a replicated or shared consciousness. But our critical attention is at least as occupied with the stylishly ironic presentations of these fables as it is with their allegorical sense. On the one hand, the presentation tends to destroy the credibility of even the most realistic pieces. The believable anecdotes of, for example, "Le Joujou du pauvre," "Les Yeux des pauvres," "La Fausse Monnaie," or "Le Vieux Saltimbanque" take on the appearance of fables as arbitrary and as philosophically exemplary as "Assommons les pauvres!": the narrator is far less interested in the dramatic immediacy of the anecdotes than in absorbing them into a ceremony of recitation. That is, they are worked on as they are presented so that we may see them *at once* not as life but as material for art, as an aesthetic performance. And yet, as in "Le Peintre de la vie moderne," the narrator's very refusal to adhere unambiguously to his material has the effect of transforming the material into a self-expressive speech act. In *Le Spleen de Paris,* the highest aesthetic refinement is exactly equivalent to the utterance of an individual voice.

This may be another way of saying that in each of his prose poems Baudelaire enacts a generic mutation—the novelizing of poetry, a displacement of the aesthetic from an act of representation to the deployment of a perspective. Perhaps nowhere is Baudelaire more modern than in this mutational activity, this tribute to the great literary form of the nineteenth century, a form—as Henry James might have put it— reverberating with interpretations of consciousness. Finally, however, the individuality of the ironic narrative voice of *Le Spleen de Paris* goes no further than its capacity for self-consciousness; it has nothing to express but that. In other words, individuality is a function of self-apprehension. Irony in Baudelaire's prose poems is individuating without being psychologically expressive. The individual subject thus appears in art without violating a fundamental condition of art: that it represent modes of being distinct from particular histories. In the Baudelairean universe of correspondences and fusions, individuation is achieved as the *phenomenon* of a perspective purified of selfhood. In each relational move by which particular individuals "complete" themselves by connecting to the eternal, or the ideal individuals, already within them—more generally, in each move by which the *moi* corresponds to the *non-moi* that it can only ecstatically remember—there is now, perhaps always, an ironic third. There is the subject conscious of those moves, the existential awareness of its own metaphysical supplements—an awareness that, most strangely of all, naturalizes and particularizes the metaphysical itself.

Nietzsche

Art never represents individuals. This premise is central to *The Birth of Tragedy,* although it might also be thought of as running counter to Nietzsche's most celebrated argument in that book. In contrast to "primordial unity," associated with Dionysus—a unity in which the boundaries between individuals as well as between humanity and nature have been erased or, more exactly, have not yet been drawn—there is Apollo, "the glorious divine image of the *principium individuationis,*" which "knows but one law . . . the delimiting of the boundaries of the individual."[40] And it is this individuating principle that "calls art into being"; the Apollonian impulse is an "impulse toward beauty." There is Dionysian art; nonetheless, art is born as a kind of release or discharge of the Dionysian in an Apollonian world of distinct images. And yet Nietzsche—in a move that should remind us of the distinction between what I have called *l'individuel* and *l'individu* in the Baudelairean aesthetic— vehemently warns against any confusion of the individual in art with the subjective. "We know the subjective artist only as the poor artist, and throughout the entire range of art we demand first of all the conquest of the subjective, redemption *(Erlösung)* from the 'ego,' and the silencing of the individual will and desire" (48).[41] Individuality in art does not constitute human subjects. Not only that; it is a major thesis of *The Birth of Tragedy* that the *principium individuationis* is also a *redemptive* principle. Nietzsche's first book—which Nietzsche himself would later call a "questionable book," even "an impossible book" (17, 19)[42]—is a brilliant if at times confused philosophical condensation of the problems we have been considering, more specifically of the relation between the individual (both in the sense of a nonpsychological, relational *individuel* established by correspondences and in that of a constituted self) and the redemptive claims of art. Most startlingly from the perspective of my argument about the authority of art in a culture of redemption, *The Birth of Tragedy* simultaneously attacks that culture and raises the possibility of a metaphysical legitimizing of an aesthetic of redemption.

Nowhere is the apparent paradox of a nonsubjective individuality more evident than in the "I" of the lyric poet. Nietzsche uses the early Greek poet Archilochus—called "the first 'subjective' artist" in contrast to Homer, "the first 'objective' artist"—to raise the question of how the "lyrist" is even "possible as an artist—he who, according to the experience of all ages, is continually saying 'I' and running through the entire chromatic scale of his passions and desires." Nietzsche answers this question by positing a nonrepresentational "I." "In the first place, as a Dionysian artist [the lyrist] has identified himself with the primal unity, its pain and contradiction." We will come back to that "pain and contradiction" (can they be defined?). For the moment I want to focus on the act of identification itself, on the fact that the lyrist "has already surrendered his subjectivity," has given up his "I" before he utters it (48–49). To whom, then, does the lyrist's "I" belong, if indeed it belongs to anyone?

An "inchoate, intangible reflection of the primordial pain" is first of all given in the lyrist's music, which is a "primordial re-echoing," "a repetition and a recast of the world." ("The most important phenomenon of all ancient lyric poetry," Nietzsche writes, is that the ancients "took for granted *the union,* indeed the *identity, of the lyrist with the musician.*") But then that reechoing separates or differentiates itself from that which it repeats; "a second mirroring" is produced that takes the form of "a specific symbol or example *(Gleichniss oder Exempel.)*" The lyrist now sees "his identity with the heart of the world"—an identification from which all individual identity is absent—in "a dream scene that embodies the primordial contradiction and primordial pain, together with the primordial pleasure of mere appearance." The lyrist's "I" is one of the actors in this scene; it helps to constitute a dramatic symbol or example. More exactly, there seem to be two "I"s in the lyrist's work. The first "sounds from the depth of his being"; it is, we might say, the "I" whose nonexistence *as a distinct "I"* the dream scene symbolizes. But there is also a persona within the poem who says "I," a dreaming, passionate figure whose subjectivity, however, is a "fiction" (49). Note that this fiction may or may not be identical to the lyrist's empirical self. Given the fictive nature of *any* "I", there is no representation of the subject that would be more real, more faithful to its referent or origin, than any other representation. Because there is, profoundly, *no* "I," any number of "I"s is possible. Thus the subjective passion of the lyric poet in his poem has no representational obligation whatsoever toward the passions of the poet Archilochus. The "I" within the lyrist's work is not pointed toward the man writing the work, for the latter is no more original than the former. Indeed Nietzsche imagines that the lyric poet may use his empirical self as just one of the images in his poem, an image that is no truer, no more real than any of the others:

> Now let us suppose that among these images he also beholds *himself* as non-genius, i.e., his subject, the whole throng of subjective passions and agitations of the will directed to a definite object which appears real to him. It might seem as if the lyric genius and the allied non-genius were one, as if the former had of its own accord spoken that little word "I." But this mere appearance will no longer be able to lead us astray, as it certainly led astray those who designated the lyrist as the subjective poet. For, as a matter of fact, Archilochus, the passionately inflamed, loving, and hating man, is but a vision of the genius, who by this time is no longer merely Archilochus, but a world-genius expressing his primordial pain symbolically in the symbol of the man Archilochus—while the subjectively willing and desiring man, Archilochus, can never at any time be a poet. It is by no means necessary, however, that the lyrist should see nothing but the phenomenon of the man Archilochus before him as a reflection of eternal being; and tragedy shows how far the visionary world of the lyrist may be removed from this phenomenon which, to be sure, is closest at hand. (50–51)

Nietzsche's discussion of all this is far from unambiguous. The "world-genius expressing his primordial pain symbolically in the symbol of the man Archilochus" is, in the sentence preceding the paragraph just quoted, also called "the only truly existent and eternal self *(Ichheit)* resting at the basis of things." This is presumably a nonsubjective self, one present in all the lyrist's images, images that are "only different projections of himself, so he, as the moving center of this world, may say 'I'" (50). But all the figures of any dramatic literary work are "only different projections" of the author's self, that is, of his subjective self. Self-dispersal is not necessarily the sign of a nonsubjective "I." Nietzsche's argument is weakened by his attempt to imagine and to favor a nonsubjective self, the lyrist's real self, the self "resting at the basis of things." For the main thrust of his argument is that there can be no self at the basis of things. The problem might be defined as a linguistic one. Language itself is part of the symbolic dream scene; it already belongs to, indeed may constitute, a register of being that posits a self alien to the selfless being at "the heart of the world." What Nietzsche calls an "I" from the depths of the lyrist's being is not an "I," but a condition of being to which the very possibility of naming a delimited subject is absolutely alien. But even by saying this we of course demonstrate the possibility of a kind of critical transcendence of language by language (a transcendence implicitly designated but not performed by Nietzsche here), in which, first of all, the anomalous use of "I" referred to would be recognized. Even more crucially, that critical move would allow us to see the problematic status of what Nietzsche presents as an example and as a symbol (perhaps more accurately, simile: *Gleichniss*), or "a reflection of eternal being." The principal difficulty he faces is to imagine how one order of being can reflect or exemplify or be like a wholly different order of being. For the symbol here is by its very nature (as a distinct, individual image) incommensurable with the nonindividuated being it is said to symbolize.[43]

There is, as we shall see, perhaps another way to formulate this passage from primal being to the world of phenomena. The interest of the section I am discussing lies in the claim it makes for the purely contingent nature of subjectivity both in and outside art. A self is always an image or a fiction, and while Nietzsche seems more comfortable making this argument by opposing "the man Archilochus" to Archilochus as world-genius or as "the only truly existent and eternal self resting at the basis of things," his definition of "the basis of things" should lead us to conclude that images of the self never refer to an identity. There is no identity at the basis of things. And the lyrist as a persona in his poems recognizably different from the lyrist's real self is actually no more of a fiction than the lyrist himself. The latter is nothing more than the phenomenon "closest at hand," but no less of a phenomenon for that. Life, then, has no special authority as the referent of art. And while Nietzsche makes immense claims for art, art also loses its traditional authority as a superior version of life.[44] Or, rather, art *is* superior to life, but life itself can be viewed as art, and this superiority has to do with a certain superficiality or lack of reality. Life and art are both fictions; what we will have to see is how a certain type of fiction can be redemptive.

Both art and life *as* art are superior to "the subject, the willing individual that furthers his own egoistic ends" and that "can be conceived of only as the antagonist, not as the origin of art." Art teaches us nothing and does not improve us; as moral and psychological subjects, we can't even claim to be the creators of works of art. Human pride claims that art mirrors—and reveals the profound sense of—human existence. Nietzsche, on the other hand, strips art of everything except its relation to the metaphysical. And that relation has nothing profound about it; it consists in the reduction of phenomena to the status of mere images and "artistic" projections for the true author at the basis of things, for the primal unity. Nietzsche's original and intricate move here is to make a claim for the metaphysical nature of art (and, consequently, for the metaphysical significance of life viewed *as* art) by eliminating all meaning from art beyond its mere appearance as projected images. It is at once humbling and exalting for human beings to realize that their existence can have no greater dignity than to be simplified (desire and will are gone, the moral life is gone, knowledge is gone) to a merely metaphysical sense. All this is said in one of the most famous passages of *The Birth of Tragedy:*

> For to our humiliation *and* exaltation, one thing above all must be clear to us. The entire comedy of art is neither performed for our betterment or education nor are we the true authors of this art world. On the contrary, we may assume that we are merely images and artistic projections for the true author, and that we have our highest dignity in our significance as works of art—for it is only as an *aesthetic phenomenon* that existence and the world are eternally *justified*—while of course our consciousness of our own significance hardly differs from that which the soldiers painted on canvas have of the battle represented on it. (52)

*   *   *

How do we become art? And, in art, what is the metaphysical individual, the individual whose psychological and moral attributes have no significance? In his reading of Greek tragedy, Nietzsche dismisses all interpretations based on the idea of its cathartic effect or the hero's tragic flaw:

> Never since Aristotle has an explanation of the tragic effect been offered from which aesthetic states or an aesthetic activity of the listener could be

inferred. Now the serious events are supposed to prompt pity and fear to discharge themselves in a way that relieves us; now we are supposed to feel elevated and inspired by the triumph of good and noble principles, at the sacrifice of the hero in the interest of a moral vision of the universe. I am sure that for countless men precisely this, and only this, is the effect of tragedy, but it plainly follows that all these men, together with their interpreting aestheticians, have had no experience of tragedy as a supreme *art*. (132)

Oedipus' pride, for example, is ethically neutralized by Nietzsche. Sophocles' hero is guilty neither of parricide and incest nor of an arrogant confidence in his own wisdom or in his ability to escape his predicted fate. It is Oedipus' wisdom itself that is his "crime," but the crime is not a moral one. "The myth seems to whisper to us that wisdom . . . is an unnatural abomination," but this remains an extremely enigmatic statement of ethical norms (except in the vague and moralistic sense that wisdom encourages unnatural and destructive pride), unless we interpret it, as Nietzsche does, to mean that wisdom violates the conditions that allow for creation. In Oedipus' case, wisdom is of course associated with riddle solving and with "prophetic and magical powers [that] have broken the spell of present and future." Prophecy and magic do not trivialize the notion of wisdom; on the contrary, they can be thought of as its highest forms. Far from being content with a passive understanding of the boundaries and constraints imposed on human existence, true wisdom knows how to lift those constraints, to overstep those boundaries. The wisdom that merely comprehends boundaries is second-best, the prize given to the defeated. The wisdom of prophets and magicians, on the other hand, includes knowledge that time itself—"the spell of present and future"—has made impossible. It has thus broken "the rigid law of individuation," which in this context refers not to human individuation but to the articulation of the eternal itself into temporal succession (68).

This kind of wisdom—which Nietzsche calls "Dionysian wisdom" because it tends to collapse difference back into the primordial unity—is the "unnatural abomination." Such knowledge—and there is hardly any rhetorical exaggeration here—"plunges nature into the abyss of destruction," into a *simultaneity* ontologically incompatible with creation. Such a sage must therefore "suffer the dissolution of nature in his own person"—in the case of Oedipus, the crimes of parricide and incest. Those crimes are, from the Nietzschean perspective, identical to the crime of knowledge (he speaks of "some enormously unnatural event—such as incest—[which] must have occurred earlier, as a cause," but perhaps also as a corollary of the "prophetic and magical powers" manifested in Oedipus' life). In particular, incest, like prophecy, violates "the rigid law of individuation"; it is a denial of separateness, a return to the original oneness of two. Oedipus' sexual union with his mother is a "dissolution of nature in his own person," not merely in the sense of a violation of "the most sacred natural orders" but—more literally, more corporeally—a dissolving of the boundaries of his distinct being in this fusion with the (m)other (68–69).

The Oedipus plays give us "the glory of passivity," but it is "the story of activity" that illuminates Aeschylus' *Prometheus* (69). Still Nietzsche interprets the two heroes in essentially similar ways. Prometheus' crime can also be said to be against the law of individuation, but now the crime is one of deed rather than of consciousness. It is the power of Oedipus' mind that is transgressive; prophecy and magic are knowledge no longer constrained by the conditions of created being. Prometheus, on the other hand, steals fire, which might be called a transgression of spatial individuation. "The presupposition of the Prometheus myth is to be found in the extravagant value which a naive humanity attaches to *fire* as the true palladium of every ascending culture. But that man should freely dispose of fire without receiving it as a present from heaven, either as a lightning bolt or as the warming rays of the sun, struck these reflective primitive men as sacrilege, as a robbery of divine nature" (71). There is an interesting if primitive reflection here: since I see fire in the heavens, it must belong there, and if I appropriate it for the earth, the universe might no longer be recognizable. This is not the sophisticated Sophoclean sense of a possible and dangerous incommensurability of mind with creation, the sense of mind as so powerful that it will overturn the very conditions of knowledge in creation. The Aeschylean intuition of a collapse of boundaries is almost entirely perceptual: to bring the attributes of the sun to the earth is to attack the clarity of the most fundamental distinction in our universe.

Rather than seeing Oedipus and Prometheus as individuals, Nietzsche considers them as participants in dramas *about individuation*. Now to the extent that the impulse to art is identified with the Apollonian in Nietzsche's first book, his subject—the birth of tragedy—is a somewhat paradoxical illustration of his central argument. Tragedy works against the *principium individuationis*. "In the heroic effort of the individual to attain universality, in the attempt to transcend the curse of individuation and to become the *one* world-being, he suffers in his own person the primordial contradiction that is concealed in things, which means that he commits sacrilege and suffers" (74). It is important to remember this when we read the famous passages in *The Birth of Tragedy* about the Apollonian state as the reposeful contemplation of individual forms, of redemptive appearances. It is true that the Dionysian chorus "discharges itself in an Apollinian world of images." On the other hand, "being the objectification of a Dionysian state," Greek tragedy "represents not Apollinian redemption through mere appearance but, on the contrary, the shattering of the individual and his fusion with primal being. Thus the drama is the Dionysian embodiment of Dionysian insights and effects and thereby separated, as by a tremendous chasm, from the epic" (65). We will have to understand how, from a Dionysian perspective, individuation is *both* redemptive and "the primal cause of evil" (74). Oedipus and Prometheus are the symbolic appearances through whom Apollo "interprets to the chorus its Dionysian state:"

> In truth, however, the hero is the suffering Dionysus of the Mysteries, the god experiencing in himself the agonies of individuation, of whom wonderful myths tell that as a boy he was torn to pieces by the Titans and now is worshiped in this state as Zagreus. Thus it is intimated that this dismemberment, the properly Dionysian *suffering,* is like a transformation into air, water, earth, and fire, that we are therefore to regard the state of individuation as the origin and primal cause of all suffering, as something objectionable in itself.

The tragic myth simultaneously punishes the transgression of boundaries and holds out the promise of "a rebirth of Dionysus," that is, "the end of individuation." From this perspective, individuation is an original Fall, the fall into creation itself. And perhaps the most profound interpretation Nietzsche proposes of Greek tragedy is not that it warns humanity against the temptation to transcend the individual, but rather that—given the fundamental knowledge it embodies "of the oneness of everything existent"—individuation is a crime against Being and that, the fate of the tragic hero notwithstanding, Greek tragedy encourages "the joyous hope that the spell of individuation may be broken in augury of a restored oneness" (74).[45]

Redemption, then, may be a two-way street. Yet if redemption is both through and from individuation, it is achieved neither by nor for individuals. Nietzsche is, I think, describing a movement between the physical and the metaphysical, and the difficult notion of an ontological redemption will be intelligible only if we rigorously banish not only the category of subjective selfhood but also that of art as symbolic or exemplary. The very use of Dionysus as the mythic incarnation of oneness corrupts the notion of the Dionysian itself with a mythologically delimited figure. Thus a oneness that by its very nature cannot be figured is named Dionysus or, as we have seen, is referred to as "the only truly existent and eternal self resting at the basis of things," as a "world-genius" or "the only truly existent subject" or the "primordial artist of the world." Having thus figured the Dionysian, Nietzsche can speak of the heroes of

Greek tragedy as "symbolic appearances" of Dionysus—as if a distinct figure could symbolize or project that which is not a transcendence of it but which can be understood only as its annihilation.[46]

Indeed, Nietzsche's discussion of Greek tragedy suggests something far more interesting than a view of Oedipus and Prometheus as symbols of the Dionysian. As Nietzsche was to say in his critical preface to the 1886 edition of *The Birth of Tragedy*—and it is said in order to indicate what he still admires in the book—"art, and *not* morality, is presented as the truly *metaphysical* activity of man" (22). If we are to take that claim seriously—and it is the conceptual foundation on which the relation between the Apollonian and the Dionysian is built—then we must say that art is not symbolic or illustrative of metaphysical reality; rather it *constitutes* that reality. It is only in art, or as art, that the human subject becomes a metaphysical being. The interpretation of art is, then, a commentary on metaphysics. And this is precisely the mode in which Nietzsche reads Greek tragedy. Oedipus and Prometheus enact the improbability of their own confinement within the names and figures of Oedipus and Prometheus. Their lack of measure *is* the metaphysical dimension of consciousness; through them, Sophocles and Aeschylus represent what might be called the affinities of consciousness with realities beyond the subjectivity and the place that contain consciousness but that consciousness always exceeds. They represent, in other words (to return to a Baudelairean vocabulary), those correspondences through which the "I" loses itself in the "non-I."

Nietzsche philosophically relocates what an ethical criticism would call the pride of the tragic hero as a morally neutral violation of the boundaries of being. The only function of the ethical from the Nietzschean perspective is as an imperfect metaphor for the incompatibility of those violations with the conditions of individuation. It is not moral laws that govern the universe, but rather ontological contradictions, contradictions inevitably appropriated by the all too available language of moral laws. If these contradictions can be represented only in art (and not in a treatise on metaphysics), this is because the metaphysical itself can only be enacted as a representation—not as a symbolic representation but as that of a *figure dissolving its own figured state*. The figures of art are necessary for their always imminent immolation in the fusions and simultaneities of being that can never be figured in art.

*   *   *

The metaphysical in Nietzsche's argument is thus always played or performed in a drama of individuation. But I have been giving a biased view of Nietzsche's metaphysical aesthetic by leaning so heavily on his own major example. The "world of images" in art is always an Apollonian world, even though, as in Greek tragedy, that world does not represent "redemption through mere appearance but, on the contrary, the shattering of the individual and his fusion with primal being" (65). Music may be essentially Dionysian, which means that—especially in "the emotional power of the tone, the uniform flow of the melody, and the utterly incomparable world of harmony" (40)—it is "a repetition and a recast of the world," a "copy of this primal unity" (49). But inasmuch as the impulse to articulation is central to all art, then art must be considered as the highest—most deliberate and most developed—manifestation of the Apollonian. In his 1886 preface, Nietzsche defines the "artists' metaphysics" in *The Birth of Tragedy* as positing "a 'god,' if you please, but certainly only an entirely reckless and amoral artist-god who wants to experience, whether he is building or destroying, in the good and in the bad, his own joy and glory—one who, creating worlds, frees himself from the *distress* of fullness and *overfullness* and from the *affliction* of the contradictions compressed in his soul" (22). This is indeed "artists' metaphysics" in that the account it gives of the creation of the universe is an inference from the human creation of works of art. In art, created being is implicitly defined as a redemptive release from "overfullness."

The anthropomorphic projection of this meaning in art onto the creation of the universe is not a way of affirming some original Creation, but is perhaps the only means of designating the metaphysical nature of artistic sense. The transcendental inference should be thought of as a metaphysical metaphor, which allows us to visualize the deeply ambivalent impulse to appearance that is the significance and the subject of art. Art in fact confirms the nonnecessity of the divine in the constituting of a metaphysical dimension; the imagination of fusions and correspondences irreducible to individual identities is the phenomenon of a human consciousness perhaps inherently unsituated, unlocated. The Apollonian is the impulse to save consciousness from the nonidentity, the overfullness of those fusions, of an always potential oneness of being. In Nietzsche's terms, "primal unity" *needs* "rapturous vision" or "pleasurable illusion" or "mere appearance." Apollo is "the apotheosis of the *principium individuationis,* in which alone is consummated the perpetually attained goal of the primal unity, its redemption through mere appearance *(das ewigerreichte Ziel des Ur-Einen, seine Erlösung durch den Schein)*" (45).

We can perhaps interpret this to mean that the *principium individuationis* rescues consciousness from the distress of nonidentity. But it is important to see that this individuation is as metaphysically conceived as its complementary and menacing oneness. Individuation, far from being a return to the empirical, is an affirmation of the individual *in spite of* the empirical. The individual cannot be characterized; it is actually the activity of "delimiting the boundaries of the individual, *measure* in the Hellenic sense." It is true that this measure has its moral corollaries: "Apollo, an ethical deity . . . requires self-knowledge," makes the demands "know thyself" and "nothing in excess" (46). In its essence, however—as an aesthetic principle—the *principium individuationis* enacts nothing more than the possibility of bounded being. It separates; it delimits. And this is the source of aesthetic calm, of that "will-less contemplation" which "the strictly Apollonian artists" evoke in us (130). "Apollo wants to grant repose to individual beings precisely by drawing boundaries between them" (72). Because the source of that repose is in the perception of the boundaries, Apollonian individuality is unrelated to the individuals who, aesthetically, are merely traced by the drawing of those boundaries.

In our response to characters in literature or to human figures in painting and sculpture, we must therefore be like the epic poet who can enjoy Achilles' "angry expression . . . with the dreamer's pleasure in illusion," precisely because "even the image of the angry Achilles is only an image to him" (50). We might extend the logic of Nietzsche's thought and say that the angry Achilles—Achilles as a particular psychological subject—is already too general to serve as a representation of the *principium individuationis*. Indeed, the most profound characteristic of the psychological and the moral—which may be why they have been privileged in a long "anti-Nietzschean" aesthetic tradition—is their aptitude for being universalized. The psychological and the ethical self, however carefully it may be particularized by the artist, is easily recognizable as a communal, even universal self. It has traits that all men and women may recognize, and while this has often been presumed to be the sign of great achievement in aesthetic characterization, it is for Nietzsche what disqualifies "character" as an aesthetic phenomenon. The self must be erased for the Apollonian individual to be perceived. The Apollonian in art is the condition of possibility of the empirical; it is at once a release from the overfullness of undifferentiated being and a rejection of the always imminent generality of psychological and ethical character. It is as if we could *see pure demarcation*. Thus—and quite paradoxically—the Apollonian is, like the Dionysian (but for wholly different reasons), a threat to appearances—a threat to that in which it is grounded. Since all particular figures are potentially generalizable, for the absolutely individual to appear we must see only the boundaries that trace figures or, even more problematically, the appearances of figures divorced from their content.

*   *   *

In what sense is the *principium individuationis* redemptive? "Art," Nietzsche writes, "is not merely imitation of the reality of nature but rather a metaphysical supplement of the reality of nature, placed beside it for its overcoming *(ein metaphysisches Supplement des Naturwirklichkeit . . . zu deren Ueberwindung neben sie gestellt)*" (140). Art does not refer to life; it supplements it. That supplement should not, however, be understood as a correction. The later sections of *The Birth of Tragedy* analyze a profound mistake "that first saw the light of the world in the person of Socrates: the unshakable faith that thought, using the thread of causality, can penetrate the deepest abysses of being, and that thought is capable not only of knowing being but even of correcting it" (95). Nietzsche attributes this illusion to the "theoretical man," but it is obviously relevant not only to the history of philosophy but also to the ways in which we have been trained to think of art. In a view of art as a superior version of life—superior by virtue of the form and significance it presumably discovers in the life it imitates—art is enslaved to the objects it also annihilates and transcends. Art redeems the catastrophes of experience—of individual and collective histories—by the violence of its symbolic reconstructions of experience.

This redemptive aesthetic is inherently sacrificial, as we can see if we reread tragedy from a non- (even anti-) Nietzschean perspective. (And though I have of course been arguing for Nietzsche's interpretation, the spirit of Nietzschean thought requires that we entertain the most antagonistic theories as corresponding to the shifting appearances of sense within, for example, Greek tragedy.) The tragic hero—and we might include here not only Oedipus but also Lear, Othello, and Racine's Phèdre—dies (or loses his worldly power) at the moment of self-comprehension. He is sacrificed to his understanding of himself. Oedipus' life is simultaneously destroyed and corrected by his knowledge of that life. A catastrophic error or defect is somehow made up for by the hero's (the victim's, the sinner's) consciousness of his defect. Life is redeemed by an act of cognition. And as spectators, we are purified—vicariously purged of life itself—by this ascension into knowledge, an ascension that rescues us from the hero's tragic fate. This is the ethical reading of tragedy that Nietzsche scornfully rejects when, in a passage quoted earlier, he refers to "the sacrifice of the hero in the interest of a moral vision of the universe." To see the hero in this way is to "react merely as moral beings when listening to a tragedy" (132).

From this perspective, the life of the tragic hero also traces a familiar theory of sublimation. The relation of the wise blind Oedipus to his catastrophic existence metaphorically theorizes the relation of this tragedy, and of all art, to life. In Kleinean terms, sublimations are symbolic reparations of damaged experience; they are spectral replications of experience, entirely bound to the shattering and shattered fantasies they repair, but at the same time liberated from those fantasies by virtue of repeating them as knowledge, without affect. Fundamentally, what needs to be repaired in those fantasies are the individual identities they have shattered. The projections, introjections, and identifications studied by Klein gravely problematize the formation of a bounded ego; what she called the restitutive tendencies of sublimation are tendencies to give back to the subject—and to the objects of the subject's love and hatred—their securely traced boundaries. The redemptive role of knowledge—its ethical value—is thus inseparable from a primarily cognitive and adaptive view of ego formation that, as we have seen, is implicitly repudiated by Freud's hypothesis, at the beginning of his essay "On Narcissism," of egoconstitution as identical to egoshattering. In this view, sublimation, precisely because it is an ego activity, must be a sexualizing activity. The constitution of psychic boundaries originates as the narcissistic project of reliving a self-shattering jouissance incompatible with psychic boundaries. But this, as I have argued in Chapter 2, is denied in Freud's later theory of the ego. The repudiation of his own hypothesis is reinforced by a view of the ego's desexualization as that which makes it worthy of the superego's approval. So too the ego activities of sublimation are defined as desexualizing activities, thus counteracting that other view of sublimation (outlined most explicitly toward the end of chapter 1 in Freud's book on Leonardo da Vinci) according to which cultural symbolizations are always invested with unrepressed sexual energy.

In these later Kleinean and Freudian views of sublimation, as in the aesthetic I have outlined on the basis of an anti-Nietzschean reading of the tragic hero's fate, art and cultural symbolizations in general are the work of an ego purified of its dependence on the body. The hero's death is the dramatic figure for this purifying sacrifice. As Proust's narrator suggests, only by dying can he truly begin to live—to live, that is, as a uniquely aesthetic self. Thus the redemptive aesthetic posits—like the aesthetic of *The Birth of Tragedy*—a constitutive link between art and individuation. But, unlike the Nietzschean version of this, the Proustian and psychoanalytic versions of the individual in art (an individual both responsible for artistic creation and represented in works of art) are visions of the *empirical self cognitively and morally perfected* rather than of the individual as the metaphysical articulation and differentiation of being. In the culture of redemption, the passage into art is a ritual of sacrificial transcendence.

In the Nietzschean aesthetic, on the other hand, redemption should probably be understood as a kind of release of being rather than as a moral rehabilitation. The "pleasurable illusion" given to us by Apollo is that being is commensurate with appearance. "I feel myself impelled,"

Nietzsche writes, "to the metaphysical assumption that the truly existent primal unity, eternally suffering and contradictory, also needs the rapturous visions, the pleasurable illusion, for its continuous redemption" (45). This can be reformulated as a phenomenon of consciousness with which our study of Baudelaire has made us familiar. "Primal unity" would express an intuition of consciousness about being: the intuition that being consists of mobile fusions and correspondences—or, in other terms, that being is not reducible to identities. Consciousness itself would be both the subject and one of the objects of this "understanding"; it would, as it were, know the difference between itself and the subjectivity to which it is bound. Each "I" would lodge an intrinsically universal "non-I," a "non-I" that would "be" nothing but its continuously shifting contacts, affinities, and positions. It is perhaps consciousness as untraceable correspondences that needs the unique cognitive release of the *principium individuationis*. This release cannot be provided by the subjectivity with which consciousness is already too familiar. Subjectivity is, on the one hand, too restrictive (too exclusively human) an individuating principle to provide the necessary guarantee of *l'individuel* in the universe and, on the other, not individual enough by virtue of the generalizable nature of psychological and ethical attributions. What saves (or releases, redeems) consciousness from its inability to posit an identity for itself is not an identity *for consciousness* (which could perhaps only be a subjectivity) but rather a kind of visionary (necessarily nonperceptual) experience of traces, lines, demarcations.

Yet lines delineate forms, and forms, as Baudelaire suggests, always move toward those other forms with which they correspond. The *principium individuationis* is therefore not exactly a formalizing principle. It stops operating before forms are solidified; it can be nothing more than *the appearing of their appearance*. What is absolutely individual dies at the moment of being defined; what Apollo give us is not definite forms but rather, as Nietzsche says over and over again, "mere appearance *(Schein)*." The redemptive power of the Apollonian is indissociable from its impoverished nature. The poet's, and our, "rapturous vision" is not of the too defined character of Achilles (a character is always too defined) but rather of a denuded Achilles, an Achilles stripped of selfhood, Achilles as the pure appearing of the individual that is the condition of possibility of the character Achilles.

But how can we see such appearing? We cannot. It is nothing but an illusion, appearance *as* illusion, illusory because it appears. What I have interpreted as the appearing of appearance can never give us the evidential security encouraged (if not really authorized) by perceived forms. It is something that had to take place without ever taking place; it is, exactly, the *principle* of individuation in which all individual forms are grounded.

This, Nietzsche suggests, is what art deceives us into thinking we see. Art saves us from the distress of overfullness not by the perhaps equally distressful variety of its individual figures, but by making those figures somewhat doubtful—by partially derealizing them, by moving them back to that stage of being where they are nothing more than a kind of impersonal confidence in the possibility of their realization.

In this ascetic triumph of the individual as merely the appearing of appearance, Apollo is poor. Redemption, as I have said, turns out to be a two-way street. Nietzsche insists so often on the primal unity's need for redemption through appearance that we may underestimate the importance of his claim that the Dionysian, or "intoxicated reality," "seeks to destroy the individual and redeem him by a mystical feeling of oneness" (38). The highest effect of Greek tragedy is one "that transcends *all Apollinian artistic effects*. In the total effect of tragedy, the Dionysian predominates once again." The spectator "sees the tragic hero before him in epic clearness and beauty, and nevertheless rejoices in his annihilation" (130–131). Mere appearance is redeemed by the fullness of primal unity, by undifferentiated being. The individual figure in art is, then, menaced both by the *principium individuationis* that reduces it to the possibility of appearance itself and by a Dionysian yearning for ever mobile fusions. Like the Apollonian, but for wholly different reasons, the Dionysian makes the identity of figures doubtful—because each figure, even while staying in place, is somewhat departicularized as it designates its correspondences with a magnetic field of other figures. The Dionysian saves us from the redemptive illusion of the individual; it cancels out, and redeems, Apollo's crime of cutting into being, of defiguring it with figures, with lines and forms.

Can it be, finally, that this return to the Dionysian is a way of mythologizing the self-shattering that is the consequence of narcissistic self-contemplation? Let us end with a speculation by no means authorized in *The Birth of Tragedy:* it is the "rapturous vision" of the Apollonian that shatters Apollonian calm. And let us consider this speculation as a psychoanalytically inspired homage to Nietzsche's own repudiation, later in his life, of the idea of art as inspiring "pure contemplation devoid of interest" (48). Psychoanalysis reformulates the Nietzschean tension (it is not an opposition) between the Dionysian and the Apollonian as the inevitable movement in the human subject between the self-shattering jouissance of the sexual and the desexualizing tracing of an ego's boundaries. But if the ego is originally constituted in order to be shattered, then the ego's consciousness of its boundaries may always include the possibility of a boundless self-interest that will explode boundaries. This interest is not a *desire for* something; it is a desire *to be* with an intensity that cannot be contained—held in or defined—by a self. In a sense, such desire is indeed characterized by a disinterestedness generally associated with art. But this disinterestedness is the sign not of a lack of affect but rather of a drive so pure that it covets no objects. If it is true that "Apollo wants to grant repose to individual beings precisely by drawing boundaries between them," the reposeful contemplation of those boundaries perhaps necessarily generates the intoxicated distress of the Dionysian. The Apollonian pleasure in boundaries is of course a specular pleasure: the rapturous vision of the *principium individuationis* at work in art confirms, for a time, the bounded nature of the enraptured consciousness, its own singleness. But it is precisely that pleasure, that rapture, which signals the annihilation of the individual in the painful ecstasy of the Dionysian. Our "rejoicing" in the tragic hero's annihilation is our participation in jouissance, the sign of our truly disinterested (and aesthetic) readiness, as Nietzsche writes, to silence "the individual will and desire." Yet the silencing is the effect of a narcissistic passion, although the effect of this passion may be to destroy its object. Art plays with these boundaries—to the point even of reflecting upon that play in its moves along the boundaries between the bounded and the unbounded. It is, then, these risks of disappearance and of appearance—the risk of a dying at once more insignificant and infinitely more consequential than our personal death—that we accept when we "enter" art.

CHAPTER 4

Literature and History:
Malraux and Bataille

What is literature's responsibility toward history? And how have writers expressed, or possibly repudiated, the idea of a relation between the imaginary and the historical? In order to begin answering these questions, I will be looking at two modern novels that refer to some of the most dramatic political events of our century: André Malraux's *La Condition humaine* and Georges Bataille's *Le Bleu du ciel*. Malraux's novel—which takes place mainly in Shanghai in 1927—documents an especially critical moment in modern Chinese history, the break between Chiang Kai-shek and his Communist allies in their common revolutionary struggle. The political contexts of *Le Bleu du ciel* are at least as highly charged: the year is 1934, we have several images of a recently triumphant Nazism, and about half the novel takes place in Barcelona on the eve and day of a workers' insurrection. But while Malraux's characters are thoroughly committed revolutionaries or counterrevolutionaries, Bataille's protagonists—with the exception of the rather brutally satirized leftist woman Lazare—seem either only remotely aware of the momentous events taking place around them or, in the case of the novel's central figure (and narrator) Troppmann, their political interests seem limited to a cynical observation of the political interests of others (especially those of the dirty, cadaverous virgin Lazare). *Le Bleu du ciel* appears to be a wholly personal account of what Troppmann calls the unhappiest period of his life, a year that coincidentally is one of great fascist and communist unrest in Europe, whereas *La Condition humaine* is about people whose most intimate consciousness of themselves seems almost indistinguishable from their political passions.

But just how political *is* Malraux's celebrated novel? Malraux gives us, several years before Sartre formulated the concept, an image of the irreproachably engagé writer, of that historically conscious and responsible novelist capable of rescuing fiction from what Sartre was to analyze as the corrupting essentialism of fiction from Balzac to Mauriac. It is, how-

ever, the anticommunist entrepreneur Ferral (anticommunist and ideologically the enemy of the novel's real heroes) who strikes the most
Sartrian note in *La Condition humaine:* "action, action alone justifies life
and satisfies the white man. What would we think if we were told of a
painter who makes no paintings? A man is the sum of his actions, of
what he has *done,* of what he can do. Nothing else . . . I am my roads."
Gisors, the former teacher whose students have become communist mili-
tants and who is the father of the novel's revolutionary hero Kyo, answers: "The roads had to be built," if not by Ferral, he implies, then
by someone else, which would indicate that "a man" (a woman too?—
that's not certain) should be defined by something quite different from
his acts. [1]

What we are is more profound—more profoundly characteristic—
than what we do. And what we are is a certain tension between what
Malraux calls our fate and our will. *Fatalité* is the key word in this presumably historical novel, and it seems to refer to the constraints to which
being human subjects us. "'All suffer,' [Gisors] thought, 'and each one
suffers because he thinks. At bottom, the mind conceives man only in
the eternal, and the consciousness of life can be nothing but anguish'"
(335; 335). The most fundamental constraint is, then, temporal, and our
inevitable, ineradicable anguish would be the result of a kind of dysfunctional inability to *think time.* This sense of an imposed fate somehow
foreign to our nature, to the very terms of our thought, is so strong in
Malraux that the fear of death seems almost to derive from it rather than
to determine it. "The essence of man," Kyo remembers from his father's
teaching, "is anguish, the consciousness of his own fatality from which
all fears are born, even the fear of death" (148; 151). The anguish born of
the idea of death would be merely the most dramatic manifestation of a
more pervasive and, we might say, more abstract anxiety: that of a human consciousness structured to perceive human existence as constraint.
Thus Gisors' deceptively superficial definition of "the will to god-head"
as an "urge to compel" or constrain, as "l'envie de contraindre."
Stronger than the desire to govern is "l'illusion du bon plaisir," the illusion of being able to do exactly as we please, and "the will to power" is
defined, with considerable originality, as nothing more than the "intellectual justification"—a sublimated version—of a more concrete compulsion to constrain rather than to be constrained. To be immortal is not
even mentioned in Gisors' definition of godhead; even that is a result of
being able—as only God is able—to have one's own way. To constrain:
that is the "visionary disease," the content of our dream of being God,
the essence of what it means "to be more than a man, in a world of men"
(228; 229).

All of this comes from Gisors, and while it is true that he serves as

Malraux's intellectual spokesman in the novel, it is also true that in his private world, dominated by opium, he is somewhat outside the main action of the novel. More surprisingly, Gisors' son Kyo, the militant hero of *La Condition humaine,* also explicitly subordinates his militancy to the most secret, ahistorical part of his being. " 'To others,' " he thinks, 'I am what I have done.' To [his wife] May alone, he was not what he had done; to him alone, she was something altogether different from her bi-ography." What, where, is this "something altogether different?" In "the inescapable aloneness behind the living multitudes," there is a kind of absolute affirmation, "the affirmation of an idiot: an intensity greater than that of all the rest." It is at the center of that mad affirmation that lovers meet: "The embrace by which love holds beings together against solitude did not bring its relief to man; it brought relief only to the mad-man, to the incomparable monster, dear above all things *(préférable à tout)* that every being is to himself and that he cherishes in his heart" (53; 57). It is not the loved one, or even love itself, that is so dear; the incompa-rable and treasured monster is a relation entirely within the self, one that takes place in the depths of an inalterable solitude. And that cherished mad self can only be a senseless "absolute affirmation" against fate and against time. The tragic disproportion of which Gisors speaks nonethe-less becomes, for the incomparable monster, an occasion of insane yet heroic self-affirmation.

On the one hand, nothing is more highly valued in *La Condition hu-maine* than the revolutionary commitment for which Kyo is willing to die. Indeed, when he swallows cyanide in order to escape being thrown alive into the boiler of a locomotive, his suicide can be judged as an "exalted act." "He had fought for what in his time was charged with the deepest meaning and the greatest hope; he was dying among those with whom he would have wanted to live; he was dying, like each of these men, because he has given a meaning to his life" (304; 304). Where is the incomparable monster at this extraordinarily moving moment? If we are to take seriously Gisors' contention that "the mind conceives man only in the eternal," then what are we to think of Kyo's intensely historical and communal consciousness just before he dies? Is he dying in the an-techambers of his being? We may be stirred by the closeness he feels to the other condemned men around him; we may be impressed by his sense of having been an actor in the greatest adventure of his time. But how can history—even the noblest history—assuage an anxiety caused by what Malraux apparently considers the anomaly of our being born into history?

This could easily strike us as a false problem, for in fact Malraux does provide some answers to these questions. In *La Condition humaine* Marx-ism historicizes the metaphysical tension between fatality and will. Gisors and his son react to this tension in opposite ways. For Gisors, Marxism "is a fatality and [he] found [himself] in harmony with it because [his] fear of death was in harmony with fatality" (333; 332). Gisors reinterprets the Marxist confidence in the triumph of the proletariat and the advent of a classless society; he responds not to the extraordinary optimism of that belief, but to its implicit subordination of human will to what it posits as the necessity of certain historical processes. Thus the most utopian aspect of Marxist philosophy is paradoxically congenial to Gisors' temperamental pessimism. But it is precisely this reliance on historical necessity that exasperates Kyo. The question is by no means an academic one in *La Condition humaine,* since the decision about whether to break with Chiang Kai-shek is largely based on the emphasis given to historical fatality. The official line is that the party should go along with Chiang, that it can use him and that, as Vologuine tells Kyo, the revolution "by its very nature . . . must become socialist. We must let it find its own way. Our job is to safeguard its birth." It is, however, this role of historical midwife that Kyo rejects, and his strongest political argument is couched in terms of the novel's fundamental dualism: "In Marxism there is the sense of a fatality, and also the exaltation of a will. Every time fatality comes before will, I'm suspicious" (136; 139).

In short, the strongest appeal of Marxism for Malraux's characters may lie in the historical intelligibility it appears to give to the very definition of their humanity. And even Kyo can respond to Marxism's relocation of fatality on the side of affirmation. For not only is the fatality liberating; the exercise of an exalted will in the service of that historical vision also allows Kyo to find a certain self-affirmation in the acceptance of his defeat. Curiously enough, the mad incomparable monster of affirmation who is wholly different from the biographical Kyo coincides with Kyo's active acceptance of fatality when, at the end, his death itself is seen as the supreme—priceless, if in a sense useless, even mad—expression of his will.

Thus Malraux's impressive consistency. And yet: if Marxism historicizes a tension inherent in the very condition of being human, it is also what might be called a secondary option within that condition. It presents itself to Malraux's characters—as do all political commitments—as a choice to be made, as a step into history that can be freely taken (and perhaps taken back). Nothing seems more natural, and most of us have been trained to admire writers who, like Malraux and Sartre, both moralize politics (it is a responsibility) and make it something of a luxury (it is a field in which to exercise our freedom). Surely nothing is further from Malraux's intention than to make politics a luxury. Still the political is essentially irrelevant to his novel's most profound subject: "la condition humaine." Thus Gisors, after his son's death, finds himself "thrown outside of time," brought back to his atemporal human essence, an essence from which life itself is merely a distraction: "He felt the basic suffering trembling within him, not that which comes from creatures or from things, but that which gushes forth from man himself and from which life attempts to tear us away" (313–314; 314). And in thus being removed from history, Gisors finds himself where his son in the heat of his revolutionary activism had always, deeply and secretly, been: in the realm of that incomparable monster about whom nothing biographical can be said.

Whether one finds in that realm fundamental suffering or absolute affirmation is perhaps secondary to its positioning. It is from there that one enters history—life itself—in Malraux, which means that, instead of being historically determined, human beings themselves determine the time, the nature, and one might even say (we could of course begin to speak of Malraux's different political careers here) the number of their entrances into history. If history is lucky, so to speak, there will be certain analogies or "agreements" between the forms it takes and our perception of the human condition; but the most intensely lived political involvement is always a kind of superfluity or even degradation of being. We do not, that is, create the political immediately and continuously; we confront history—as if it existed apart from us, as if its origins were not exactly human, as if it came to us like an alien object—and if we enter it, that very step confirms our tragic fate, the fate of a mind attuned to eternity but condemned to the constraints of life in time.

The peculiar but entirely logical correlative of this inner distance from history is the unintended psychologizing of the metaphysical. Malraux makes an important point of the difference between Kyo's activism and that of the terrorist Tchen. For Tchen, who discovers in the novel's famous opening scene the erotically irresistible horror of terroristic violence, the boundaries between politics, metaphysics, and sex are hopelessly blurred, and that is why he is doomed. Tchen remarks that he scorns those he kills less than "those who don't kill: the virgins" (my translation; 58; 62), and, in trying to explain to Kyo why he wouldn't want anyone else to organize Chiang's assassination, he says: "Because I don't like the women I love to be screwed by other men" (my translation; 149; 152). Because he uses the revolution to act out his sexual and metaphysical anxieties (the *possession vertigineuse* [151] of himself that he seeks in death is a kind of defiant embrace of fatality), Tchen is politically unreliable and fundamentally expendable. The major fact about Kyo, on the other hand, is that he has earned the right to be in history. And this also means, as his father suggests in saying that for Kyo "individual problems existed . . . only in his private life," that Kyo has earned the right to a nonpsychological treatment. His revolutionary activity can have the simple authenticity of a struggle "to give to each of those men whom famine, at this very moment, was killing off like a slow plague, the sense of his own dignity" (64; 68).

But how valid is this distinction? First of all, the relation between the sexes in *La Condition humaine* is a psychological replay of the characters' metaphysical power struggle. Ferral, Tchen, and to a certain extent even Kyo seem to think of the woman's role in love as the sexual equivalent of being passively victimized by fate. Woman lends herself to being constrained, and in a sense she is an anomaly within the human condition. It is as if, within the intimacy of her jouissance, she renounces all struggle, all her will and freedom, all the mad but precious affirmation against fatality. Tchen is the most extreme example in the novel of male fury against this treacherous submission to "fate"—fury and also excitement. If woman betrays her humanity by her humiliating acquiescence to constraints, she also allows man to play the role of fate, to drop his heroic if crushed protest and to become, momentarily, himself the crusher. In a sense, sexual excitement—for the man, at any rate—is inherently necrophilic; it consists in the vengeful and wildly stimulating power of having reduced the other to a nonresistant thing. Sex is always a kind of assassination (even if it is only a character assassination). In his angry jealousy over May's having gone to bed with another man, Kyo imagines the man as now thinking of her as "cette petite poule" (54), and assassination is inevitably associated with sex.

Sexual desire is, then, another manifestation of the will to godhead that Gisors calls our "maladie chimérique." Especially with the light on (Ferral insists on this with his mistress Valérie), man can enjoy "l'illusion du bon plaisir," the double pleasure of "having his way" and, more secretly, of imagining himself as being had by himself, of savoring his omnipotence by sharing the woman's helpless desire to be its victim. Or perhaps we should say that the "volonté de déité" is the coverup—the symptomatic sublimation—of Ferral's hermaphroditic fantasies and Tchen's association of sex with murder. But it is unnecessary to determine priorities here. The congruence between the sexual and the metaphysical in Malraux does not necessarily mean that the latter derives from the former, although it is true that the intended transcendence of the historical risks being translated as a psychological origin of both the historical and the metaphysical itself. It is, at any rate, disturbing—at least from the point of view of Malraux's obvious intentions—that a psychological language adequately covers both levels of being. Gisors' discourse on the "volonté de déité" and Tchen's necrophilic terrorism are both adequately covered—made perfectly intelligible—in a psychological discourse on constraints.

What can it mean, then, to say that Kyo has earned the right to be in history and to be understood, by Malraux and the reader, in nonpsy-chological terms? Kyo's reasons for being in the revolution are as per-sonal—or, more exactly, as nonpolitical—as Tchen's. The discourse on fatality in *La Condition humaine* sublimates a cruder discourse on the re-lation between the sexes; even without assigning priority to one or the other, we have to recognize that they both belong to the same fantasmatic network. In Malraux, man produces the sexual and the metaphysical, and this is to be expected; what is not to be expected—given Malraux's reputation—is how little he is inclined to produce the political. Political history in Malraux comes along, quite conveniently, to solve other prob-lems. And the great illusion in this writer who has been thought of as providing us with the very model of political and historical fiction is that not only can we stand outside history but also that, whatever our politi-cal choices may be, we are, in the deepest part of our being, alienated from and indifferent to those choices.

In this book I have been arguing that, in a culture of redemption, sexu-ality and history are catastrophes that art has the task of repairing and redeeming. Reparative cultural symbolizations repeat those catastrophes in order to transcend them, which means that they scrupulously reenact the failures they are meant to make not happen. The mood produced by this intended spectralization of pervasive personal and historical failures is one of noble and eloquent melancholy, a mood common to such dif-ferent writers as Malraux and Proust. *La Condition humaine* (like *L'Espoir*) is the record of what Malraux clearly thought of as a historical disaster: Chiang Kai-shek's elimination of his Communist allies and the conse-quent loss of any socially revolutionary gains from the civil war in China. And yet this disaster seems to matter less than its symbolic trans-figuration. The novel's coda is a comparatively somber scene between Gisors and May months after Kyo's death; its climax, however, is Mal-raux's exalted account of that death. It is not that Malraux's art simply cancels out the suffering of his revolutionary heroes or the historical tragedy of which they are the victims. Indeed Malraux appears to reject any such use of art to deny suffering in his somewhat ambiguous presen-tation of the Japanese painter Kama, for whom "Everything is a symbol. To go from the symbol to the things symbolized is to explore the depth and meaning of the world, it is to seek God" (187; 190). In this aesthetic, art discovers truth or essences, and this transcendence of the phenomenal, the transformation of things into signs, is, as Clappique sees, a negation of the reality of pain. But, precisely, this insight comes from Clappique, a character defined as a sort of clown and, as we know more conclusively from Malraux's books on painting and sculpture, it is not the final word on art as a denial of death. Furthermore, Gisors at the end returns to Japan and takes refuge in Kama's home, where—again somewhat ambi-

guously—he associates his host's art with the dissipating of human suffering in the evening light: "Humanity was dense and heavy, heavy with
flesh, with blood, with suffering, eternally clinging to itself like all that
dies; but even blood, even flesh, even suffering, even death was being
absorbed up here in the light like music in the silent night" (336; 336).

Malraux's complicity with Gisors' mood can be detected perhaps less
in the eloquent rhythms of this sentence than in a certain stylistic appeasement throughout the novel of the conflicts and the suffering that are
its subjects. I am thinking of all those pauses, or dead moments, when
Malraux gives us sensitive descriptions of the city fog, or of the strange
mixture of a cricket's "tremulous cry" and "the last vibrations of the
shadows" on the faces of a group of men (13; 18–19), and especially of
all the "interesting" patterns of reflected light on people and on the city's
surfaces. Several awkwardly, self-consciously poetic passages create a
kind of compositional quietism at odds with the historical turbulence
being recorded, and with the characters' sense of urgency, as if in art that
turbulence can be absorbed, made to disappear, just as the signs or symbols of pain disappear in Kama's *approfondissement* of their sense.

In the climactic scene of Kyo's and Katow's deaths, Malraux explicitly
looks forward to the redemption of their suffering in the legends that
will spring up about them: "A death saturated with this brotherly qua-
vering, an assembly of the vanquished in which multitudes would recognize their martyrs, a bloody legend of which the golden legends are
made!" (304; 304). In the admittedly attenuated legend-making genre of
modern fiction, it is of course *La Condition humaine* itself that seeks to
perform the transfiguration from bloody to golden legend. Malraux's
exalted récit approves and consecrates that dismissal of history implicit
in his militant heroes' refusal to be defined by their heroic militancy.
Revolutionary struggle is the contingency, the constraint, in short the
fatality against which Malraux's art struggles. *La Condition humaine,*
thereby illustrating Gisors' account of the human mind, seems unable to
think history except as a fall—albeit a redeemable fall—from eternity.

*   *   *

Compared to the grown-up seriousness of Malraux's book, *Le Bleu du
ciel* can easily appear trivial and adolescent. During the unhappy year he
writes about, two very different women played important roles in the
narrator Troppmann's life: the rich, beautiful, apolitical Dirty (short for
Dorothea), whose astonishing excesses seem to have plunged Troppmann into a kind of anguished ecstasy (the novel's introduction is an
account of her drinking, belching, vomiting, passing air, water and
stools in a luxurious room at the Savoy in London); and the ugly, revolutionary virgin Lazare. It would be difficult to speak of any of these

figures as novelistic characters in a traditional sense or of the work itself as having a plot. Troppmann's constantly reiterated unhappiness is manifested in Herculean bouts of drinking, crying, and vomiting, and in an illness from which apparently he nearly died. Troppmann's language is unrelentingly excessive (he is always referring to himself as in a state of nausea and vertigo, as empty, lost, beside himself), but none of these states is reduced to psychological intelligibility, and *Le Bleu du ciel* maintains a kind of portentous and aristocratic vagueness about the excesses it describes. (Of the time he spent with Dirty in London, for example, Troppmann writes: "Drunkenness had committed us to dereliction, in pursuit of some grim response to the grimmest of compulsions.")[2] The gravity of all this anguish is at once emphasized and made somewhat doubtful by Troppmann's clownish Don Juanism, practiced even on his deathbed and including considerable boasting about his necrophilic tastes (tastes finally satisfied when he is cured of his impotence with Dirty by rolling naked with her in the muddy soil near a cemetery, a position that allows him to equate entering her body with penetrating a freshly dug grave). Everything is anguish and excess, but anguish and excess are themselves something of a joke, as are the novel's defiant references to the Don Juan legend and especially to the don's punishment—an irresistible and obsessive joke nonetheless, relegating the historical contexts of *Le Bleu du ciel* to the margins of the characters' frenzied self-absorption.

In short, Bataille's novel appears to be continuously flaunting its indifference to the realistic seriousness that *La Condition humaine* so scrupulously respects. So it is all the more unexpected and significant that Bataille, in his 1957 foreword to the novel, announces what might seem to be a commitment to the high seriousness of literature. "To a greater or lesser extent, everyone depends on *stories (récits)*, on *novels,* to discover the manifold truth of life." But if these récits have the unique privilege of "confronting a person with his fate," the truth they reveal is apparently compatible with a certain failure of attention on the reader's part and, even more unexpectedly, with a certain failure of control on the writer's part. The novels most important to us are "read sometimes in a trance," and "a story that reveals the possibilities of life is not necessarily an appeal but it does appeal to a moment of fury *(le récit qui révèle les possibilitiés de la vie n'appelle pas forcément, mais il appelle un moment de rage)* without which its author would remain blind to those possibilities, which are those of *excess.*" "An anguish to which I was prey" was, Bataille remembers, at the bottom of the "freakish anomalies" of *Le Bleu du ciel,* which, we are told, he wrote in 1935, put aside and more or less forgot, and finally published in 1957 at the insistence of friends "affected *(émus)* by a reading of the manuscript." And while Bataille is quick to point out that he is far from considering such anguish as a sufficient guarantee of the novel's value, his creative disarray naturally evokes that "moment of fury" or, as he also calls it, the "intolerable, impossible ordeal" that "can give an author the means of achieving that wide-ranging vision that readers weary of the narrow limitations imposed by convention are waiting for" (153–155; 381–382).

There is, then, a creative corollary to Troppmann's frantic anxieties. Bataille takes the trouble to invent a fictional narrator at the same time that, when he finally decides to publish the novel, he remembers himself writing *Le Bleu du ciel* in terms that can also describe his hero: "Un tourment . . . me ravageait." This does not mean that Bataille "is" Troppmann, but it does alert us to the author's compositional complicity with his narrator. That is, we find no attempt to provide a controlling perspective on Troppmann's perspective, to suggest that the material is being organized by anyone else. There is, first of all, the novel's lopsided structure. The five pages describing Dirty's antics at the Savoy are called an introduction, and what is apparently the novel proper is divided into two parts.[3] But part one, which is entirely italicized, takes up a page and a half, while part two, nearly one hundred pages long, is divided into five sections, each of which has its own title and is itself divided into chapters. We might call this a spurting-motor structure: after what could seem like a couple of false starts, Troppmann's *récit* goes on without any important structural interruptions. The narrative mode of the introduction—a scene with identifiable characters—will be picked up again in part two, in the body of the novel, while part one, written by an unidentified "je" (Troppmann? Bataille?), is a kind of lyrical interlude—which might have been an epilogue or even an introduction. The narrator begins by announcing the imminence of his dishonorable but desired death, then relates a terrifying visit from the Commander (of the Don Juan legend) after which, condemned to solitude but moved by a "blind anger," he asserts that he would invite the old man again, and this time it would be the Commander's corpse that would be carried off, and finally, moved by an insolence that has "blinded and transfigured [him] with a happiness that defies all reason," ends with the exclamation: "I have prevailed! *(Je triomphe!)*" (24; 395–396).

We should be less interested in determining what these shifts of mood might mean—or even in fully exploiting the references to the Don Juan legend—than in registering the effects of Bataille's extraordinarily mobile juxtapositions. The page and a half that constitutes part one, by being called part one, carries an enormous structural weight: it is as if those few lines were in some way as important as the subsequent ninety pages or so of part two. It is, however, difficult to say exactly what that importance consists of. The differences in narrative mode between parts one and two are partially undermined by a couple of anecdotal references in part one: "Today, I am overjoyed at being an object of horror and repugnance to the one being I am bound to," and the narrator insists twice that the Commander's visit "really" took place, "not in any nightmare . . . not in any dream." The elements of a whole new story are evoked in the first of these remarks, and the Commander's visit is treated as if it had the same sort of reality as the scene in the Savoy or the lovemaking above the cemetery outside Trier in the Moselle valley. And yet the story is never told (who is that other person for whom the narrator has become "an object of horror and repugnance?"), and the Commander's visit, which took place in the middle of the night (there was, incidentally, a "second victim"—who?—lying next to the narrator that night; "the utter repugnance on her lips made them resemble the lips of a certain dead woman. From them dribbled something more dreadful than blood"), obviously resembles a dream more than a real event (23–24; 395). Dreams play an important role in part two, and they are identified as such. For all Troppmann's frantic confusion, he keeps the boundaries between dreaming and waking life perfectly clear; *Le Bleu du ciel* has no surrealist blurring of those boundaries, no poetic derealizing of objects and people so that, as in a dream, they appear as mere extensions of the subject's anxieties and desires. And yet part one, mysteriously and provokingly, seems to violate that distinction, even though it does so in a particularly hard-nosed way with, again, none of the surrealist's trembling doubt about states of being: here is a supernatural event that "really," "really" took place.

The more we talk about Part One, the less we are able to make sense of it. The easy way out would be to settle for a reading that sees this italicized interlude (which is also structurally half of the novel) as the main indicator of a thematic center: the subversion of the legendary use of the Commander-Father as a punishment for Don Juan's erotic sins. In *Le Bleu du ciel* Troppmann will perhaps defeat the Commander by bringing sex to the cemetery, by insisting that sex is sustained by death. Interesting as this might be (and important as it would be in a discussion of Bataille's work on eroticism),[4] Bataille's reworking of the Don Juan legend is not enough to account for the renewal of the novel that, in the introduction, he speaks of as the object of passionate pursuit. From this perspective, what is perhaps most disorienting—and most original—about part one is the presence of a certain number of notations that distract us from the thematically central assertions of the narrator's insolent triumph over the Commander. The references to a "second victim," as well as to "the one being I am bound to," in addition to the perverse insistence on the reality of the Commander's visit (and the consequent shift of the récit to the level of a literal supernaturalism)—all of this goes beyond what we might take to be the passage's thematic function. And through that lack of proportion, Bataille appears to be confirming the analogy, or even the identity, between Troppmann's disarray and the anguish in which he, Bataille, wrote *Le Bleu du ciel*. He is arguing, from the very start, for *an abdication of the novelist's mastery over his material*. It is not only Troppmann who is frenetically restless; *Le Bleu du ciel* has trouble settling on its own sense, and this is largely how it revolutionizes the practice of writing novels.

Bataille is one of the first writers to reject the great modernist project of a domination of life through art. In its most extreme form (in Proust, Joyce, and the Mallarmean image of the Book), the culture of redemption dreams of the erasure of history in art through a massive, encyclopedic, and transfiguring absorption of history into the artist's work. The modernist project frequently includes the seeds of its own undoing; but on the whole *Ulysses* and *A la Recherche du temps perdu* have little patience for structurally unassimilated material or false starts. They seek to exclude the kind of repetition that makes visible within the work itself the actual process of working, the discovery of sense as a succession of always threatened, always local achievements. In this respect, Bataille's predecessor is D. H. Lawrence, for whom art was also a tormented encounter with sense rather than the occasion for repudiating experience by monumentalizing its meanings. In his foreword to *Women in Love* Lawrence wrote that the "struggle for verbal consciousness should not be left out in art. It is a very great part of life. It is no superimposition of a theory. It is the passionate struggle into conscious being"—the sign, in art, of the writer's struggling "with his unborn needs and fulfillment," with the "new unfoldings" struggling up "in torment in him, as buds struggle forth from the midst of a plant."[5] The Lawrentian struggle—the word is repeated five times in the short paragraph I've been quoting from—is perhaps not too far from that "intolerable, impossible ordeal" without which, for Bataille, no "wide-ranging vision" can be achieved. Most important, for Lawrence and Bataille, these struggles and ordeals are made visible in the very work of their writing, with the result that their fiction is compelled to abdicate any authority for resolving the dilemmas it poses, any superior point of view that could justify a broader cultural claim for art as a vehicle of truth.

"How," Bataille asks in the foreword to *Le Bleu du ciel*, "can we linger over books to which their authors have manifestly not been *driven*? (*des livres auxquels, sensiblement, l'auteur n'a pas été* contraint?)" (153; 381.) The emphasized word brings us back to Malraux, with the significant difference that an unacceptable if inevitable insult to human freedom has become an indispensable creative principle. Fatality and will: it is as if *Le Bleu du ciel* took up the central dualism of *La Condition humaine* in order to reverse the value attributed to each term. What I have called Bataille's compositional complicity with Troppmann is a way of suggesting that a certain type of *corrective will* cannot operate in this novel. Compare this to Proust, in whom the reparative intention is inscribed in the narrative point of view. At every moment in *La Recherche* we are to be aware of the gap separating Marcel's experience in the past from the redemptive alchemy to which that experience is now being submitted. And in works by Henry James, Gide, and Mann, the corrective intention becomes the novel's hidden subject. (What does James want us to think of the Governess in *The Turn of the Screw?* Can we trust Jérôme's account of his attachment to Alissa in *La Porte étroite?* To what extent does Mann share Serenus Zeitblom's perspective on Leverkühn in *Doctor Faustus?*) In its most pedagogical manifestations, the culture of redemption produces epistemological detective stories, stories that incite us to a kind of critical gymnastics in the discovery of truth, that force the reader to perform the central operation of art—the operation of corrective vision.

In *Le Bleu du ciel* no provision is made for the reader (or the author) to know more than Troppmann knows. The novel is written—as Troppmann's life is lived—under a kind of constraint, which means that *it has to be performed before a technique for dominating its sense has been worked out.* Another way of expressing this would be to say that the novel is somewhat like a dream. Since we are encouraged to make this connection by the detailed accounts Troppmann gives us of several of his dreams, it is all the more important to get the terms of that connection right. If Troppmann himself often seems to have the impression of "walking around in a dream," his narrative is anything but dreamlike. He gives us precise, matter-of-fact descriptions of both his waking life and his dreams, with the result that the material reality of the former is never dissipated and the interest of the latter is never merely atmospheric. Nor is it ever suggested that dreams give us the key to the significance of things—that they either reveal Troppmann's depths or provide symbolic condensations of the novel's historical contexts. Rather, dreams offer a particularly striking model of the mobility of inaccurate replications; in dreams, identities continuously repeat themselves in different forms.

Thus in the dream in which Troppmann finds himself, with several other people, in front of a coffin placed on a "four-poster canopy bed—a kind of wheelless hearse," the corpse revealed when the coffin's plank slides off and disappears "like a theater curtain or the lid of a chess set," goes through several metamorphoses: it is at first a pink wax figure resembling a wax doll (with its feet cut off) which Troppmann had seen in a nightclub a couple of nights before, then becomes a giant marble corpse with an immense mare's skull for a head (covered with a military helmet), a fishbone (or an enormous half-toothless jawbone) for a body, and the footless "long, gnarled stumps of a horse's legs," then a frantically agitated statue of Minerva "in gown and armor, erect and aggressive beneath her helmet," who rushes toward Troppmann to attack him with her whirling "marble scimitar." "I quickly grasped," Troppmann writes, "that, in this dream, Dirty (now both insane and dead) had assumed the garb and likeness of the *Commendatore.* In this unrecognizable guise, she was rushing at me in order to annihilate me" (55–57; 418–420). But this interpretation, far from reducing the dream to a single meaning, destabilizes it even more. Troppmann has merely added two more terms—Dirty and the Commander—to an already fantastically incongruous equation: the wax doll is an animal marble corpse, is a statue of the Roman goddess of wisdom, is Dirty, is the Commander. It would be absurd to say that Dirty is the underlying term of all these equivalences, except in the sense that Dirty herself is precisely this sort of horrifying but tantalizing succession of discontinuous identities. The dream's incoherence is in no way reduced by Troppmann's brief explanation; instead it is Dirty herself who is illuminated by that incoherence. Her monstrous excess, her inability to stop throwing up her being, is figured in the dream by its defiance of the discontinuities it theatrically performs. In what Troppmann calls her limitless avidity, which is identical to a limitless pouring out of her self, Dirty sullies the distinctness of her humanity, as if she were seeking to spend herself into death or transgress the boundaries of her species.

The night before Dirty arrives in Barcelona, Troppmann, standing under a starry sky on a city street, has an epiphanous experience that gives to the novel (and to the section in which the experience is related) its name. First he is again a child, waiting under this foreign sky for "for some unknown, impossible event." Then he thinks that he has to wait until two in the afternoon, when Dirty's plane is scheduled to arrive. "Deux heures" leads to another memory:

> I remembered: it was about two in the afternoon, beneath a brilliant Paris sun, and I was standing on the Pont du Carrousel, when I saw a butcher's van drive past. The headless necks of flayed lambs protruded from canvas coverings; the butchers' blue-and-white striped smocks were spotlessly clean; the van was slowly moving forward in open sunlight. When I was a boy, I loved the sun; I used to shut my eyes and let it shine redly through my lids. The sun was fantastic—it evoked dreams of explosion. Was there anything more sunlike than red blood running over cobblestones, as though light could shatter and kill? Now, in this thick darkness, I'd made myself drunk with light; and so, once again, Lazare in my eyes was merely a bird of ill omen; a dirty, trivial bird. My eyes were no longer lost among the stars that were shining above me actually, but in the blue of the noon sky. I shut them so as to lose myself in that bright blueness. From it, fat black insects spouted forth in buzzing swarms: just as, next day, there would

emerge at the blazing high point of the day, at first as an imperceptible speck, the plane that was bringing Dorothea . . . I opened my eyes. The stars were still covering my head, but I was maddened with sunlight. I felt like laughing: next day, that plane, too small and distant to attenuate the sky's blaze even minimally, would appear to me in the likeness of a noisy bug; it would be harboring Dirty's preposterous fantasies inside its glassed-in cage; and as I stood there on the ground, it would, to my tiny human mind—at a moment when pain would be rending deeper than habit within her—assume the aspect of an impossible, adorable "outhouse fly."—So I had laughed, and it was no longer merely the gloomy boy with his cruel pen who was walking through the night hugging the walls: I had laughed the same laugh as a child, convinced that one day, since such a lucky insolence was sustaining me, it was I who was bound to turn the world upside down—turn the world, quite ineluctably, upside down. (107–108; 454–455).

This passage is, we might say, prudently non-hallucinatory. Memories are clearly distinguished from perceptions. Troppmann never forgets that Dirty won't arrive until the next day, and although he asserts that his eyes were lost "in the blue of the noon sky," that "in this thick darkness, I'd made myself drunk with light," he reminds us twice of the real hour and the real setting ("the stars that were shining above me actually," "the stars were still covering my head"). And yet, though the distinction between waking and sleeping is never lost, we move among seemingly incongruous identities with the same ease as in the dream of the multiple-identity corpse. The man becomes the boy, night becomes day, the stars are replaced by the sun. And the sun is blood; its light is explosive, murderous, evoking the butchery of animals and blood flowing on a pavement. But something less sinister and more fanciful is also in that blue sky: fat black insects appearing in Troppmann's closed eyes just as Dirty's plane will appear the next day in the sky above Barcelona. Finally, because the plane will be carrying the suffering Dirty's "preposterous dreams" ("rêves démusurés"), Troppmann knows that it will appear to him as "an impossible, adorable 'outhouse fly.'" A certain unity is given to these disparate memories and impressions by Troppmann's happily insolent and conquering laugh—as if the anticipation of that adorable outhouse fly gives him the strength to knock everything over.

Such, then, is Dirty's most exhilarating metamorphosis: wildly dreaming and suffering even more deeply than usual within the belly of a toilet fly. In a sense it is Dirty who is the butchered animal of *Le Bleu du ciel,* the sacrificial victim of Troppmann's, and Bataille's, dreams of a stupefying excess, of a self-expenditure of unimaginable psychic waste, exploding the limits of the spent self. Like the lambs in Troppmann's memory, Dirty has lost her head, the features that might make her reliably identifiable. Much more than Malraux's sensitive souls, it is she who deserves to be called the "incomparable monster": monstrous in the way she lets her self go, incomparable by virtue of the fact that we can't locate her long enough to make of her a term of comparison. Dirty is the lost focal point of *Le Bleu du ciel*'s violence, a violence that—and now we approach the elusive but profound political dimensions of *Le Bleu du ciel*—may distill Nazism.

*   *   *

I first characterized Dirty as apparently apolitical. But if, unlike Lazare, she shows no signs of a political commitment, in another sense she can't help being as political as her sister in dirty-ness. In Bataille, the political (like the sexual) is not a choice; it is constitutive of the human. The closest Dirty comes to a political statement is when, in the train between Coblenz and Frankfort, she admits to Troppmann that "I sometimes wish there would be a war," and that she has the fantasy of announcing both the advent of war and the death of his children to "a really nice man." She comes to the man wearing a black dress and when she leaves him, "There's a puddle of blood where I've been standing." "What about you?" Troppmann asks:

> Her breath issued from her like a moan, as if she were suddenly beseeching: "I love you."
> She pressed her cool mouth against mine. I was in a state of intolerable joy. When her tongue licked mine, it was so wonderful I might have wished my life over.
> In my arms (she had taken off her coat), Dirty was in a bright red silk dress—the red of swastikaed flags. Her body was naked under the dress. She smelled of wet earth. (147–148; 484)

It is impossible to separate the excitements and anxieties of the sexual from those of the political. This does not mean, as it does in the case of Tchen, that the political is derived from the sexual, or that public commitment is merely a cover for private anxiety. For Malraux, the possibility of demystifying a political commitment depends on a belief in the possibility of being "authentically" political, in a relation to history uncontaminated by the sexual. Bataille suggests that the political is always related to the sexual, but their interconnectedness implies no priority on one side or the other. Politics cannot be reduced to sex because neither is imagined as ever being independent of desiring energies, of a fundamentally erotic (but not necessarily specifically sexual) self-expenditure. Our historicity is part of our fatality and not—as it is for Malraux—a possible transcendence of fate. It is as if human life were a kind of continuum in which Troppmann and Dirty having sex above a cemetery repeats both something as private as Troppmann's dream, elsewhere in the novel, of everything he has loved in his life rising like a cemetery that is also a brothel ("The funereal marble was alive. In some places it had *hair* on it" [76; 433]), and something as public as Dollfuss' assassination in Vienna and the workers' uprising in Barcelona. I realize how difficult it is to imagine in what way such disparate events can be said to repeat one another if their relations are not derivative. What is being repeated is not some transcendental nature; instead we should think of various expenditures of energy shaped by the materials available in each spending occasion. In Dirty we see war emerging as a possible consequence of the anguished desire to live beyond oneself. In war, that wish crystallizes as the monstrous appetite for a community of blood, for bodies shattered in a movement of universal destruction. The principal question raised by *Le Bleu du ciel* is how to control the historical precipitates of that desire without denying our inescapable implication in the passion for violence.

On the last page of the novel, just after Dirty leaves him in Frankfurt and before the departure of his own train, Troppmann listens to an orchestra of Nazi children playing on the steps of a theater in a large square near the railway station:

> They were playing with such ferocity, with so strident a beat, that I stood breathless in front of them. Nothing could have been more abrupt than the beating of the side drums, or more caustic than the fifes. As they faced the vast, empty, rain-drenched square and played for occasional passersby, all the Nazi boys (some of them were blonde, with doll-like faces) seemed, in their sticklike stiffness, to be possessed by some cataclysmic exultation. In front of them, their leader—a degenerately skinny kid with the sulky face of a fish—kept time with a long drum major's stick. He held this stick obscenely erect, with the knob at his crotch, it then looked like a monstrous monkey's penis that had been decorated with braids of colored cord. Like a dirty little brute, he would then jerk the stick level with his mouth; from crotch to mouth, from mouth to crotch, each rise and fall jerking to a grinding salvo from the drums. The sight was obscene. It was terrifying—if I hadn't been blessed with exceptional composure, how could I have stood and looked at these hateful automatons as calmly as if I were facing a stone wall? Each peal of music in the night was an incantatory summons to war and murder. The drum rolls were raised to their paroxysm in the expectation of an ultimate release in bloody salvos of artillery. I looked into the distance . . . a children's army in battle order. They were motionless, nonetheless, but in a trance. I saw them, so near me, entranced by a longing to meet their death, hallucinated by the endless fields where they would one day advance, laughing in the sunlight, leaving the dead and the dying behind them. (151; 486–487.)

It is tempting to emphasize the signs of Troppmann's revulsion in this description: the children are "stiff as sticks," their leader is "a degenerately skinny kid with the sulky face of a fish," he is "a dirty little brute" and conducts the music as if he were a monkey performing fellatio on his own enormous penis. The spectacle is "obscene" and "terrifying," and all these "hateful automatons" seem to be playing a hymn to war and murder. But this would be a partial reading of the passage. We are far from the childlike vulnerability of Dirty, and yet this final scene obviously has a symmetrical relation to the novel's introductory scene, in which we had seen a drunken and convulsed Dirty first in a London dive squeezing her naked thighs and biting on a dirty curtain and then letting herself go on a chair in her room at the Savoy: "While the urine was gathering into a puddle that spread over the carpet, a noise of slackening bowels made itself ponderously evident beneath the young woman's dress—beet-red, her eyes twisted upwards, she was squirming on her chair like a pig under the knife" (17; 389). We begin with a pig and end with a monkey; this sliding from the human to the animal is by no means necessarily meant to inspire revulsion, and Dirty's metamorphosis in the first scene even gives rise to a "feeling of purity" in Troppmann, to the desire to throw himself at Dirty's feet in fearful worship of so much "candor" (14; 387). There is also the "exaltation" of those obscene children (Troppmann first describes their music as "magnificent, ear-rending in its exaltation") and their hallucinated anticipation of the endless fields where, "laughing in the sunlight," they would leave "the dead and the dying behind them."

As we have seen, the sun has already been associated with violence and death, but by no means in a negative way: in the "bleu du ciel" passage, the sun makes Troppmann drunk with a happy insolence, the insolence of a conqueror, of someone who would "turn the world quite ineluctably upside down." Dirty, harbinger of death and adorable toilet fly, would appear in the sun-drenched sky over Barcelona the next day. In the earlier passage, the sun was already "terrible," reminiscent of an explosion; "was there anything more sunlike," Troppmann had asked, "than red blood running over cobblestones as though light could shatter and kill?" It is difficult not to feel that those obscene little Nazis at the end profit from such associations. Indeed, immediately after his description of their orchestra Troppmann calls this "rising tide of murder far more incisive *(acidique)* than life," and he parenthetically adds: "Because life is not as resplendent with blood as death" (my translation; 151; 487). One might almost say that the sun-child Dirty (referred to earlier as a "sunlike skeleton") engenders Hitler's murderous children; and to laugh in the blue of noon is the exalted privilege of the murderers, of those who can overturn everything and who, like Troppmann, know that death has more light—the blood-red light that also illuminates Dirty's dress and the Nazi flag—than life.

The function of art, Bataille seems to suggest, is not to take a stand against this monstrosity with the noble detachment of a Malraux-like *engagement,* but rather to insist, even somewhat nastily, that we can't avoid being implicated in it. The courageous self-sacrifices of Malraux's heroes—sacrifices made in the name of human dignity—are perhaps tragic self-deceptions if they are not accompanied by the recognition of our complicity in abjection, a complicity that Kyo, interestingly enough, both recognizes and repudiates in what he calls his dependence on the fascinated horror he feels at a prison guard's sadistic cruelty toward an insane fellow prisoner. It is this "loathsome part" of himself that, "with a joy whose violence surprised him," he leaves behind when he goes to the apotheosis of his legend-inspiring death. No such epic-inspiring shedding of abjection and violence is possible in *Le Bleu du ciel.* For Bataille, a false perspective on Nazism gives an account of it solely in terms of other political events, in terms of historical antecedents and contexts, cut off from the desiring energies that produced it. Nazism is thus reified and enjoys the enormous prestige of a historical "object" that somehow sets itself against an antithetical, overwhelmed, and yet to a certain extent heroic human will. In its avoidance of this reifying seriousness about History and Politics, Bataille's art of vertiginous replications is designed to make us feel that we are already everywhere in history, and that an ethos of political engagement is grounded in the illusion that we have not produced the violence against which we struggle.

There are no images of any such struggle in *Le Bleu du ciel.* I would nonetheless argue against what has seemed to some readers a highly disturbing conclusion about the novel's political sympathies, and I make this argument on the basis of the very repetitions that allow Nazism to benefit from the exaltation of solar violence. If *Le Bleu du ciel* is one of the books that, as Bataille says of those novels that reveal "the manifold truth of life," are "read sometimes in a trance," it is perhaps because of the destabilizing and destructuralizing effect of its repetitions. Certain words and objects continuously reappear. We have just seen some of the reappearances of the solarity motif: in the fantasies of conquest that Troppmann projects on the Nazi children, in the "bleu du ciel" passage (where the sun shines on the butcher's van, as well as in the Barcelona night sky where it eclipses the stars, and in the afternoon sky in which Dirty's plane will arrive the next day), in the description of Dirty as a "sunlike skeleton"—to which might be added the "insolent look," the "sunlike look," of the beggar who stares at Troppmann on a sun-drenched street in Barcelona (126; 468). The most prominent object in the novel is the black banner hanging over a Vienna street in honor of Dollfuss' death, which "becomes" the dark rug thrown from the floor above outside the window of Troppmann's sickroom in Paris, and both of which make him think of the Commander and specifically of the black tablecloth spread on Don Juan's and the Commander's supper table. I could also mention the doll series: the broken wax doll in the Paris nightclub, its reappearances in Troppmann's multiple-identity corpse dream and in the description of the Nazi children as "blonde, with doll-like faces."

But the most interesting point to be made about these repetitions is that they obscure the sense of a motif in the very process of appearing to constitute one. Criticism has generally used repetition as a guide to sense-making patterns. The critical search for deep structures—whether the particular approach be thematic, phenomenological, psychoanalytic, or Marxist—relies on what it assumes to be networks of intelligibility created by various types of recurrence in the literary work. Bataille defeats such critical intentions by suggesting that repetition is at once inevitable and aleatory. Terms will always recur, but their recurrence produces what might be called nonstructurable continuities. The Commander's death-announcing black tablecloth shows up as an image alongside the black banner honoring Dollfuss, but it is unnecessary to strain toward some significant identity between the punishment of Don Juan's libertinism and a political assassination in Vienna. Our repertory of images is vast but finite; the resemblances that encourage us to place one thing next to another may range from what Proust calls shared essences (a fundamental identity of being) to chance affinities of form in a universe where richness is largely a function of unpredictable reappearances.

More is of course at stake in the continuity between Dirty or Troppmann's insolence and Nazism. Nazism involves the calculated mechanization of violence, and it would be true—but perhaps a little too easy—to say that Dirty could not recognize her own uncontrollable prodigality in the "hateful automatons" who mesmerize Troppmann. It would be better to emphasize the continuities between the image of Nazism at the end of the novel and both Dirty's excesses and Troppmann's exhilaration in the "bleu du ciel" passage. That is, we can consider the opposition between calculation and spontaneity as a secondary difference within a more profound resemblance; but, having done this, we can argue for a form of self-repetition in which the terms are so disproportionate as to make imperative a movement of self-rejection. Nazism is the monstrously inaccurate replication of the solarity that Troppmann nearly worships; it is a repetition of Dirty in which Dirty gets lost, in which she can only fail to find herself.

It is much more than a question of merely exculpating Dirty, Troppmann, or for that matter Bataille. To what extent do the monstrously inaccurate self-replications initiate effective forms of political *resistance?* Nazism is a form of violence to which, Troppmann predicts in his final paragraph, "it will be impossible to set anything but trivialities—the comic entreaties of old ladies." And yet from within those repetitions that Troppmann accepts with such a dizzying casualness, and that irreversibly implicate him in the murderous solar laugh of his fantasized Nazi butchers, he experiences what he calls a "black irony," an unavoidable separation of himself from what is his own solar madness. "Inordinate laughter was making my head spin. As I found myself confronting this catastrophe, I was filled with the black irony that accompanies the moments of seizure when no one can help screaming" (152; 487). Dizzy, nearly hysterical, on the point of abdicating all control and all will in the face of this phenomenon whose appeal is precisely to multiply the occasions of a spasmodic loss of self, Troppmann discovers the self-restorative virtues of blackness. His irony partially annuls his mad jouissance, and its blackness is the assertion of a normalizing light, one that dims the blood-red light of the sun. If it is impossible not to be drawn to solar violence, it is equally impossible not to hold a domain of the self at a certain distance from it, in the same way, Troppmann suggests, that a certain arresting attention inevitably accompanies the spasms and cries of a seizure or perhaps of a sexual climax.

It is as if a negativizing movement of self-reflexiveness—itself a kind of spasm of being—were an inescapable retreat and protection from the intrinsically totalitarian nature of ecstatic violence. Or, to put this another way, if Bataille's resolutely nonredemptive art, far from making sense of life, initiates us to the pleasures of an uncritical participation in the text's own trance of agitated repetitions, it also cultivates an ironic reserve toward its own excesses. Thematically, this reserve takes the form of Troppmann's somewhat foolish Don Juanism. His erotic calculations (especially with Xénie) both cheapen and save him from the unguarded excesses of Dirty (he thinks of her as "too voracious to go on living" [149; 485]). The seducer's plotting is thus vindicated as a sign of what is at stake in his erotic play; indeed it may save him from being the lost victim of the violence of his own eroticism.

More generally, black irony can be thought of in terms of a pervasive self-consciousness, the consciousness of a text continuously attesting to its own distance from the anguish or torment that may have inspired it. Language remains inescapably discrete at every moment of its attempt to represent the loss of all discretion. Politically, it is true, Troppmann's black irony is also the sign of a radical impotence; in one sense it is merely the way he registers his notion that nothing (not even the war in which the "rising tide of murder" will finally be stopped) can defeat the catastrophically exciting violence that, from Dirty in the Savoy to the Nazi children's orchestra, *Le Bleu du ciel* has so ambiguously figured. Bataille's novel implicitly mocks the limitless bad faith of a society that looks to art for its salvation. But in demonstrating, even in monstrously exaggerating, art's propensity to undo the formalizing and sense-making projects of a redemptive culture, *Le Bleu du ciel* resolutely refuses to dominate its mobile, muddled positions. It has, that is, the courage to leave us with the wholly undeveloped—but possibly precious—suggestion that spasmodic irony may be the beginning of political and cultural realism.

PART II

Encyclopedic Fictions

CHAPTER 5

Flaubertian Rhythms of Knowledge

Unable to agree on either the subject or the compositional principles of the novel they have decided to write, Flaubert's Bouvard and Pécuchet turn to "the science called aesthetics." After receiving a list of books on the subject, the two friends go to work. First they study the nature of the Beautiful. Then, Flaubert reports:

> They tackled the question of the sublime.
> Certain objects are sublime in themselves, the thunder of a torrent, deep darkness, a tree struck by a storm. A character is beautiful when it triumphs, and sublime when it struggles.
> "I understand," said Bouvard, "the Beautiful is the Beautiful, and the Sublime the very Beautiful." How can they be distinguished?
> "By intuition," answered Pécuchet.
> "And where does that come from?"
> "From taste?"
> It is defined as special discernment, rapid judgement, the ability to distinguish certain relationships.
> "What it comes to is that taste is taste, and none of that tells you how you get it."
> Conventions must be observed, but they vary, and however perfect a work may be it will not always be above reproach. Yet there is an indestructible Beautiful, whose laws we do not know, because its origin is mysterious.
> Since an idea cannot be translated by every form, we must recognize limits between the arts and, in each of the arts, several genres; but combinations arise in which the style of one will enter into another, or else miss the target, fail to be true.
> The Truth too slavishly applied impairs Beauty, and preoccupation with Beauty impedes Truth; however, without an ideal there is no truth; which is why the reality of types is more continuous than that of portraits. Besides, art only deals with verisimilitude, but that depends on the observer, is something relative, transitory.[1]

Does Flaubert mean to be satirical here, and of what and of whom? It may be of Bouvard and Pécuchet's deficient intellectual method or habits of reading, or it may be of the books they read—but what are those books? Flaubert usually names some of the authors his protagonists consult in their studies (just before the lines quoted he mentions five writers on aesthetics) without, however, mentioning the particular source of each theory or set of facts. The passage on aesthetic theory is typical in this respect: it condenses a mass of quite different theories into a single page of theoretical pronouncements with no attributions whatsoever. And yet stylistically that page could be a direct quote from a single author, for in this version of free indirect discourse Flaubert has reduced the distance between the narrator and his nearly quoted referent by using the present tense. It is, in other words, as if aesthetic theory were speaking directly—not a particular theorist of aesthetics, but the sourceless theory itself.

The passage is, however, distinguished by a certain type of stylistic performance that, far from speaking the truth of aesthetic theory or of the characters immersed in that theory, is repeated throughout the novel regardless of the changes in epistemological reference. In the quoted passage there are numerous examples of Flaubert's rhythmical "signature." I am thinking, for example, of the ternary construction: in the first paragraph, "the thunder of a torrent, deep darkness, a tree struck by a storm," then the one-sentence paragraph on definitions of taste, and, in what might be considered a variation on that construction in which the second and third syntactic units decrease in size (the third is a single word), "but that depends on the observer, is something relative, transitory." There is also a prodigious use of directional shifts: note the interruptive nature of "but," "yet," and, peculiarly enough, "and" in the paragraph on Conventions and the Beautiful, and, especially, the zigzagging effect in the final paragraph on Truth of the first sentence's opening two clauses and of the subsequent "however," "besides," and "but." All these are of course swerves and negations of thought; but given the rapidity with which we pass from one thought to the next (each originally complex theory gets only a few words), we tend to experience intellectual inconsistency and confusion here as an almost purely rhythmical agitation, as a linguistic approximation of musical repetitions, variations, and abrupt shifts in thematic lines. In other words, the passage—and the novel as a whole—is really not "about" the deficiencies of either Bouvard and Pécuchet's understanding or of the state of human knowledge in a particular area. Instead Flaubert's work performs an erasure of the very conditions of being that would allow for such critical intentions in the first place. Human knowledge is cut off from both its sources and its reception; it is reduced—or elevated (these oppositions are meaningless

applied to such mutations)—to intellectually and psychologically insignificant rhythms.

Bouvard and Pécuchet themselves undergo the same mutation as the
books they devour. If in the course of the novel Flaubert nearly eliminates the distance between himself and his *bonshommes,* it is not, as some
critics have said, because they become more intelligent or that Flaubert
comes to feel more sympathy for them, but because he wants to eliminate them. Consider the following account of Pécuchet's ideas for religious reform:

> "The world has expanded, the earth is not the centre any more. It turns
> among the infinite multitude of worlds like it. Many exceed it in size, and
> this shrinking of our globe brings about a more sublime ideal of God."
>
> So, religion had to change. Paradise is something childish with its blessed
> ones always rapt in contemplation, always singing and looking down on the
> tortures of the damned. When you think that the basis of Christianity is an
> apple. (249; 362)

Our first impression is that Flaubert stops quoting Pécuchet in order to
continue quoting him. Except for the dropping of quotation marks, the
change from direct discourse to free indirect discourse is indicated by a
single tense shift: "Donc la religion devait changer" transposes Pécuchet's
saying: "Donc la religion doit changer." The rest of the paragraph continues in the present, and if the whole passage were put in quotes and
"devait" became "doit," we would certainly not feel that Pécuchet is
speaking "out of character." Having made Pécuchet's speech nearly indistinguishable from his own, the narrator's move into free indirect discourse is therefore primarily experienced not as a strategy of point of
view (which these moves largely are in *Madame Bovary*) but rather as the
expression of an ontological preference. The narrator continues Pécuchet's speech by eliminating him as its source; Pécuchet as a thinking
subject merely provides the anecdotal term for an anonymous performance of the imaginary. Nothing subsists of Pécuchet except his speech
as sourceless style—speech that, by virtue of its essence, can no longer
be considered as quotation.

Human knowledge and human character are neither evaluated nor performed in their essential being in *Bouvard et Pécuchet;* they undergo a
change in ontological status. This operation is the same throughout the
novel; what happens to horticultural or jam-making expertise is identical
to what happens to theological doctrine. What we might be inclined to
consider as the tics of Flaubert's style are perhaps the excessively visible
signposts of the mutation I am discussing; the stylistic sameness they
produce suggests—in a way that contradicts Flaubert's own notions of
style, at least as he expressed them in letters written during the compo-

sition of *Madame Bovary*—the epistemological indifference of art to its objects. Furthermore, once the model of these mutations is given, their repetition is unnecessary. The encyclopedism of *Bouvard et Pécuchet*—Flaubert's massive reading for the novel notwithstanding—is somewhat illusory. What we have is the appearance of an encyclopedic novel, an accumulation of facts and theories from the most diverse fields of knowledge in order to discredit the claims of art to any epistemological validity whatsoever.

In *Bouvard et Pécuchet* Flaubert makes a perhaps unexpectedly modest claim for the authority of art. If the novel ceaselessly repeats an operation that might be thought of as requiring a single demonstration (since the effect of the operation will not be changed by the use of new material), this is because Bouvard and Pécuchet are themselves in a tensely frictional opposition to the narrator's mutational work. By resisting their total absorption into the Flaubertian free indirect discourse, Bouvard and Pécuchet keep open another option: that of consciousness at work in the world. If they lack both the believability and the psychological density we associate with the characters of realistic fiction, they nonetheless have a marked specificity as characters—more precisely, as philosophical characters. The relation of Bouvard and Pécuchet to knowledge is highly practical; if Flaubert has satirical intentions toward them, it is not because they are intellectually mediocre but because they would put knowledge *to use*. As their studies proceed, they develop "a need for truth in itself" (121; 188), but their philosophy always takes the form of applied philosophy, of innumerable experiments (on themselves and on others) and tireless attempts to enlighten themselves and their neighbors. These inveterate lecturers are extraordinarily restless; they always have to do something with knowledge, and they must have an audience. A suitable climax to the careers of such eminently practical and public philosophers, Flaubert suggests, might have been in urban planning and adult education.[2]

Flaubert's letters are full of generous praise for those writers (Rabelais, Shakespeare, Cervantes) who—unlike himself, at least as he magnanimously imagines them—could afford not to worry about each turn of phrase because they had the gift of excess. But this is what Flaubert himself finally produced in *Bouvard et Pécuchet*: a work that, as it proceeds, erases its concessions to its own readability within a tradition of fiction that Flaubert himself helped to solidify. *Bouvard et Pécuchet* is a hybrid masterpiece, a crossing of social realism and philosophical allegory, a mutation of fictional anecdote and biography into a kind of heroic struggle between the concerns of philosophy (philosophy as always concerned) and the epistemological indifference or neutrality of art. By their excesses, Bouvard and Pécuchet come to figure the sublimity of a civilization without art, a civilization devoted exclusively to the use of knowledge to bridge the gap between human consciousness and its environment. At this level of emblematic significance, the quality of Bouvard and Pécuchet's learning is irrelevant; intelligence itself is finally irrelevant to the boundlessly energetic will to make the human mind ideally consequential, to *realize representation*.

Against this temptation, Flaubert's narrative performs a highly seductive derealization: the mere *representation of representation*. Bouvard and Pécuchet rush into the world with their representations of it; Flaubert, by severing their knowledge from its sources,[3] its reception, and its possible uses, simply repeats it as nothing more than a series of moments in the life of an errant, unidentifiable, unusable consciousness. Bouvard and Pécuchet ceaselessly work against the imaginary nature of the mind's representations; Flaubert just as ceaselessly emphasizes the autonomy of representations, thus suggesting that the effect of our inclination to represent the real is, necessarily, to alienate us from objects of representation. The comedy of *Bouvard et Pécuchet* depends on the two friends being defeated by this opposition to their projects; they are, that is to say, saved from the world's persecution by the erasure of their projects *as* projects. But it is of course impossible to speak of them as if they themselves merely opposed such erasure. The energetic will to live with knowledge in the world has already been invalidated by the primary representation of that will—by the very precondition of our being able to recognize it, the writing of *Bouvard et Pécuchet*. Before the quotation marks of their speech have been removed, they are already not there, although it is of course one of the tricks of literature—and especially of realistic fiction—to make us believe in its multiple contacts with the world. In art, the price of comic relief is always the inconsequential nature of both catastrophe and salvation.

*   *   *

And yet the Flaubertian move into the imaginary—which Sartre saw as a rejection of history and politics—should, I think, also be seen as a political strategy. The alienation I have been describing is a form of resistance. First of all, the practice of an *inapplicable discourse* can be thought of as a defense against the manipulative seductions of political language. In the famous "Comices agricoles" scene in *Madame Bovary,* Flaubert renders the sexually and politically pornographic language of Rodolphe and Lieuvain impotent merely by juxtaposing the two discourses, by letting each of them cut into or interrupt the other. The juxtaposition of Rodolphe's amorous rhapsody with the sous-préfet's praise of agriculture and civil obedience reveals important rhetorical similarities between the two. Each speech is designed to seduce its audience, and the superficial differences of content (the spiritual opposed to the basely material, passion against manure) hide a common intention: that of making the listeners passive and obedient (sexually and politically). This intention is realized through "literary" means, through metaphor, antitheses, rhetorical questions, and more generally a pleasantly numbing musicalizing of the brutal message. I have spoken of the dominance of certain rhythms in Flaubert's writing as the sign of language being severed from any such intentions, of its participating in the disinterested, purposeless activity of the imaginary. We should, however, see that Flaubert recognizes the potential *uses* of verbal musicality and that he implicitly distinguishes between art and the persuasive potentialities of rhetoric. Art occurs only as a kind of rhetorical ascesis, when rhetoric itself renounces its persuasive or seductive powers. And this seems to occur principally through a type of self-reflexiveness, or ironic move. Rodolphe's and Lieuvain's representations of love and the nation are neutralized—and, it is implied, authentically aestheticized—simply by being themselves represented, repeated within a different musical structure—one of alternating blocks of discourse—which preempts the shorter persuasive rhythms and reduces (or elevates) both discourses to the status of artistic display.

The representation of representation can therefore be a politically defensive move. The aestheticizing repetition of Rodolphe and Lieuvain operates almost as a pedagogical model of how to elude the immediacy of seductive speech. It is not exactly a question of a critical analysis of such speech, but of a perhaps more potent invalidating strategy: a kind of distancing repetition or reenactment in which the manipulative agent's discourse is deprived of any subject who might profit from its effectiveness. Flaubert's art suggests ways in which the aestheticizing of discourse can operate *outside art* if only as moments of resistance within networks of political or sexual power. It is of course true that neither Emma nor Lieuvain's peasant listeners nor finally—but this is more ambiguous—the protagonists of *Bouvard et Pécuchet* profit from such ironic repetitions. Yet they are models of how a certain type of appropriation of language can, at least momentarily, protect us from its coercive designs. In *Bouvard et Pécuchet,* however, Flaubert goes so far as to save the realistic novel itself from its collaborative participation in such designs. The instability of Bouvard and Pécuchet as characters—the process by which they are "replayed" as the subjectless rhythms of a depersonalized narrative—points to a kind of resistance to strategies of power that would no longer be dependent on the spectacle of defeated (if heroic) characters. As long as the novelist acquiesces in, say, the very possibility of Emma Bovary as a psychological subject, the novel that presents itself as an ironic repetition of her fate can resist this fate only if it presents art as a retreat from the phenomenal to the imaginary. *Bouvard et Pécuchet* raises the more exciting possibility of the imaginary as *politically aggressive*. The incoherence of Flaubert's bonshommes is perhaps the novel's most precious achievement, for it suggests that the *errance* of the imaginary dissolves the identities that coercive strategies must assume in order to be effective. On the one hand, Bouvard and Pécuchet are so uncompromisingly definite in their projects that they become easy targets for an antagonistic community; on the other, the very excess of their philosophical and proselytizing energy is constantly undoing their projects, giving them a kind of crazy mobility that may, had Flaubert completed the novel, have allowed them to escape their countrymen's wrath and enjoy the ambiguous freedom of harmless madmen. This may not seem like much in the way of political aggressiveness, and yet it is potentially more radical than any reformist project. For it proposes the aesthetic as a strategy for eluding definitions and identifications, and in so doing it suggests, paradoxically, the political uses of art's uselessness in any struggle for a free society.

Flaubert's brief mutational résumés of vast areas of knowledge suggest that, far from being condemned to cultural insignificance if it does not somehow account for the encyclopedic knowledge of its time,[4] art is by definition an ontological relocation of the materials of philosophy and science. *Bouvard et Pécuchet* does not imply—as, say, *Ulysses* does—that its own performance can redemptively replace all those materials, but it does propose what we might think of as a salutary interference with the processing of knowledge as power. At the price of a certain indifference to the beneficial effects of thought's mastery of nature (including its own nature), art cultivates a deliberately fragmentary, unusable, even ignorant relational play with the entries of its culture's encyclopedia. Flaubert's treatment of all the books devoured with such anxiety by his heroes is to convert their subjects into a few occasions of purposeless pleasure. For the Flaubertian writer this pleasure involves certain rhythmical preferences. He sensually repeats the knowledge of his time in the form of his musical prose, a prose continuously returning to, and playing with, its preferred rests and measures. Bouvard and Pécuchet—not to speak of the hostile world of Chavignolles—retain just enough resistant presence to remind us that the world is still there, that the narcissistic luxury of art is always a momentary delay in the necessary work of civilization.

Flaubert, for all his presumed idolatry of art, therefore implies that, far from having a secure place or a central role in that accumulation of knowledge by which civilizations achieve historical mastery, the artist is content to repeat himself in the margins of such work. The language of every page of *Bouvard et Pécuchet* obtrusively reenacts that turning away from objects (and by objects I mean here the entire fictional world of the novel: the two friends, the books they read, the community they live in), the solipsistic play that psychoanalysis invites us to see as intrinsic to sexuality and to art. Indeed, art could be put on the side of sexuality in the Freudian opposition between civilization and pleasure. But if the narcissistic aestheticizing of Bouvard and Pécuchet's studies suggests that art transforms discursive communications into the privacy of a verbal jouissance, the very blocking of the message in art limits the political uses of knowledge. Flaubert defines both the limitations and the necessity of art. In *Bouvard et Pécuchet,* style caresses an encyclopedic culture out of its projects of mastery and into a liberalizing impotence.

*   *   *

We may, finally, be happy about Flaubert's failure to complete his work. In the unwritten second volume, his bonshommes were apparently to return to their work as copyists, and this part of *Bouvard et Pécuchet* would have been an encyclopedic mass of quotations, a stupefying documentation of human stupidity. Passages from the innumerable books Bouvard and Pécuchet have read would replace the narrative summaries of part one, summaries that, as we have seen in the one-page condensation of several works of aesthetic theory, effect a mutation that is the principal operation of Flaubert's work. But Flaubert was hesitant to reduce part two to mere quotation; his notes for the unwritten volume show him moving toward an additional narrative presence, or even explicitly critical interventions, in, for example, the form of including other readers' notes that Bouvard and Pécuchet would find in the margins of certain passages, or simply of comments from the two copyists themselves.[5] The *Dictionnaire des idées reçues*—a project Flaubert was working on for years before he began writing *Bouvard et Pécuchet*—would also have found its way into volume two. The *Dictionnaire* could also be thought of as a work of quotation, but here the sources are anonymous: this strangest (and perhaps most cherished) of Flaubert's projects either quotes a common cliché about one of its entries ("ARTISTS: They earn huge sums but squander them. Often asked to dine out . . . What artists do can't be called work" [294; 489]) or indicates, often with obvious irony, how to use the term in the most acceptably mindless way ("NE-GROES: Express surprise that their saliva is white and that they can speak French" [318; 542]).

It is tempting to think of volume two as merely continuing—with other, more direct means—the encyclopedic review of human knowledge begun in volume one. But the "other means" change everything. From all the indications we have, volume two would have been a brutally satirical work, by virtue of its citational nature. It is as if Flaubert had lost faith in the mutational power of his style, as if the mass of contradictory and cliché-ridden opinions securely passing themselves off as knowledge could be dealt with only by lighting them up, by letting them speak for themselves, by accumulating and stuffing them into the readers' minds until they are violently rejected, thrown up by a finally sickened intelligence. This enterprise has fascinated many of Flaubert's critics, but it seems to me that the stakes have become considerably less important with volume two. *Bouvard et Pécuchet* becomes virulent satire, the "encyclopedia of human stupidity" that Flaubert thought at one point of using as a subtitle for the entire novel. Perhaps Flaubert himself had become the victim of a realistic illusion that the first nine chapters work to destroy: angered by his heroes' defeat, Flaubert, like them, becomes the vengeful mirror of the community's meanness and imbecility.

A *Dictionnaire des idées reçues* is an act of revenge, but perhaps also one of redemptive annihilation: the artist's classification of mental garbage replaces it, and the detritus of consciousness, repeated in literature, is at once transmuted and immortalized. But the transmutation depends on a superstitious belief in the redemptive power of art, a belief starkly illustrated by the nearly literal reduction of art to copying. Within this magical system, the *work* of art has become unnecessary. It is merely a question of transporting the materials of experience into the area of the book; once there, it will be invested by virtues inherent in art, metonymically transfigured. Nothing could be more different from the processes I have attempted to describe in discussing the first (and, in fact, only) section of *Bouvard et Pécuchet*. There art is not lying in wait, like a divine receptacle, to receive and redeem experience; rather, art is a mode of being produced by a certain type of human work. In suggesting its preference for this more modest role, the realized *Bouvard et Pécuchet* accomplishes its own impressive mutations, mutations that depend on—and remind us of—the extraordinary plasticity of consciousness, its capacity to make something we call art from a narcissistic lingering over its own representations or, in other words, from a preference for representational play over representational truth.

CHAPTER 6

Incomparable America

Should America be orphaned? Can you become an orphan if you already know who your parents are? Put in these terms, the problems inherent in the resolve of nineteenth-century American writers to forge a great national literature freed from parental European influence may begin to seem not merely grave but unsolvable. One of the most stirring and militant versions of this call for an independent American literature can be found in Herman Melville's "Hawthorne and His Mosses," an essay written for the *Literary World* in the summer of 1850, during the composition of *Moby-Dick*. The fact that Hawthorne is extravagantly praised in the first part of the essay, even though Melville—"to be frank (though, perhaps, rather foolish)"—admits in the second part (written a day later) that he hadn't yet read all the stories in *Mosses from an Old Manse,* suggests that Hawthorne himself may not be exactly central to the argument he inspires. If Hawthorne is compared to Shakespeare in this essay, and if Melville defiantly defends the comparison against those who may be shocked "to read of Shakespeare and Hawthorne on the same page," it is in order to move beyond Hawthorne, to suggest that while Hawthorne himself is not as great as Shakespeare, someone else will soon appear to rival the greatest English writer. "If Shakespeare has not been equalled, give the world time, and he is sure to be surpassed, in one hemisphere or the other." Actually Melville has already been much more precise geographically. "Believe me, my friends, that men not very much inferior to Shakespeare, are this day being born on the banks of the Ohio." Shakespeare will be surpassed, that is, by an American. But if America is to produce writers at least equal to the greatest European writers, it will not be by imitating European models. American literary greatness requires an originality that carries within it the danger of failure, a danger that, in the most remarkable passage of the essay, Melville happily embraces:

But it is better to fail in originality, than to succeed in imitation. He who has never failed somewhere, that man cannot be great. Failure is the true test of greatness. And if it be said, that continual success is a proof that a man wisely knows his powers,—it is only to be added, that, in that case, he knows them to be small. Let us believe it, then, once for all, that there is no hope for us in these smooth pleasing writers that know their powers. Without malice, but to speak the plain fact, they but furnish an appendix to Goldsmith, and other English authors. And we want no American Goldsmiths; nay; we want no American Miltons. It were the vilest thing you could say of a true American author, that he were an American Tompkins. Call him an American, and have done; for you can not say a nobler thing of him,—but it is not meant that all American writers should studiously cleave to nationality in their writings; only this, no American writer should write like an Englishman, or a Frenchman; let him write like a man, for then he will be sure to write like an American. Let us away with this leaven of literary flunkyism towards England. If either must play the flunky in this thing, let England do it, not us. While we are rapidly preparing for that political supremacy among the nations, which prophetically awaits us at the close of the present century; in a literary point of view, we are deplorably unprepared for it; and we seem studious to remain so. Hitherto, reasons might have existed why this should be; but no good reason exists now. And all that is requisite to amendment in this matter, is simply this: that, while freely acknowledging all excellence, everywhere, we should refrain from unduly lauding foreign writers, and, at the same time, duly recognize the meritorious writers that are our own;—those writers, who breathe that unshackled, democratic spirit of Christianity in all things, which now takes the practical lead in this world, though at the same time led by ourselves—us Americans. Let us boldly contemn all imitation, though it comes to us graceful and fragrant as the morning; and foster all originality, though, at first, it be crabbed and ugly as our own pine knots. [1]

This unashamed expression of an intense national pride at once creates and obscures considerable problems. America is preparing to assert its "political supremacy among the nations." Only "in a literary point of view" are we lagging behind; the great American writer will, then, give to his country a cultural authority equal to its political authority. This authority rests, however, on a form of government that subverts its very basis: the democratic idea of equality makes somewhat problematic Melville's comfortable, indeed emphatic promotion of nondemocratic cultural and political relations between America and the rest of the world. A society that asserts both the limits and the provisional nature of authority is about to dominate other societies, and Melville is so excited by that idea that he wants no form of domination to be left out. The American spirit of equality has to be first everywhere in both letters and politics.

Moby-Dick both represents and seeks to evade the difficulties raised by the imperialist militancy of the democratic spirit. We can already see Melville's predilection—also confirmed by the rhetoric of *Moby-Dick*—for concepts whose terms appear to cancel each other out. The proven value of the democratic ideal justifies America's accession to supreme power in the nondemocratic relations among countries (relations consonant, in the case of other states, with their internal hierarchies of power). This entire section of "Hawthorne and His Mosses" is characterized by its conceptual incompatibilities. Not content to say that an original failure is better than a successful imitation, or even that a man must have risked failure to attain greatness, Melville asserts, in a significant logical jump from the two previous propositions: "Failure is the true test of greatness." Most important, this habit of thought makes it nearly impossible to imagine how the great American work might be produced. Melville's invocation of American greatness is almost obsessively comparative. Hawthorne is not "greater than William of Avon, or as great. But the difference between them is by no means immeasurable. Not a very great deal more, and Nathaniel were verily William." This fidelity to, and meticulous quantifying of, the notion of greatness continues in the comparison between Shakespeare and all other writers, both past and present. "This, too, I mean, that if Shakespeare has not been equalled, give the world time, and he is sure to be surpassed, in one hemisphere or the other." But the condition of such surpassing seems to be the erasure of the continuities allowing us to recognize, for example, that Shakespeare has been surpassed. The passage is most remarkable for its extravagant—and perhaps peculiarly American—expression of an impossible dream: that of a literature without debts, which would owe nothing to the past.[2] How is original American greatness to be measured (since it is apparently to be measured) or even identified? The answer is defiant, but scarcely illuminating: "no American writer should write like an Englishman, or a Frenchman; let him write like a man, for then he will be sure to write like an American." The question should probably be reformulated as: Is it possible to write *like* nobody—without, however, eliminating the possibility of writing *better* than anyone else or being favorably compared with those to whom one owes nothing? American originality will write a glorious new chapter in the history of world literature only if it rejects its place in that history.

Moby-Dick, in extraordinary ways, accepts and struggles with the pressure of these contradictions. It is clear that Melville has no intention of waiting for those men just being born on the banks of the Ohio to prove their genius. *Moby-Dick is* the great original American book invoked in "Hawthorne and His Mosses"; or, at the very least, it squarely meets the challenge of that essay. Melville will take an American subject—even a provincial American subject: the industry of whaling—and show that the greatest literature can be made from that subject. It is not a question of proving that a lot can be made out of a little, but rather of showing that what may seem to be a little is already a lot. "To produce a mighty book," Ishmael declares, "you must choose a mighty theme. No great and enduring volume can ever be written on the flea, though many there be who have tried it" (379). Whaling is inherently a mighty subject, and to embrace it is to try to hold something that itself reaches out and connects to everything else in human time and cosmic space. Ahab may be crazy to assign evil intentions to a dumb brute, but the pursuit of Moby Dick can't help being a hunt for sense. A whaling expedition is inevitably an adventure in reading; the whale is a primary text of nature itself. Not only that: even as Melville's novel goes along, it is constantly being submitted to a vigilant comparison to other cultural models. There is a cultural encyclopedism in *Moby-Dick* as well as a cetological encyclopedism. It is not that the entries exhaustively treat any subject, but the encyclopedic intention—which is perhaps all the encyclopedic novel ever gives us in any case—is obvious with respect to foreign cultures as well as to whaling. It is as if the great American novel had constantly to be measuring itself against the highest achievements of other cultures, and in *Moby-Dick* this means testing the American book's capacity to appropriate a vast field of cultural reference. Melville's splendidly arrogant claim is that almost everything in world culture might be made to serve his subject. The "comprehensiveness of sweep" of Ishmael's thoughts of Leviathan reaches out, most notably, to the Bible, to Shakespeare, and to Greek tragedy, and these illustrious references lose some of their autonomous worth in order to serve *Moby-Dick,* to become mere aids to intelligibility—analogical satellites—in an American drama. It is not merely that *Moby-Dick* is worthy of being compared to either *King Lear* or *Oedipus Rex.* Instead it must be compared to both at the same time; only an encyclopedic range of cultural reference can do justice to Melville's mighty theme. His book reenacts several biblical dramas (Ahab, Ishmael, Ezekiel, Rachel, and others), the Greek tragedies of fatality, and Lear's tragic intimacy with nature and madness. *Moby-Dick* is therefore not only as great as any one of these references; in needing them all to explain itself, it also proposes to surpass them all. Cetological erudition in *Moby-Dick* is only the first step in an enterprise of cannibalistic encyclopedism. Like its monster-hero, Melville's novel opens its jaws to devour all other representations from Lear's Fool to Vishnoo the Hindu god.

And yet all this is something of a joke (although one that can also turn on itself and make another kind of joke of joking):

> Friends, hold my arms! For in the mere act of penning my thoughts of this
> Leviathan, they weary me, and make me faint with their outreaching com-
> prehensiveness of sweep, as if to include the whole circle of the sciences,
> and all the generations of whales, and men, and mastodons, past, present,
> and to come, with all the revolving panoramas of empire on earth, and
> throughout the whole universe, not excluding its suburbs. (379)

"Not excluding its suburbs"? Something, obviously, has gone awry. The
hyperbole of the first part of this passage may already have made us
somewhat suspicious, but how are we to place that phrase about the
universe's suburbs in a serious claim about *Moby-Dick*'s mighty theme?
Much has been written about the humor in Melville's novel, especially as
a counterpoint to Ahab's monomaniacal pursuit of the whale. The possibility of sinister and far-reaching significance in the whale is often dissipated by all the mocking allusions to the philosophical profundity
necessary to uncover that significance. Besides, the last thing a whaling
ship needs is a serious philosophical mind. Indeed, this is the explicit
lesson of "The Mast-Head" chapter, where Ishmael warns Nantucket
shipowners to beware that "sunken-eyed young Platonist [who] will tow
you ten wakes around the world, and never make you one pint of sperm
the richer" (139). The cultural appropriations meant to authenticate
Moby-Dick's claim to greatness are exposed as both laughingly inappropriate to the book's subject and even somewhat ridiculous in themselves.
Not only that: in spite of what might seem like a heavy dose of cetology
for a work of fiction, Ishmael actually encourages us to be distrustful of
his research and presumed knowledge about the whale. The book's cetological erudition—based on remarkably partial sources—is often nothing more than a parody of the erudition of others, and the "proofs"
offered of the whale's extraordinary powers most frequently consist (as
in "The Affidavit" chapter) of hearsay and assertion.[3] More is at stake
here than Ishmael's resistance to Ahab's monomania, more than a presumably viable humanistic alternative to interpretive madness. It is as
if the writing of *Moby-Dick* became for Melville the eerie process of
dismissing the very ambitions that the novel also seeks so strenuously
to realize, as if a kind of leveling indifference had taken over or—
most interestingly—as if the notion of American literary greatness were
dropped in order to be reinvented, but reinvented *as* something lost,
indefensible, abandoned.

*   *   *

What is it, in *Moby-Dick*'s primary project, that might explain Melville's
apparent indifference toward it, even his subversion of it? In *Moby-Dick*
the political implication of the contradictions hinted at in "Hawthorne
and His Mosses" becomes inescapable. More exactly, the notion of

American literary greatness is politically represented in *Moby-Dick,* and this means trying to give some coherence or plausibility to the idea of a democratic greatness.[4] The "august dignity I treat of," Ishmael writes in the early section introducing Ahab and his mates,

> is not the dignity of kings and robes, but that abounding dignity which has no robed investiture. Thou shalt see it shining in the arm that wields a pick or drives a spike; that democratic dignity which, on all hands, radiates without end from God; Himself! The great God absolute! The center and circumference of all democracy! His omnipresence, our divine equality!
>
> If, then, to meanest mariners, and renegades and castaways, I shall hereafter ascribe high qualities, though dark; weave round them tragic graces; if even the most mournful, perchance the most abased, among them all, shall at times lift himself to the exalted mounts; if I shall touch that workman's arm with some ethereal light; if I shall spread a rainbow over his disastrous set of sun; then against all mortal critics bear me out in it; thou just Spirit of Equality, which hast spread one royal mantle of humanity over all my kind! (104–105)

Nothing in this passage suggests a rejection of the principle of aristocratic privilege. On the contrary: Ishmael promises a multiplication of the signs and accoutrements of a society based on privilege. He will ascribe "high qualities" to the heroes of his narrative, "weave around them tragic graces," touch them with "ethereal light" and lift them to "exalted mounts"; "pearl" and "finest gold" translate the genius of Bunyan and Cervantes, and Andrew Jackson is imagined as having been "thundered" higher than a throne. "Democracy" here consists in the fact that none of this preeminence is predetermined: in a democratic society, anybody can be lifted to royalty. The principles that determine places within a hierarchy have been changed, but the hierarchical structure has remained intact. It is simply that now the "champions" will come from "the kingly commons." In *Moby-Dick* the rhetoric of democracy has become oxymoronic: in a democracy, equality founds and legitimates inequality.

Ahab's "irresistible dictatorship" perfectly represents this conversion of democracy into royalism. His absolute domination of the crew provides a democratic sanction of despotism. It is true that to a certain extent "the paramount forms and usages of the sea" reinforce a captain's authority independently of his intrinsic merit. In this sense a ship is less like a democracy than a monarchy, and can even call to mind those "royal instances" when "external arts and embellishments" have "imparted potency" to "idiot imbecility." But having granted this, Ishmael insists that the greatness of Ahab owes nothing to the prestige of inherited forms, that—and we can add: like the greatness of America itself or that of the American literary works invoked in "Hawthorne and His Mosses"—it is a wholly original greatness, one without history or traditions. Unlike the "tragic dramatists" who, wishing to "depict mortal indomitableness in its fullest sweep and direct swing," never forget to lend their heroes the persuasive power of "external arts and embellishments," Ishmael sees his captain Ahab as moving before him

> in all his Nantucket grimness and shagginess; and in this episode touching Emperors and kings, I must not conceal that I have only to do with a poor old whale-hunter like him; and, therefore, all outward majestical trappings and housings are denied me. Oh, Ahab! What shall be grand in thee, it must needs be plucked at from the skies, and dived for in the deep, and featured in the unbodied air! (129–130)

Far from being a democratic rejection of emperors and kings, *Moby-Dick* proposes a unique expansion of the monarchic principle. Ahab will earn his right to be called King Ahab, to have his meals with his three mates compared to "the Coronation banquet at Frankfort, where the German Emperor profoundly dines with the seven Imperial Electors." Ahab embodies and realizes the ambition of the novel itself: to have a royal pre-eminence over European literature without borrowing anything from European models of literary greatness.

And yet the very condition of this success is of course a massive borrowing from those models. The justification of Ahab's kingship is perhaps original and democratic; but the implicit argument for kingship itself comes from abroad, and this condemns Ishmael to analogical proofs of Ahab's greatness. That is, his royal nature will be confirmed by both passing (the German emperor) and sustained (Lear) comparisons between him and other royal natures, by continuous assertions that no royal example is too high to describe him. Melville defines the idea of greatness itself—both for his book and his tragic hero—by constant appeals to our cultural recognitions, thus destroying the argument for originality with its proofs. Or, to put this another way, originality turns out to be nothing more than multiplication of the same. *Moby-Dick*'s greatness is unlike that of any other book, and Ahab's royal nature is not to be thought of as comparable to that of other kings and emperors precisely because they can be compared to so many other books and kings. Originality occurs, as it were, after a certain threshold of absorption has been passed, and *Moby-Dick*'s cultural encyclopedism is a peculiarly American attempt to quantify quality, to produce originality through mass. Once again we are forced to recognize the novel's oxymoronic argument: democracy produces the greatest kings, and analogy authenticates originality. Thus Melville wins his argument for Ahab by destroying the very reason for making the argument in the first place: the unassimilable, unrecuperable uniqueness of the democratic personality.

If the democratic ideas of intrinsic worth, and of equal opportunity to assert that worth, are shown to have oligarchic consequences, these consequences are also vindicated in the novel's metaphysical terms. Although Ahab's monomania is most explicitly defined as his transferring the idea of (and, in an even madder way, the responsibility for) "all evil" to Moby Dick, there are hints in the novel that he may also see the whale in terms closer to those used by Ishmael in the central chapter on "The Whiteness of the Whale." Then Moby Dick would not only embody "that intangible malignity which has been from the beginning" (160); more subtly, and more terrifyingly, he would figure the absence of any intentionality whatsoever outside the human mind. This, as we shall shortly see, is the basis for what I will call the crisis of interpretation in *Moby-Dick*. Ahab's defiant invocation to fire in "The Candles" best indicates this shift of metaphysical emphasis: "In the midst of the personified impersonal, a personality stands here. Though but a point at best; whencesoe'er I came; whereso'er I go; yet while I earthly live, the queenly personality lives in me, and feels her royal rights" (417). From this perspective, the pursuit of Moby Dick is perhaps less mad; it is precisely because the whale *is,* as Starbuck says, merely a dumb brute that its power to do so much harm is intolerable. It may *unintentionally destroy.* To be attacked by the whale is not to encounter an enemy; rather, as Ahab at least suggests, it is to have the catastrophic experience of personality's contingency in the universe. Even more intolerable than Moby Dick's intelligent malignity would be its lack of any design at all, for then Ahab's pursuit would be a madly (and comically) incongruous motivation in a universe where purely physical laws govern the movements and meetings of objects. Ahab's assertion of personality—even more, his assertion of royal prerogatives for his "queenly personality"—would then be at once senseless and heroic, a necessarily unheard protest against his having been thrown into the wrong universe, against *this* universe's metaphysical uncongeniality.

Self-assertion is, then, vindicated in *Moby-Dick* as the most profound manifestation of a metaphysical pathos. The value given to personality in a democratic society might be thought of as the political corollary of the novel's philosophical bias in favor of political and metaphysical and literary self-assertions. Against those aristocratic societies where individual personality is largely irrelevant to a hierarchy of power determined by inherited privileges and reinforced by external arts and embellishments, Melville argues for a society (if not a universe) where the individual personality counts, indeed is determinant, in the distribution of power. But it is the very assertion of the rights of self which risks destroying those conditions allowing for it in the first place. In the terms of an unrelenting logic enacted by *Moby-Dick,* democracy ultimately promises the unintended and politically tragic consequence of its own extinction. Melville persuasively expresses the thrill of the democratic promise, both for the individual and for literature, but that thrill is perhaps inseparable from the prospect of unlimited power. The excitement *about* Ahab in *Moby-Dick* is provoked by the spectacle of what might be called an earned despotism. The *Pequod* is the social realization of a fantasy of intrinsic kingship. The opportunity for self-expression and self-assertion in a democratic society is, Melville's novel suggests, existentially translated as a will to power; despotism is the social logic within an argument for the rights of personality.

*   *   *

But we also have Ishmael and the *Pequod*'s crew. Another type of society is—or so it appears—constituted in the margins of Ahab's rule. There seems to be a social space in *Moby-Dick* outside the circle of fascinated subjugation to Ahab's monomania. And this space would be defined by a kind of democratic camaraderie in shared work.[5] There is, for example, the convivial atmosphere during the hoisting, cutting, and lowering of the whale's blubber, a task accompanied by fraternal swearing and the transformation of part of the crew into a "wild" operatic chorus. See especially the famous description of the men squeezing lumps of sperm back into fluid, an activity that frees Ishmael "from all ill-will, or petulance, or malice of any sort whatsoever":

> Squeeze! squeeze! squeeze! all the morning long; I squeezed that sperm till I myself almost melted into it; I squeezed that sperm till a strange sort of insanity came over me; and I found myself unwittingly squeezing my co-laborers' hands in it, mistaking their hands for the gentle globules. Such an abounding, affectionate, friendly, loving feeling did this avocation beget; that at last I was continually squeezing their hands, and looking up into their eyes sentimentally; as much as to say,—Oh! my dear fellow beings, why should we longer cherish any social acerbities, or know the slightest ill-humor or envy! Come; let us squeeze hands all round; nay, let us all squeeze ourselves into each other; let us squeeze ourselves universally into the very milk and sperm of kindness. (348–349)

The fraternal warmth engendered by this communal activity seems to be the best antidote to Ahab's mad isolation. It is, in terms of the book's major metaphorical opposition, a return from the dangers of sea to the security of land. Ishmael goes on to interpret what he has just described in precisely such terms. Having learned that "man must eventually lower, or at least shift, his concert of attainable felicity; not placing it anywhere in the intellect or the fancy; but in the wife, the heart, the bed, the table, the saddle, the fire-side, the country," he is "ready to squeeze case eternally" (349). But this is a tame and pious conclusion to what we have just read, and it is difficult to see what wife, fireside, and country have to do with the "strange sort of insanity" that leads Ishmael—made drunk by the touch of "those soft, gentle globules of infiltrated tissues" and the "uncontaminated aroma" of "that inexpressible sperm"—to begin squeezing his comrades' hands and gazing "sentimentally" into their eyes, dreaming of an ecstatic loss of self in a universal melting squeeze. I don't mean simply that the need to place happiness in wife and fireside seems a strangely inappropriate lesson to be drawn from such an obviously homoerotic experience, but rather that the homoeroticism itself is merely the secondary expression of a comically anarchic sensuality. Ishmael's coworkers allow for the momentary focusing and socializing of a sensuality that is so idiosyncratic, so frankly irreducible to any viable social bond—in Ishmael's own words, so insane—that it can only be *described*—accommodated by language—as a joke. The joke is emphasized by the corny, decidedly nonpious vision at the end of the passage: "In visions of the night, I saw long rows of angels in paradise, each with his hands in a jar of spermaceti."

Much has been made of homoeroticism in *Moby-Dick,* and this is not astonishing in view of the novel's hints in this direction.[6] The major piece of presumed evidence is of course the Ishmael-Queequeg relation, in which Ishmael seems not at all reluctant to portray himself as the huge savage's contented wife. On the one hand, as a couple Ishmael and Queequeg both prefigure and personalize the fraternal feelings in such tasks as cutting into the whale's blubber and reconverting its sperm into liquid. On the other hand, Ishmael gives a highly eroticized account of the friendship. After their first night together in the same bed at the Spouter Inn in New Bedford, Ishmael awakes to find Queequeg's arm thrown over him "in the most loving and affectionate manner," as if he "had been his wife" and were being held in a "bridegroom clasp" (32–33). The next night they seal their friendship, once again in bed, with "confidential disclosures," just as man and wife often choose their bed to "open the very bottom of their souls to each other." "Thus, then," this passage ends, "in our hearts' honeymoon, lay I and Queequeg—a cosy, loving pair" (54). During the voyage, when they are both tied to the same monkey rope (in the "humorously perilous business" of Queequeg's going over the side of the ship to insert a blubber hook into the whale's back, where he must remain during the whole stripping operation), they are not simply "inseparable twin brother[s]" but are "for the time . . . wedded" (271).

There is no ambiguity whatsoever in all these eroticizing allusions. They clearly instruct us to think of the bond between Ishmael and Queequeg as not unlike marital bonds, and it can be argued that they do this with no suggestion of homosexual desire. I say this somewhat tentatively because we might also say that homosexual desire is precisely what is signified by those conjugal signifiers. But where exactly is the signified? Is there a *subject* of homosexual desire in *Moby-Dick?* Far from representing either unequivocal homosexuality or surfaces of heterosexual desire troubled by repressed homosexual impulses, Melville's characters have no sexual subjectivity at all. Critics readily admit how little the wholly improbable soliloquies of Melville's characters conform to the discursive parameters of realistic fiction; they have more difficulty recognizing that those soliloquies adequately represent the essence of the characters. Interiority in *Moby-Dick* is almost entirely philosophical; each character is a certain confluence of metaphysical, epistemological, and social-ethical positions. Homoeroticism can enter the novel so easily because, psychologically, there is nothing at stake. In Balzac, Gide, and Proust, homosexual desire is a fact of great psychological significance, whereas it may be a peculiarity of American literature—Cooper, Twain, and Hemingway come to mind—that it frequently presents homosexual situations that are psychologically inconsequential, unconnected to characterization. Ishmael's marital metaphors reveal nothing about him because there is nowhere in the novel an Ishmael about whom such metaphors can be revealing.

This does not mean that they are unimportant: their very significance depends on *not* providing an intelligible alternative to Ahab's despotism. Each time the novel spells out any such alternative, it is in terms that do little more than negatively repeat what they oppose. Thus the land is opposed to the sea, and Ahab's unhappy solitude is set against the quiet joy of domestic ties. Starbuck is the principal advocate of intelligible alternatives to Ahab, such as wife and family, the land, fraternal compassion, and a democratic respect for the rights of others. But if Ahab's tyrannical rule enacts the ultimate logic of the privileges that democracy would accord personality, then perhaps the very principle of oppositional couplings cannot be trusted. Only something that does not enter into logical opposition can be "opposed" to Ahab. Politically this means that in order to escape the antidemocratic consequences inherent in the democratic ideal, a type of social relation must be imagined that is neither autocratic nor democratic.

Ishmael's response to Queequeg and the crew is the testing of this other relation, although each time he tries to analyze it he also banalizes it, as in the Starbuck-like contrast between the intellect and the fireside. But, just as Ishmael's insane ecstasy while squeezing blobs of sperm is irreducible to any of these terms, so the introduction of homoeroticism into the novel prevents his representation of Queequeg and the crew from being one of a society united in the bonds of friendship created by communal work. This homoeroticism, however, never settles into what would be merely another type of oppositional grouping. By figuring what I have called a nonpsychological homosexuality, Melville proposes a social bond based not on subordination to the great personality embodied by Ahab, not on the democratic ideal of power distributed according to intrinsic worth, not on those feelings binding either two friends or the partners in a marriage, not, finally, on the transgressed homage to all such legitimated social bonds in conventional images of homosexual desire. (Proust serves as a good example of the homosexual writer unable, for the most part, to account for his own desires except as transgressive replications of the socially accepted bonds they only superficially exclude.)

The casual humor of both the early section on Ishmael's "marriage" to Queequeg and the description of sperm squeezing helps to transform the representation of both friendship and homoeroticism into an inconceivable social bond. In so doing it evokes, in an unexpected way, the originality of American society, which Melville is both attached to and unable to describe. Ishmael's humor is a way of simultaneously proposing and withdrawing definitions and identifications, of using what are, after all, the only available categories, social and linguistic, to coax into existence as yet unavailable terms. Even the most inappropriate descriptions can serve this dislocating function. Thus, though I may have been right to argue that the reference to wife, heart, and fireside is a taming irrelevance in the squeezing-sperm chapter, the terms also disturbingly suggest an unformulated relation between a kind of anarchic sensuality and a socially viable domesticity. Similarly, far from being a parodistic version of normal marriage or a domesticating of homosexual bonds, the Ishmael-Queequeg marriage enacts a sensuality that cannot be reduced to the psychology of either heterosexual or homosexual desire, a sensuality at once nontransgressive and authorized by nothing beyond Ishmael's mode of addressing it.

Lest this begin to sound like an argument for the socially unthreatening nature of homoeroticism, I want to insist on the absence of authorization. Melville makes it clear that the society in which these new relations are being tested is a society wholly outside society. From the very first pages, going to sea is presented as a letting go of all social, conceptual, and sexual familiarity. The first chapter of *Moby-Dick* is an extraordinarily haunting invocation of seagoing as a "substitute for pistol and ball," a deliberate removal from life itself. A whole city is transformed into a collective suicidal longing when Ishmael evokes thousands of men "posted like silent sentinels all around the town" and "fixed in ocean reveries." We should keep in mind this powerfully oneiric image of a humanity thronging "just as nigh the water as they possibly can without falling in," anxious to abandon the ship of society for the magnetizing and original death promised by the sea. The first chapter clearly warns us not to consider any bonds or fellowship that may develop or, in the case of Ishmael or Queequeg, be confirmed on board the *Pequod* as compatible with the society of the land.

Is the *Pequod,* to the extent that it functions outside Ahab's domination, the image of an authentically democratic work society? Perhaps—but the workforce is constituted by a hybrid collection of exiles and outcasts. Not only does the biblical name by which the narrator invites the reader to address him in the novel's first line resonate with such connotations; the latter aptly describe the crew of the *Pequod.* Ishmael's emphasis on all the countries and races represented on the ship invites us to see the crew as a kind of international fraternity of men united in harmonious and useful work. But there is an equally strong emphasis on the wild, untutored, asocial nature of the men in that fraternity. "They were nearly all Islanders in the Pequod. *Isolatos* too, I call such, not acknowledging the common continent of men, but each *Isolato* living on a separate continent of his own" (108). It is, as Starbuck says, "a heathen crew . . . whelped somewhere by the sharkish sea" (148), a crew, as Ishmael puts it, "chiefly made up of mongrel renegades, and castaways, and cannibals" (162). Indeed whalers in general are "floating outlaws," manned by "unaccountable odds and ends of strange nations come up from the unknown nooks and ash-holes of the earth" (198).

Ishmael himself must be thought of as belonging to that group; he is its expression.[7] He is so casual in his dismissals of ordinary assumptions about social bonds that we may easily miss his readiness to reject the values of the land. "For my part," he announces in chapter one, "I abominate all honorable respectable toils, trials, and tribulations of every kind whatsoever." In context, this is playfully perverse hyperbole; but it also belongs to what amounts to a systematic rejection of the civilized ethics of a democratic and Christian land society. Honorable respectable toils are abominated; the chapter on Fast-Fish and Loose-Fish is a Swiftean mockery of legal systems in which rights to ownership are often identical to the brute force necessary to claim possession; and Christianity itself is implicitly dismissed in the comparison of images of physical "robustness" in art ("in everything imposingly beautiful, strength has much to do with the magic") to "the soft, curled, hermaphroditical Italian pictures" of Christ, which "hint nothing of any power, but the mere negative, feminine one of submission and endurance, which on all hands it is conceded, form the peculiar practical virtue of his teaching" (315). The *Pequod* is not, however, a reconstitution of politics, morality, or religious beliefs on some presumably more natural basis. Queequeg's

religion is as unsatisfactory as Christianity, and Ishmael's infinite tolerance, far from being grounded in a faith where tolerance is preached as a
virtue, merely expresses his unwillingness to be intolerant in the name of
any faith whatsoever. Nor is Ishmael willing to swear allegiance to the
Pequod's society of savages as a type of social organization. "I myself am
a savage, owning to no allegiance but to the King of the Cannibals, and
ready at any moment to rebel against him" (232).

Is the *Pequod* an image of America?[8] It is the settlement of America
reenacted, but uncompromisingly radicalized. The "unaccountable odds
and ends" from all over the world who ended up in America were of
course not only castaways and cannibals; nor were they all, for that matter, unaccountable. But by insisting on the *Pequod*'s nearly total break
with the land and the past, Melville simultaneously evokes the origins of
America as a house for exiles from everywhere and makes those origins
absolute. That is, he evokes the possibility of exile as a wholly new beginning and brutally deprives it of the comforting notion of loss. There
is no dream that has been frustrated, no second chance for forms of life
imagined, but then blocked in their realization, somewhere else. The sea
is wildness and anarchy; it opposes to both Ahab's despotism and the
democratic vision a kind of social suicide. Thus Melville's novel dreams
metaphorically of that absolute break with Europe which of course never
took place, of a risky willingness to "come to America" with no social
vision at all, with nothing but an anxious need to die to society and to
history. Far from fulfilling a European dream, America would therefore
have to be invented by those "thousands upon thousands of mortal men"
who at first wanted nothing more than to flee from the land but who,
having joined the crew of exiles and renegades from all over the hated
world, now find themselves suspended in their dying and are obliged to
redefine the social itself.

I have argued that, principally through Ahab, *Moby-Dick* dramatizes
the oxymoronic impasse of democracy: the great man's despotism realizes the democratic dream of equality. But *Moby-Dick* also reinvents that
politically infernal rhetoric as a political promise: it dreams a society owing nothing whatsoever to known social ideas. What this society after
social death might actually be, we can say no more than Melville (or
Ishmael) himself can. What can be said is only what has already been
said, and Ishmael's way of coercing all that used speech into unimagined
significances is to withdraw humorously from nearly all his propositions.
He can say what he means only by refusing to mean what he says.
America's history will take place in the space at once cluttered and blank
where all imaginable social bonds have been simultaneously figured and
dissolved. Melville's America is a historical meta-oxymoron: it defeats

the defeating oxymoron of a democracy ruined by the fulfillment of its own promise by erasing all promises in order to make the wholly unauthorized promise of an absolutely new society.

*   *   *

The representation of Melville's America is thus inseparable from a crisis of meaning. On the one hand, the interpretive faculty is associated with madness. It is not only that "all evil" is personified in Moby Dick, but also that Ahab sees evil omens and portents everywhere. The mass of information given to us about whales and whaling is obviously designed to counteract this madness; here the encyclopedia functions as an antidote to overreading, as a source of reliable facts, as a comfortable and necessary myth of a collection of knowledge unaffected by the collector's passions. "So ignorant are most landsman of some of the plainest and most palpable wonders of the world, that without some hints touching the plain facts, historical and otherwise, of the fishery they might scout at Moby Dick as a monstrous fable, or still worse and more detestable, a hideous and intolerable allegory" (177).

But this is somewhat disingenuous. The most persistent and extravagant sign reader in the novel is Ishmael. His allegorical wisdom, it is true, is of fairly modest quality; nor does he hesitate to mock it himself. What is interesting, as others have noted, is the interpretive habit itself or, more strangely, the inability to stop reading, even though the object to be read may be unreadable. *Moby-Dick* is full of enigmatic texts. First and foremost, there is the whale, both as a species and in its individual features and behavior. There is also the doubloon, with its "strange figures and inscriptions"; in chapter 99, Ahab, Starbuck, Stubb, Flask, the Manxman, Queequeg, Fedallah, and Pip all perform interpretively— producing little more than self-characterizations—in front of the gold coin. If Ahab interprets "in some monomaniac way whatever significance might lurk" in the doubloon's markings, "some certain significance," Ishmael nonetheless adds, "lurks in all things, else all things are little worth, and the round world itself but an empty cipher, except to sell by the cartload, as they do hills about Boston, to fill up some morass in the Milky Way" (358). Even Queequeg's tatoos are described as hieroglyphics containing "a complete theory of the heavens and the earth, a mystical treatise on the art of attaining truth"; and looking at that unsolvable riddle, Ahab wildly exclaims: "'Oh, devilish tantalization of the gods!'" (399). Most remarkably, however tragically frustrated or humorously tentative all such readings may be, the very course of events in the novel spectacularly confirms the power of reading. Not only do all the omens and portents turn out to be omens and portents of what actually happens to the *Pequod* and its crew; Elijah's dire prophecy also accurately prefigures the voyage's tragic end ("'Good bye to ye. Shan't see ye again very soon, I guess; unless it's before the Grand Jury'" [91]); and the demonic Fedallah's prediction—one doesn't even know what text he reads—of how he and Ahab will die is fulfilled with uncanny precision.

Moby-Dick is a chaos of interpretive modes. As a drama of interpretation, Melville's novel appears to center on Ahab. But Ahab represents only one type of interpretive activity, and in a sense it is the crudest and the easiest to discredit. For him, Moby Dick is a symbol of evil that, in its vicious attacks, fittingly partakes of the nature of what it symbolizes. Ahab is guilty of a double mistake of logic: he unjustifiably infers an agent or course of evil from the observable phenomenon of human "sufferings and exasperations," and then he identifies a possible manifestation of that evil with its essence. Having done that, he—and with him now the crew—begins to see all things as signs. Although the symbolic reading is particular to Ahab (nothing indicates that the crew shares Ahab's philosophically sophisticated madness of attributing the sum of human woes to the whale they are chasing), a degraded form of symbolic interpretation manifests itself as the superstition of signs. Instead of symbols, we have portents: the darting away of "shoals of small harmless fish . . . with what seemed shuddering fins," the "tri-painted trinity of flames" when the ship's three masts are set on fire by lightning during the typhoon, and the seizing of Ahab's hat from his head by a savage sea hawk. Symbolism is a vertical mode of interpretation (Moby Dick is transcended by the metaphysical reality he points to), but the ominous sign can be thought of as a metonymic slip. It is as if part of a pattern of catastrophe had been detached from the pattern and moved ahead of its realization in time. The omen announces the events to which it belongs; it is the beginning of a catastrophe that has not yet begun.

There is, more generally, the interpretation of the entire novel as a philosophical parable in which going to sea figures the risky movement of speculative thought, of thought unanchored, set loose from all evidential "land" securities. I also spoke earlier of the interpretive analogies meant to authenticate Melville's "mighty theme." The very syntax of analogy ("just as . . . so . . . ") suggests the equal status of this strange and isolated incident in the annals of whaling and the most memorable moments of human history and culture. Finally, the local descriptive metaphor in *Moby-Dick* can even work in the opposite direction, to normalize and domesticate the drama aboard the *Pequod*. In describing the crew's transfixed horror when, during a lightning storm, the ends of the three tall masts catch fire and silently burn "like three gigantic wax tapers before an altar," Ishmael writes: "From the arched and overhanging rigging, where they had just been engaged securing a spar, a number of the seamen, arrested by the glare, now cohered together, and hung pendulous, like a knot of numbed wasps from a drooping, orchard twig" (415–416). This astonishing comparison assimilates a moment of crazy panic on the *Pequod* to an ordinary rural scene, and in so doing it casually naturalizes melodrama, making the sailor's terror into—asking us to read their terror as—something as unexceptional as immobile wasps on a twig. Thus the most melodramatic of scenes is domesticated, and the exceptional scenes of human tragedy are reintegrated into the vast tableau of nature, where relations may be constituted by nothing more meaningful than the visual resemblance between two distant points in space.

Ishmael's principal function is, however, less to add to interpretive modes than to be the hermeneutical ground of *all* modes of interpretation. That is, he defines the conditions of possibility for all interpretive activity in *Moby-Dick,* and we can define that condition as Ishmael's invalidating tolerance of the search for meanings. If the interpretive process cannot be stopped, if the novel is a relentless, nearly grotesque compulsion to read significance into all objects and events (a compulsion ranging from Ahab's mad symbolism to Ishmael's allegorizing speculations on the thickness of the whale's blubber), Ishmael's humor simultaneously withdraws all credibility from the sense he ceaselessly proposes. Thus the principal question we face in reading this encyclopedic demonstration of interpretive processes is how to read the deployment of those processes. Next to that problem, Ahab is comparatively simple to understand; indeed, his immediately recognizable tragic stance, and his monomaniacal madness, may delay our recognition of the far greater radicality of Ishmael. For the reader, the primary enigmatic text is not Moby Dick, but Ishmael's relation to the possible readings of Moby Dick. Is there any view of the story, or any interpretive mode, that escapes Ishmael's repeated retreat from all points of view? We might think of this retreating move as one of irony; Ishmael's ironic humor interprets interpretation by a noncritical but no less effectively destructive step back from all interpretations. Humor is the tonal sign of this step; it gives a voice to that suspensive move of consciousness which invalidates its objects without erasing them, merely by reflecting them at a certain distance. This move can, finally, consist in the erasure of the tonal sign of humor itself—as in "The Fountain" chapter, which Ishmael ends on a serious note, stepping back from the humor just preceding the end and making of his very seriousness the lightest mode of thought, merely another sign of consciousness in retreat.

The consequence of all this is that *Moby-Dick* becomes a novel unavailable to the culture it still manages to define (while making the generous, even utopian assumption that such readings as the one I am proposing *are* available to that culture). Melville's novel is the literary equivalent of that "dumb blankness full of meaning" which is what

Ishmael finds so awesome in the whale's whiteness. We may continue to speak of *Moby-Dick* (as the novel itself demonstrates, criticism is unstoppable), but we can at least hope for an appropriately impoverished reading, one that principally describes how the narrative anticipates, entertains, and withdraws its assent from all our interpretive moves. The chapter on "The Whiteness of the Whale" analyzes the symptoms of a mind afflicted with an oxymoronic perception of the universe. Reality is an infinitely meaningful absence of meaning, and *Moby-Dick*—a novel of metaphysical realism—repeats that textuality in its own apparently unlimited capacity to entertain unauthorized interpretations. But this type of textuality—in which unreadability is identical to a limitless availability to interpretation—may be the condition of the novel's originality. American literature can be great not by being as good as or even better than European literature; it must be, in the full force of the term, incomparable. Thus Ishmael will not only destroy the terms of comparison; he will also invalidate the very process of comparison—the unrelenting analogical habit—to which he appeals in order to validate his project of writing a "mighty book." *Moby-Dick* outdoes the cultural references it appropriates by dismissing itself; the simultaneous proposal and erasure of sense produces a book bloated with unaccepted sense. The extraordinary originality of Melville's work is that it somehow subsists—materially—as a book orphaned by its content.

The only surviving analogy of this shipwreck of sense is the analogy with America itself. Not only does the *Pequod*'s crew reenact the origin of American society as a break with the very idea of the social; the hermeneutic suspension of every interpretive move in the novel gives a kind of plausibility to the difficult idea of an historical originality.[9] It suggests that the originality of America cannot consist in a chimerical absolute break with its European past, but rather in what might be called an encyclopedic nonendorsement of that past. In America, as in Melville's novel, the massive borrowing from other cultures is identical to a self-distancing from other cultures. Sense is borrowed without being subscribed to, and the very indiscriminacy of the borrowing should produce a society without debts, one that never holds what it nonetheless greedily takes. *Moby-Dick* is at once politically, aesthetically, and economically utopian in that it invites America *to dissipate its capital*. This is not, I believe, merely another capitalistic or liberal mystification: far from merely offering the illusion of a break with established orders (an illusion so comforting that it would actually weaken our resistance to those same orders), *Moby-Dick* proposes no object of loyalty or of desire except the continuously repeated gesture of not receiving the wealth it appropriates.

The encyclopedism of *Moby-Dick* is, then, in no way redemptive. Never using either its cetological erudition or its cultural borrowings to monumentalize the truly raw materials of the American life, Melville's novel takes the same risks as the country it finally honors, not by taking the lead in world literature but by repeating its impoverished beginning, its utopian negations. *Moby-Dick* is indeed our mighty book, not because it makes a whole of the fragments of America but rather because, in its sheer massiveness, it never stops demonstrating (as if to inspire courage) the sustaining, self-renewing powers of historical and cultural orphanhood.

CHAPTER 7

Against Ulysses

Let us approach *Ulysses* as naively as possible, while admitting that this decision can be little more than a ruse. The ruseful naiveté I have in mind will consist in our pretending not to have any extratextual information about the novel—especially information about Joyce's elaborate scheme of Homeric correspondences and about the geography and history of Ireland's capital city. In saying this, I expose our naiveté as, precisely, a decision: it is only because we know how important Homer and Dublin are in *Ulysses* that we can refer to a reading ignorant of that importance as naive. I do not mean that it is natural to read any novel in a state of cultural ignorance. I do, however, want to suggest that it would not be naive to set about reading *La Chartreuse de Parme, War and Peace,* or *Moby-Dick* without, in the cases of Stendhal and Tolstoy, more than a fairly general, nonspecialist's knowledge of Napoleon's campaigns in Belgium and Russia, and, for Melville's work, cetological expertise. This also means that the difficulties of these novels cannot in any way be resolved by consulting sources external to them. Our ideally uninformed readers of *Ulysses,* on the other hand, may very well be overcome with embarrassment to discover, upon opening their first work of criticism, that what they had been thinking of quite simply as chapters 8 and 10 are universally referred to as "Lestrygonians" and "Wandering Rocks," or that wholly impenetrable passages have in fact the most satisfying transparency to cognoscenti, say, of nineteenth-century records of Gaelic legends or of theater programs and journalistic *faits divers* in turn-of-the-century Dublin.

Naiveté, then—when it is not the sophisticated and artificial luxury I propose we briefly enjoy—becomes a retroactive judgment: how could I have read *Ulysses* without at least trying to exploit the clue provided by the novel's title, and—what is even more humiliating—how could I have mistaken cryptic or truncated allusions to the minutiae of Dublin life around 1900 for passages of textual ambiguity or complexity? The title itself, in addition to furnishing an important clue, is after all also a clear warning against the perils of innocence: the Latinized version of Odysseus alludes to one of world literature's most resourceful and wily heroes, and—as if that weren't enough—Buck Mulligan draws our attention on the novel's very first page to Stephen Dedalus' "absurd name, an ancient Greek,"[1] the name, that is, of the cunning artificer who both constructed and escaped from Minos' labyrinth.

In short, we have only to glance at the title and read page one of *Ulysses* to be forewarned: trickery and cunning are the novel's first connotations, and the possibility is thus raised from the very start that those qualities not only belong to certain characters within the novel but, much more significantly, that they define an authorial strategy. And in that case naiveté is tantamount to walking into a trap. We would therefore do well to take trickery and cunning as hortative and not merely psychologically predictive connotations: they propose the ideal-reader response to *Ulysses* as one of extreme—or extremely nervous, perhaps even somewhat paranoid—vigilance.

The tensest vigilance will, however, allow us still to approach *Ulysses* with what may at first have seemed like dangerous naiveté. For we may now go on to suspect that the connotative cluster of trickery may itself be part of a superior trickery. Might it be possible that Joyce wastes no time in encouraging us to find the novel more complicated, more devious, than it actually is, and that a comparatively simple and uninformed reading may not be so inappropriate after all? An intentionally or unintentionally naive reading of *Ulysses* can perhaps reveal things about the novel that our inevitable loss of readerly innocence will obscure. Since my emphasis will be mainly on the nature and consequences of the ideally informed reading of *Ulysses,* we should begin by doing justice to the insights of ignorance, the interpretive gains to be had from the assumption that *Ulysses* can be read as if it were a nineteenth-century realistic novel.

Those gains are far from negligible. If we were unaware of the avant-gardist claims made for Joyce's novel, we would, I think, have little hesitation in speaking of it as a psychological work, as a novel of character. We might of course be bothered by what an old-fashioned critical discourse has called a disproportion between the technical machinery and the psychological or "human" content, machinery that frequently obscures our view of what is happening.[2] For it is undeniable that a certain type of story—rather, a story *tout court*—has awakened in us certain desires by which the second half of the novel seems embarrassed and to which the most chic contemporary critics of Joyce implicitly claim to be immune. *Ulysses* is an exceptionally detailed study of character—especially of the character of Leopold Bloom, but also of Stephen

Dedalus, Molly Bloom and even of Gerty MacDowell, who appears in only one episode.[3] We know these characters inside out, and both from the inside and from the outside. There is much evidence of how they look to others, and long sections of internal monologue and free indirect style make us familiar with their most intimate habits of mind. There is even an entire episode—"Eumaeus"—written in the manner of Bloom, that is, in the style he would presumably use were he to try his hand at writing (a possibility he himself raises in this very chapter). Since the style of "Eumaeus" also suggests—not unpainfully—why Bloom will always prefer talking to writing, the episode can be considered still another characterizing technique. This very late section (it is episode 16) lets the reader know the character even more intimately than before by temporarily turning the narrator into the dummy-double of a ventriloquistic Bloom.

Has any fictional character ever been so completely known? Warmhearted, commonsensical and unfanatic in politics and religion, a loving son, father, and even husband, full of enterprising (if unrealized and impractical) commercial schemes, slightly but not unappealingly pretentious intellectually, horny and a bit guilty sexually, garrulous but a stylistic outsider in a city of besotted skilled rhetoricians, perhaps a bit tight-fisted by Dublin pub standards (where the one unpardonable sin is failing to pay your round), something of a loner (but by no means a rebel or an outcast) with his daydreams of travel in exotic Eastern lands, Bloom is eminently appealing and eminently ordinary. In one of the exchanges that constitute the impersonal catechism of "Ithaca," Bloom is called "Everyman or Noman." In any case, he is a Sweet Man, and if Joyce has inspired a kind of attachment and anecdotal curiosity (about him, about the streets of Dublin) evocative of that affection for Jane Austen which was for so long an obstacle to her being thought of as a serious writer, it is largely because of his success in creating Bloom. The Joyceans are quite a bit raunchier that the "Janeites," but the extraordinarily prosperous Joyce industry (with organized visits to the holy spots in Dublin and Zurich) largely depends, as in the case of Austen, on the by no means unfounded or inconsiderable pleasure of recognition. The Blooms are an identifiable couple, and it is an extraordinary tribute to Joyce's power of realistic evocation that all the fancy narrative techniques of *Ulysses* are unable to dim the vivid presence of Poldy and Molly. For hordes of aficionados, June 16 will always be celebrated as Bloomsday, and it would be not only snobbish but critically wrong to suggest that the innovative power of Joyce's novel lies in a questioning or breakdown of traditional novelistic assumptions about personality.

*   *   *

But there are, from the very beginning, certain knots, or certain gnats, in the narrative that disturb our relaxed reading and easy appreciation of *Ulysses'* rounded characters. Much of the novel's difficulty, especially in the early sections, is the result not of our having to learn to think about novelistic names (such as Stephen Dedalus and Leopold Bloom) in nonpsychological terms, but rather of the uncompromising nature of the mimetic techniques. An "accurate" rendering of a character's consciousness presumably requires that the narrator do nothing to help us follow the moves of that consciousness. Confronted with characters at once vivid and obscure, the reader may be inspired to take on the exegetical task of reducing the obscurity, of getting to know Bloom, Molly, or Stephen even better by completing their sentences and explaining their allusions. Far from destroying a mimetic effect that may seem to depend on a certain degree of maintained obscurity in the recorded consciousness, exegesis in this case is itself a secondary mimetic technique: a certain type of textual research is experienced as an investigation into real lives.

Thus we are required to complete the portraits of Bloom and Stephen, an activity that includes but is very little threatened by the perception of their absorption into a variety of alien styles and nonrepresentational techniques. Indeed, in Joycean criticism the most sophisticated technical analysis comfortably cohabits with the most naive reading. John Paul Riquelme's intelligent and thorough study of mimetically disruptive techniques in *Ulysses* apparently intensified his affection for Bloom. In the midst of the most trenchant, no-nonsense point-of-view analyses, Riquelme frequently praises Bloom as a man who avoids extremes, one who "perceives what Boylan is blind to: a basis for human action in concern for others rather than primarily in self-interest."[4] Is there no relation between elaborate analysis of *Ulysses* as pure linguistic effects and a type of psychological and moral appreciation already made obsolete by the New Criticism of half a century ago? My point is, of course, that the relation is only too clear, and that Joyce's avant-gardism largely consists in forcing his readers to complete the rear-guard action that the novel itself simultaneously performs and elaborately disguises.

Filling in the blanks of consciousness is, however, only part of the game, although none of the more sophisticated moves into which Joyce maneuvers us will seriously undermine the traditional view of human identity that *Ulysses* defends. The novel is full of what has rather curiously been called stylistic intrusions, as if literature were ever anything but just that. Most frequently, these intrusions take the form of discontinuities or inconsistencies of point of view. I have in mind passages where Bloom abruptly begins to think with stylistic resources obviously not his, as well as those other moments when, as Hugh Kenner puts it, "the normally neutral narrative vocabulary [is pervaded by] a little cloud of idioms which a character might use if he were managing the narrative,"[5] or, finally, when different characters' points of view are briefly merged. The celebrated perspectival jolts and mergers of *Ulysses* include the paragraph in "Nausicaa" that abandons Bloom's limited angle of vision and takes us on a panoramic tour of the entire Howth neighborhood, the name distortions in "Scylla and Charybdis" (which may be Stephen's mental horseplay with his companions' names or the fooling around of a lexically ebullient narrator), and, in "Sirens," the subtle invasion of Bloom's consciousness by musicalizing tics of the dominant narrative style (alliterations, verbal echoes, staccato rhythms).[6]

All of this has made of Joyce one of the darlings of that branch of narratology obsessed with origins, with determining where narrators are located, over whose shoulder they may be speaking, from what temporal perspective and in whose voice they address us. In its more ambitious manifestations, this school of literary analysis moves from particular literary works to the devising of a master plan of possible narrative points of view—a model that can then serve in future readings. With a writer as perspectivally shifty as Joyce, we can easily imagine how handy, and how comforting, such pocket codes of narrative perspective can be. Now he's there and now he's not; point-of-view analysis is the literary-criticism version of hide and seek. It is the paranoid response to what might be called the irreducibility of voice in literature to locations and identities.

If point-of-view criticism is intent on getting everything straight, on putting the literary house in order (and there are academic domestic quarrels about where certain pieces of stylistic furniture belong), it can also be titillated by disorder, or perspectival inconsistencies. Only narratologists truly worth their salt will identify all the traps Joyce sets for us in *Ulysses*. One example: immediately after a passage that quotes Bloom's thoughts about Shakespeare (we know it's Bloom: he wrongly attributes Congreve's "Music hath charms to soothe the savage breast" to Shakespeare), we find, "In Gerard's rosery of Fetter lane he walks, greyedauburn" (230). This is an almost exact repetition of one of Stephen's remarks during the Shakespeare discussion in "Scylla and Charybdis," and so we go rushing back to that episode to make sure we were right to think that Bloom wasn't there. He wasn't; but the narrator was, and since he's as free as he wants to be, he has simply dropped this bit of Stephen's speech into the flow of Bloom's consciousness. There are of course cases of much greater ambiguity in Joyce's writing, one of which occurs in the description of Buck Mulligan on the first pages of *Ulysses*: "He peered sideways up and gave a long slow whistle of call, then paused awhile in rapt attention, his even white teeth glistening here and there with gold points. Chrysostomos. Two strong shrill whistles answered through the calm." Who says or thinks "Chrysostomos"? And is it the rhetorically adept Mulligan we are meant to compare to the "golden-mouthed" father of the early church, St. John Chrysostomos, or is it *Ulysses* itself? As Fritz Senn has written, the word can be taken "as the translation of a visual impression, as Stephen's internal comment, as the heralding of a new technique characterized often by the sacrifice of the syntactically complete sentence structure, as a reflection on *Ulysses* itself . . . But it *might,* after all, also be the comment of some narrator."[7] Then there are passages, such as the description of Mulligan dressing, which appear to mix not only different types of narrative reporting (third-person descriptions, internal monologue, and dialogue) but characters themselves:

> And putting on his stiff collar and rebellious tie he spoke to them, chiding them, and to his dangling watchchain. His hands plunged and rummaged in his trunk while he called for a clean handkerchief. [Agenbite of inwit.] God, we'll simply have to dress the character. I want puce gloves and green boots. Contradiction. Do I contradict myself? Very well then, I contradict myself. Mercurial Malachi. A limp black missile flew out of his talking hands. —And there's your Latin quarter hat, he said. (14)

The two sentences beginning "God, we'll simply have to dress" and "I want" seem to be Buck's speech, but with "Contradiction" we enter what David Hayman has called "a dead space between thought and action," a space that may belong to Stephen or to Buck or to both (or is it the narrator's allusion to Whitman?), one in which "the two individuals are momentarily and magically joined by the narrator whose procedures are more comprehensible on the thematic and analogical levels than on the mimetic."[8] This ambiguity, I should emphasize, in no way threatens a solidly established difference between Stephen and Buck, just as the playful transposition of the sounds of Stephen's and Bloom's names in "Ithaca" (they momentarily become "Stoom" and "Blephen") is nothing but a momentary lexical joke that has no effect whatever on differences already elaborated for well over five hundred pages by a scrupulously realistic psychology.

Joyce both provokes and soothes our critical paranoia (he provides it with exorcising exercises); the difficulty, or even impossibility, of attribution in *Ulysses* is almost always a local affair, one that takes place against a background of firmly identified and differentiated personalities. Since, for example, we could no more confuse Bloom's voice with Stephen's than we could mistake Gibbon's style for Malory's in the pastiches of "Oxen of the Sun," the intrusions, confusions, and discontinuities of point of view in *Ulysses* must, I think, be read as an important element in the strategic centering of the narrator's authority. That is, they should be read as part of his aggressively demonstrated superiority to the patterns and models of representation he insists that we recognize and analytically elaborate while he himself partially neglects them.[9]

I do not mean by this that the perspectival agitations of *Ulysses* are insignificant. The question of point of view is essentially a question of citation—whose voice is the narrative quoting?—and citation is crucial to the intra- and intertextual authority of Joyce's novel as a Masterwork. Indeed, Joyce's occasionally grand indifference to consistency of point of view should perhaps be read as a way to redirect our attention from the comparatively trivial quotations of consciousness to what I will call the quotation of essential being. And in this he brings to the mimetic tradition in literature what may be its most refined technique. Consider the first sentence of *Ulysses*: "Stately, plump Buck Mulligan came from the stairhead, bearing a bowl of lather on which a mirror and a razor lay crossed." "Bearing" instead of "carrying" is part of the "novelese" characteristic, as Kenner reminds us, of the first episode.[10] Both it and the two adjectives used to describe Buck reflect his particular rhetorical pomposity. But it is not exactly as if Buck had written that sentence; nor do we have an otherwise neutral narrative vocabulary pervaded by "a little cloud of idioms which a character might use if he were managing the narrative." Rather, Buck's verbal mannerisms are a necessary part of a wholly objective presentation of him. "Plump" somewhat deflates "stately"; it helps us to visualize the character in a way that does not exactly support the vaguer connotations of "stately." The sentence is at once seduced by Mulligan's rhetoric and coolly observant of his person. Not that Buck would have been incapable of writing the sentence (which is a rather silly issue for criticism to address at any rate); but in writing it he would already, so to speak, have stepped out of himself, would have performed himself with irony. And we could say that a complete or objective view of Buck can be given neither by a direct quote nor by an analytical description, but only by a self-performance at a certain distance from the performing self. In other words, the sentence objectifies the point of view that it takes.

It is this nonperspectival point of view that explains the peculiar and disturbing power of *Dubliners,* where Joyce characterizes not only individuals but also a kind of collective consciousness through such objectified subjectivity.[11] This impressive achievement should, I think, be considered in the light of Stephen's definition of beauty in *A Portrait of the Artist as a Young Man,* as well as the references in *Ulysses* to Aristotle's notion of entelechy and the "form of forms." In trying to understand what Aquinas means by "radiance" (or *claritas*) in his enumeration of the "three things needed for beauty" *(integritas, consonantia, claritas),* Stephen comes to the following solution: "The radiance of which he speaks is the scholastic *quidditas,* the *whatness* of a thing."[12] It is as if literature could quote being independently of any particular being's point of view. We would, that is, have the point of view of neither a narrator nor a character; instead we would have the quidditas of Buck Mulligan, and even of Dublin. The individual's or the city's point of view has been purified to its essence, to a whatness ontologically distinct from the phenomenality of having a point of view.

The somewhat comical side of this realization of Aquinas in narrative techniques of realistic fiction is evident in the following sentence from "The Boarding House," which describes Protestant Dubliners going to church on a bright summer morning: "The belfry of George's church sent out constant peals and worshippers, singly or in groups, traversed the little circus before the church, revealing their purpose by their self-contained demeanor no less than by the little volumes in their gloved hands."[13] An essence of Dublin churchgoing receives expression here not as a result of either a dramatic or an analytic approach; instead the most scrupulously impersonal description manages to raise the object of description to a kind of objectifyingly ironic self-description. The very neatness of the sentence, with its elegantly controlled but somewhat fancified syntax and its concluding succession of nouns each with a single modifier ("self-contained demeanor," "little volumes," "gloved hands"), actually speaks the activity itself as a somewhat trivial manifestation of the human taste for ritualized order.

But the language also demystifies the very idea of an essentialized self-expression by allowing us to *locate* its transcendental, nonperspectival point of view. If Dublin speaks itself in *Dubliners,* the essentializing voice itself cannot escape having a social and psychological identity. The pitiless quidditas of realistic fiction allows for the dephenomenalizing of character only *as* a phenomenon of point of view. Who can repeat Dublin with particular radiance without, however, being able to take another point of view (and another point of view would precisely, however superior it might be, destroy the essentializing repetitions)—who, if not an educated Dubliner or a Dublin schoolteacher, one who, like Stephen in the "Nestor" episode of *Ulysses,* fully assumes the continuity between his dull-witted student and himself, thereby perhaps plotting his escape from Dublin through his articulated recognition of his own Dublin-ness in art? The schoolteacher can speak only Dublinese (unless—and this is of course the difference between *Dubliners* and *Ulysses*—he borrows voices from other places): we can hear, in the second half of our sentence from "The Boarding House," those adeptly poised rhythmical designs, so receptive to hyperbole ("revealing their purpose by . . . no less than by"), which in *Ulysses* animate the endless recitation of local news in public meetingplaces. The quidditas of a Dublin church group is, then, itself a kind of secondary or occasional form within the superior, more general form of Dublin-ness. Quidditas here is manifested most profoundly as a kind of respiratory pattern in language, a pattern that then has the potential—associated by Aristotle with entelechy—to engender actualities (fictional characters and events) of the same kind, which repeat it. In Joyce, the Schoolman is reformulated as the schoolteacher; an educated but inescapable provincialism is the social precondition of an art content to give *claritas* to the artist's inherited consciousness.

*   *   *

Claritas is an effect of quotation, although, as I have been suggesting, the quote is at the level of essence and not of existence. Of course in *Ulysses* Joyce does not merely cite Dublin; the novel is an encyclopedia of references. And this means that voices are always on loan. Several critics have noted the absence of what we would call a personal style in Joyce. Stephen Heath, writing—for the most part brilliantly—as a representative of poststructuralist (and mainly French) readings of Joyce, notes: "In place of style we have *plagiarism*," and then goes on to speak of Joyce's writing as "ceaselessly pushing the *signified* back into the *signifier* in order to refind at every moment the drama of language, its production."[14] I will not linger over the satisfying spectacle of a professor praising plagiarism (high-class plagiarism, true); but the notion of a plagiaristic wandering among signifiers—of the writer as a kind of open switchboard picking up voices from all over—does deserve more attention. For it raises a question that has been of major importance in this book: the authority of literature over the materials it incorporates. In *Bouvard et Pécuchet* we have seen another encyclopedic novel that appears to indulge in massive quotation. But the intertextuality of *Bouvard et Pécuchet* is highly deceptive: the textual act of quotation is simultaneously a disqualification of the citational process. Flaubert erases our cultural memory at the very moment he awakens it. The mutations of epistemological discourses in *Bouvard et Pécuchet* remove the novel from the cultural history it nonconnectedly absorbs. Nor does the work's intratextuality create connective designs or structures; each section repeats a process of solipsistic play that cuts it off from the other sections echoed in the repetition. Finally, not only does the work of art *know nothing*, but in its incommensurability with all cultural discourses of knowledge, it can only exist in a continuous anxiety about its capacity to sustain itself, perhaps even to begin itself.

For Joyce, on the other hand, art is by definition the transcendence of any such anxiety. *Ulysses* is often hard to read but, more than any other work of literature, it is also a guidebook to how it should be read. Actually a guidebook was issued before the novel was published. Partly for reasons beyond Joyce's control (the delay of more than ten years between the publication of *Ulysses* in Paris and its appearance in England and America) and partly because Joyce wanted it that way (he sent the first known schema for *Ulysses* to Carlo Linati in September 1920—a year before Shakespeare and Co. published the book—and a second schema to Valéry Larbaud in late 1921), *Ulysses* was an object not only of discussion but also of interpretation long before its major audiences had access to the complete text. Many readers thus had lessons in reading before they had anything to read. In itself that is sufficient evidence of this great modernist text's need for a reader, of its dependence on a community of comprehension. If the modernist artist refuses to make his work accessible to a mass audience, he is, as Richard Poirier has argued, far from indifferent to being read and understood.[15] Joyce, like Eliot in his notes for "The Wasteland," helps us on the road to all those recognitions and identifications necessary for the "right" reading of *Ulysses*: recognitions of the elaborate network of repetitions within the novel, identifications of all the other cultural styles and artifacts alluded to or imitated.

There is in *Ulysses* an intratextuality meant to guide us in our intertextual investigations, to teach us how to leave the novel and, above all, how to return to it in our exegeses. Frank Budgen records pointing out to Joyce that the word "yards" would be more accurate than "crosstree" to designate the spars to which the sails are bent on the schooner Stephen sees in Dublin Bay in "Proteus." "There's no criticism I more value than that," Joyce answered, and then he went on to say: "But the word 'crosstree' is essential. It comes in later on [in "Scylla and Charybidis"] and I can't change it."[16] The repetition is not one we are likely to notice on a first reading (or perhaps on a second or third reading). It is, however, lying in wait for our recognition, and that seems to have been enough for Joyce. For he knew that even if we missed "crosstree," at least he made us expect such repetitions, and he therefore had the obligation of providing them for us even if we never see them. The training is given in a series of graduated lessons. Slightly more likely to awaken a memory are such things as Molly's allusion, in "Penelope," to Gerty MacDowell's unflattering reference to "flighty" girl cyclists "showing off what they hadn't got" (293)—Molly remembers an Andalusian singer in Gibraltar who "didn't make much secret of what she hadn't" (618)—or (farther up on the scale of visibility) the echo, in Bloom's anticipation of his bath in the last lines of "Lotus Eaters"—he "saw the dark tangled curls of his bush floating, floating hair of the stream around the limp father of thousands, a languid floating flower" (71)—of the description, in "Proteus," of the tide at Sandymount Strand: the "breath of waters" that "flows purling, widely flowing, floating foampool, flower unfurling" (41). The words in "Proteus" could be Stephen's, but the concluding passage of "Lotus Eaters" is clearly out of Bloom's linguistic range. What might in another writer be taken as coincidence (the recurrence of "crosstree"), or as forgetfulness (the repetition of Gerty's thoughts in Molly's mind), becomes in *Ulysses* an important sign of the author's virtuosity. It is as if more and more circuits were lighted as we read and reread; the movement forward, from episode to episode, is simultaneously a spatialization of the text, which is transformed into a kind of electrical board with innumerable points of light connected to one another in elaborate, crisscrossing patterns.

"Circe" condenses the activity of textual remembrance ceaselessly taking place throughout the novel. *Ulysses* is itself the hallucinating subject of "Circe"; the episode is the book dreaming itself even before it is finished (there are anticipatory echoes of things yet to come, and to some extent it is even Joyce's oeuvre both calling up moments from its past and, in certain word plays, announcing the verbal textures of *Finnegans Wake*). "Circe" is also a way for us to chéck our textual memory, to be tested on how well we have read, to find out to what extent *Ulysses* has occupied our mind. Even more: it is a model dream for the ideally occupied, or possessed, reader of *Ulysses*. "Circe" implicitly defines an absolute limit of readerly absorption. Not only would Joyce's work provide all the terms of our critical activity, it would also be the inexhaustible material of our dreams, in Freudian terms both the daytime residue and the unconscious drives. Before *Finnegans Wake,* Joyce already projects in *Ulysses* the literary textualization of the entire mind, of our day-consciousness and our night-consciousness. In so doing, he unwittingly exposes what may be the secret project behind all talk of the mind or of the world as text: the successful positing of the Book—or, more accurately, of books, of a certain type of *professional* activity—as the ontological ground of history and of desire.

The "drives" of the Book are, however, drives without affects. "Circe" hallucinates the unconscious as word play. The unconscious, it is true, never is anything but word play in literature, and though this should probably be taken as the sign of an incommensurability between mental life and the instruments of literary expression, it has recently authorized interpretations of the unconscious as a structure "in some way" analogous to that of language. Thus a sublimating bookishness domesticates the unconscious, enacting the very repudiations it purports to analyze as linguistic effects. The violations of logic and linearity, the displacements and the condensations of discourse in which we are inclined to read the operations of unconscious processes, are themselves constitutive of the vast sublimating structure of human language. That structure—perhaps thought itself, as Freud suggested—may have evolved as the result of a primary displacement of a wish—a displacement from the untranslatable terms of a drive to so-called linguistic metaphors of desire, metaphors that express drives only on the ground of their self-constitutive negation of drives.

"Circe" is Joyce's most explicit and, we might say, most Flaubertian insistence on the nonreferential finality of the signifier in literature. To a certain extent, it counters the mimetic effects I began by emphasizing. It is the episode that most openly invites a psychoanalytic interpretation, even as it compels us to acknowledge impenetrable resistance to any such interpretation. As part of a book's hallucinatory play with its own elements, Bloom's presumed masochism, for example, can only be a joke. Bloom's psychology is elaborated in "Circe"—given the dimension of unconscious drives—as it is nowhere else in *Ulysses,* but the suggestion is that, in writing, psychology can never be anything but farce. A desire with nothing more than a textual past has the lightness and unconstrained mobility of farce. In "Circe" Joyce exuberantly stages masochism with a kind of wild inventiveness—as if to insist on the profound difference between the mysterious repetition of a painful pleasure, which Freud obscurely posits as the essence of human sexuality in the *Three Essays on the Theory of Sexuality,* and masochism as an occasion for extravagantly varied scenic effects. In "Circe" the book dreams masochism without pain (or with an inconsequential pain, one that can be erased from one page to the next), and in so doing it appears to leave behind not only the "burnt up field" of *Ulysses'* own mimetic seriousness but also the devastated terrain of a more general cultural discourse.[17] Toward the other texts it quotes in various ways—especially Sacher-Masoch's *Venus in Furs,* Krafft-Ebing's *Psychopathis Sexualis,* and Flaubert's *Tentation de St. Antoine,* all textual elaborations of the perverse in human conduct—"Circe" engages in an extremely intricate operation of what we might call a resublimating desublimation. In this farcical treatment of other cultural discourses, Joyce can be understood as proposing, first of all, that the claim to truth of any cultural artifact is its primary mystification. The farcical here operates as the sign of a desublimated discourse—although it is not the sexual in this case that is revealed as the referent of an allegedly higher discourse. On the contrary: the works that "Circe" quotes claim, in different ways, to analyze or to represent sexual drives, but, Joyce suggests, the reality those claims disguise is nothing more than the arbitrary play and productiveness of the signifier. The virtuosity of desire as linguistic effects is, I think, meant to lead us to conclude that *language cannot represent desire.*

This, however, does not necessarily diminish the authority of literary language. We will have to look more closely at the resublimating aspect of the operation I have just referred to. First note that the frequently marvelous comedy of "Circe" is much more ambiguous—even suspect—than I have suggested. There is in Joyce, from *Stephen Hero* to *Ulysses,* a scrupulously serious use of techniques obviously meant to represent characters realistically, as well as the cultivation of a remarkable perspectival strategy suggesting, as we have seen, that we have the essence of a character independent of his or her point of view. Not only does Joyce frequently work within formal conventions inescapably associated with a referential bias in fiction; his departure from familiar techniques of novelistic reporting actually reinforces the illusion of referentiality. The quotation of characters in their essential being, though it violates a certain literalism in realistic point of view, suggests that characters exist outside of their novelistic appearances. The narrator quotes them at a level of reality they are themselves incapable of representing, and this means that the narrative frequently refers to, say, a Bloom or a Mulligan more real than the Bloom or the Mulligan it allows us to see and hear. Thus the reduction of Bloom's depths to verbal farce in "Circe" is countered by the very passages to which "Circe" refers us. The novel has already committed itself to illusions of truth, that is, to a belief in novelistic language as epistemologically trustworthy, as capable of recreating the density of human experience, of referring to or carrying more than its own relational play.

   This commitment is visible even in episodes that emphasize a purely rhetorical finality. To write is to experience the seductive powers of language itself, the ways in which it turns us away from the objects it designates. But that seduction is of course not limited to writing, and Joyce's interest in a milieu celebrated for its rhetorical performances allows him to represent, as an object of his own novelistic consciousness, the absorption in language that also characterizes literary consciousness. The importance of rhetorical virtuosity in Dublin talk is appreciatively recognized by Joyce in the space he gives to such talk and is also exploited as the occasion for dramatizing a general epistemological skepticism. Thus the parodies of journalistic and popular literary styles interrupting the nameless narrator's account, in "Cyclops," of what happened at about 5 P.M. in Barney Kiernan's pub are, in a sense, not really interruptions at all. The entire episode is a comic display of hyperbolic styles, and the nameless one's account, though it enjoys more space than any of the parodic asides, is merely another version of the exaggerating modes of speech (the technique here is "gigantism") characteristic of the entire episode. And this also means that, though we have a very strong sense of what is happening in this dramatic scene (Bloom is the victim of an antisemitic attack and he makes his famous defense of love as the opposite of hatred), we are perhaps also invited to doubt the validity of the narrative report. Or rather, with his customary ambivalence about such things, Joyce seems anxious both to profit from assumptions about the reliability of reporting he himself continuously exposes as naive and to give a dazzling demonstration of the epistemological finality of the report's language. Similarly, the headlines in "Aeolus" are not so much intrusions into an otherwise naturalistically rendered dialogue as a reminder that the headline itself is a modern addition to the classical repertory of rhetorical figures in this section's style. If the newspaper increases our knowledge about the world, it also significantly modifies modes of cognition, and the world we get to know better is also inseparable from the journalistic medium that may be offering little more than reports on its own resources. Displays of rhetoric are, then, an important part of *Ulysses'* referential network.

Furthermore, if Joyce somewhat fitfully makes the points I have associated principally with "Circe," they are not exactly new points. The works of Flaubert and Henry James already make the case for knowledge as a matter of style and for the self as a play of the signifier. What is original in Joyce is the use to which he puts this awareness. James's *The Europeans*—and I recognize the bizarreness of the comparison—might be read in terms not too different from those I have used for "Circe." The farce of "Circe" is a function of the melodramatic associations it evokes. Just when Bloom is to be characterized in depth, he disappears as a self, and a cultural discourse on the perverse in human nature is comically replayed devoid of a referent, as part of the more general comedy of entertaining but epistemologically insignificant mutations in the history of cultural discourse. And, at least in the immediate context of this demonstration in *Ulysses,* there is, so to speak, no one around to be affected. What interests James, on the other hand, is the effect of something like the disappearance of self on human relations. Rather than propose an extreme (and extremely theoretical) skepticism about our ability to report on anything at all, James in *The Europeans* stages a confrontation between characters who expect their inherited vocabulary to correspond to something real in human nature and a woman (Eugenia) who may be nothing but a play of styles. James suggests, with great originality, that Eugenia's lack of self may be the most morally interesting thing about her, while the Wentworths' need to know others severely limits them (they are finally compelled to label Eugenia a liar).

I will make an even more incongruous juxtaposition by suggesting that Beckett is closer to James in this respect than to his friend and compatriot. From *Waiting For Godot* to *Company,* Beckett suggests that, whereas there can no longer be "characters" in literature, that very deprivation throws into sharper relief than ever before the infinite geometry of relational play among human subjects. *Godot* demonstrates the inevitability of conversation at a cultural juncture when there may be nothing left to talk about; and the strategies for continuing talk survive the absence of psychological subjects. And *Company,* even after the elimination of a human other, performs a solipsistic sociability inherent in the grammar of language itself. (Sociability in Joyce is a function of realistically portrayed characters and not, as in Beckett, the fascinatingly anachronistic remnant of the disappearance of such characters.) Beckett's authentic avant-gardism consists in a break not only with the myths fostered by cultural discourse but, more radically, with cultural discourse itself. The mystery of his work is how it is not only sustained but even begun, for intertextuality in Beckett (the echoes of Descartes and Malebranche in the early works, for example) is not a principle of cultural continuity (as it is in Joyce, in spite of the parodic nature of the repetitions) but the occasion for a kind of psychotic raving. Cultural memories exist in the minds of Beckett's characters like fossils belonging to another age, like instruments no one knows how to use anymore. Beckett's work remembers culture as Lucky remembers the structure of a logical argument in Godot: they are played like the broken records of language and consciousness.

Joyce, for all his parodic intentions, rejuvenates the Homeric myths that, somewhat above the characters' heads, give an epic dimension to a prosaic day in Dublin life. Thus *Ulysses,* however crookedly and mockingly, resuscitates Odysseus, and Joyce's ambivalent argument against the mimetic seriousness of literature, unlike Beckett's or Flaubert's, actually works to increase literature's authority, to realize a dream of cultural artifacts as both unconstrained by and superior to life, superior by virtue of the intertextual designs they silently invite us to disengage. The resublimation of cultural discourse in "Circe" is a function of the episode's intertextuality. Joyce ultimately "saves" the other texts that "Circe" parodistically quotes, and he does this simply by putting them into relation with "Circe." Joycean parody simultaneously "scorches" the other texts to which it refers and reconstitutes them as cultural artifacts within the intertextual designs woven by *Ulysses.* Intertextuality is, of course, not a phenomenon peculiar to *Ulysses;* what is peculiar is the novel's use of the intertext as a redemptive strategy. The Joycean intertext rescues Western literature from the deconstructive effects of the intertext itself. The parodistic replays of Homer, Shakespeare, and Flaubert—not to speak of all the authors quoted in "Oxen of the Sun"—are neither subversive of nor indifferent to the fact of cultural inheritance; rather, Joyce relocates the items of that inheritance with *Ulysses* as both their center and belated origin.

This is very different from Flaubert's insistent demonstration of art's indifference to its sources. There is no pastiche in *Bouvard et Pécuchet,* which means that Flaubert never advertises his authority over other cultural texts. Flaubert's novel is deliberately monotonous and narrow, as if it couldn't do anything with the mass of human knowledge it incorporates except to submit all of it to the same, tirelessly repeated stylistic operation. The originality of *Bouvard et Pécuchet* is identical to its epistemological and cultural incompetence. In a sense, the artist is revealed (and this remark might not have displeased Flaubert) as somewhat stupid: no matter what is presented to him, he reacts with the same stylistic reflex, with a cliché. And, as I argued earlier, the writer's limited authority, even his political effectiveness, depends on this stripping away of all authority, on the recognition of the work of art as an impotent discourse. The work's solipsistic existence in the margins of history undermines, or at least helps to delay, the inevitable complicity of all art in a civilization's discourse of power.

Beckett, and not Joyce, would be the most attentive reader of the Flaubert I have been discussing. The very variety of stylistic designs in *Ulysses* reveals Joyce's designs on culture. Far from transmuting all his cultural referents into a single, recognizably Joycean discourse, Joyce scrupulously maintains the distinctness of innumerable other styles *in order to legitimize misquoting them.* The accuracy is not merely a referential scruple, just as the inaccuracies are far from being mere sloppiness. We have to recognize the sources of *Ulysses* if we are to acknowledge its superiority to them. *Ulysses* indulges massively in quotation—quotation of individual characters, social groups, myths, other writers—but quoting in Joyce is the opposite of self-effacement. It is an act of appropriation, which can be performed without Joyce's voice ever being heard. It is as if Joyce were quoting Western culture itself in its quidditas—except that the whatness of all those cultural referents is designated not as the essential property of the referents themselves but rather as a consequence of their being (mis)quoted. Joyce miraculously reconciles uncompromising mimesis with a solipsistic structure. Western culture is saved, indeed glorified, through literary metempsychosis: it dies in the Joycean parody and pastiche, but, once removed from historical time, it is resurrected as a timeless design. Far from contesting the authority of culture, *Ulysses* reinvents our relation to Western culture in terms of exegetical devotion, that is, as the exegesis of *Ulysses* itself.

Beckett, on the other hand, babbles culture, as if its cultural memories afflicted the work of art—afflicted it not because they stifle its originality but because they infect it like foreign or prehistoric organisms. The difficulty of art in Beckett is in no way connected to the encyclopedic nature of the work's intertextual range; rather it is the function of an art alienated from culture, the consequence of Beckett's extraordinary effort to stop remembering, to begin again, to protect writing from cultural inheritance. As his late work suggests, the most refined stage of Beckett's artistic consciousness is identical to a moving back, to a return to that stage of difficulty which, he may feel, he left too early: the stage at which the writer is paralyzed by the insurmountable problem of description, of saying what he sees. It is perhaps only at this stage that the writer discovers the nature of writing; "ill seen, ill said" defines nothing less than the essence of literature.

*   *   *

Ulysses is a novel curiously unaffected by its most radical propositions. Perhaps because the realistic psychology of its characters is barely affected by—to quote Heath again—Joyce's "ceaselessly pushing the signified back into the signifier in order to refind at every moment the drama of language, its productions" (this remark, however problematic we may find it today, actually does describe *The Europeans*), this pushing never engenders any oppositional pressures. To put it schematically, the finality of the signifier is at once posited and ignored. We have, however, learned from other writers that literature's greatest ruse may be to insist that language perform the function of knowledge that the writer's special intimacy with language has taught him radically to doubt. This is the ruse of a reflexive "I" conscious of an aberrant consciousness of both its inner and outer worlds, and yet skeptical of that very consciousness of error. For the epistemological nihilism that may be the consequence of our sense of the human mind as a language-producing mechanism (linguistic signifiers can proliferate independently of what they signify and what they refer to) is itself the event of a linguistic consciousness, and the most daring move of all in this "prison house of language" may be to insist that language give us the truth it falsely claims to contain.

I will name three writers who make this insistence: Proust, Lawrence, and Bataille. One can hardly imagine more different artists, and yet all three share a sense of the implausibility *and* the necessity of forging a correspondence between language and being.[18] In his foreword to *Women in Love* Lawrence writes that the "struggle for verbal consciousness should not be left out in art. It is a very great part of life. It is not superimposition of a theory. It is the passionate struggle into conscious being" of the writer's "unborn needs and fulfillment." This Lawrentian struggle—the word is repeated five times in one short paragraph—is perhaps not too far from what Bataille calls, in his foreword to *Le Bleu du ciel,* the "intolerable, impossible ordeal [that alone] can give an author the means of achieving that wide-ranging vision that readers weary of the narrow limitations imposed by convention are waiting for." "An anguish to which I was prey" was, we remember, at the origin of the "freakish anomalies" of *Le Bleu du ciel*. Thus Bataille announces his identification with his frenetically restless narrator Troppmann, and in so doing he argues, from the very start, for an abdication of the novelist's mastery of his material. *Le Bleu du ciel*—like *Women in Love* and, to a certain extent, *A la Recherche du temps perdu*—has trouble settling on its own sense, and this is how these works revolutionize the practice of writing novels. They have to be performed before any technique for dominating their sense has been worked out. Most important, the struggles and ordeals of which Lawrence and Bataille speak are incorporated into the very work of their writing, with the result that their fiction is compelled to abdicate any authority for resolving the dilemmas it poses, any superior point of view that might justify a broader cultural claim for art as a vehicle of truth.

The freakish anomalies of *Ulysses,* far from threatening the author's control of his material, are the very sign of that control. Consider "Oxen of the Sun," which may be the most difficult and the most accessible episode of the novel. Once we have identified all the referents in this virtuoso pastiche of prose styles from Sallust to modern slang, what else does the episode give us? How does its language enact its sense? While the narrator is engaging in this stylistic tour de force, several of the characters—including Bloom and Stephen—are sitting around drinking and talking in a maternity hospital, where Mrs. Purefoy is going through the final moments of a long, hard labor. With some help from a letter Joyce wrote to Frank Budgen as he was working on "Oxen of the Sun," critics have proposed a series of parallels between the evolution of English prose and (1) biological gestation and birth, (2) the development of the embryonic artist's prose style, (3) faunal evolution, and (4) Stephen's rebirth as an artist. The episode may be the most extraordinary example in the history of literature of meaning unrelated to the experience of reading and to the work of writing. What Joyce obviously worked on was a series of brief pastiches aligned in chronological order. The characters and plot of *Ulysses* provide the material for the pastiche, although Joyce wants to think of the relation between the stylistic exercise and its anecdotal context in more organic terms. And so we have a series of imitative fallacies. In what way is the historical transformation (which is of course not a development or the maturation of an organism) of English prose styles "parallel" or "analogous" to (and what do those words mean here?) the biological development of an embryo in a womb? Also the beginnings of a modern writer's work obviously in no way resemble Anglo-Saxon; the transformation of an individual prose style reflects an experience of language wholly unrelated to the reasons for the difference between Dickens and the *Morte d'Arthur*. Finally, the idea of a significant connection between Mrs. Purefoy's gestation or the history of English prose styles to Stephen's emergence as an artist is so absurd that it is difficult even to find the terms in which to object to it.

Now I may of course be taking all these analogies too seriously, and Joyce's letter to Budgen, characteristically, manages both to sound quite earnest and to strike a comic note: "Bloom is the spermatozoon, the hospital, the womb, the nurse, the ovum, Stephen the embryo."[19] (He even adds: "How's that for High?") Joyce's shifty tone suggests a wager: 'let's see how much I can be credited for, and, in the worst of cases (if my critics are uncomfortable with these analogies), it can always be argued that I proposed them with tongue in cheek.' It is true that the "Oxen of the Sun" analogies are not the sort of thing looked at too closely by the most sophisticated of Joyce's admirers, but they have, for example, led Richard Ellmann to suggest that "Mrs. Purefoy has laboured and brought forth a Purefoykin, English has laboured and brought forth Stephen," and even to say that "Mrs. Purefoy's oncoming baby" is "paralleled by the outgoing Stephen" (he leaves the hospital before Bloom, who entered first and was "hospitably received by the nurse"—who is, according to Joyce, the "ovum"), Stephen who, with his friends, can also be thought of, as they rush from the hospital to a pub, as "the placental outpouring . . . (it is the afterbirth as well as an ejaculative spray)."[20]

Such criticism is itself a joke, but my point is that it is not unauthorized by the novel (not to speak of Joyce's suggestions for reading the novel) and that authorization is itself a moment of significance in the story of how literature has been thought about. If the history of philosophy can no longer measure approximations to truth but must instead be satisfied with chronicling the mutations of fictions, and if hermeneutics can no longer provide a science of interpretation but itself becomes a stage in the history of the forms of intelligibility, "Oxen of the Sun" might be seen as one of the contributions to the literature section of such a history. Joyce initiates us to a radical separation of interpretation from the phenomenology of reading. The announced correspondences and meanings of *Ulysses'* episodes can be thought of as a way not of elucidating the novel's sense, but of forcing us to see that *sense is a series of ingenious jokes on the signifier.* It is the very prose styles of "Oxen of the Sun" that are parodied by their repetition in Mrs. Purefoy's womb. And the idea of Stephen's literary or spiritual birth in this chapter is a magnificently irresponsible way of understanding the insignificant role he plays in the episode, as well as of interpreting the possibility (suggested by Kenner[21]) of his having slugged Mulligan (and thus repudiated the sterile past connected with Mulligan) in the interval between episodes 9 and 14.

The Lawrentian (and, as I have shown elsewhere, the Mallarmean[22]) attempt to coerce language into an espousal of the moves of an individual consciousness—moves that an impersonal linguistic coherence necessarily "skips," to which such coherence is inherently alien—is rejected in

"Oxen of the Sun" as an insidious fallacy. And yet a whole set of conventional psychological and moral significances coexists quite comfortably in Joyce with a radical skepticism concerning the validity of any move whatsoever beyond the line of the signifier. (This cohabitation is quite familiar to us today. The Lacanians' ritualistic repetition of the word *signifiant* as the key to Lacan's radical rethinking of the Freudian unconscious has, for example, in no way affected the normative status, in their thought, of the psychologically and morally specific referent of a phallocentric heterosexuality.) The perception of human reality as a language effect has generally had the curious consequence of forestalling, of leaving no terms available for, the criticism of psychological, moral, and social orders elaborated by the quite different view—now seen as epistemologically naive—of language as essentially descriptive of a preexistent real. The rhetorical criticism associated with Derrida and, more properly, de Man has much to say about the deconstructive effects of the figural on political or moral assertions, and very little to say about the strategic nature of its own analytic enterprise. The decision to treat history as rhetoric must itself be deconstructed—which is of course to say *reconstructed*—as a profoundly reactionary move: it deliberately ignores how networks of power can be independent of the subversive effect presumably inherent in their own discursive practices. The resistance of language to its own performance provides insufficient friction to curtail the operational efficiency of even the most "mystified" (but powerful) linguistic performances. Foucault, it seems to me, had the great merit of seeing that effects of power are indifferent to their rhetorical legitimacy, and that a predominantly rhetorical analysis of a society's discursive practices therefore runs the risk of collaborating with those coercive intentions, even while ceaselessly demonstrating their inescapably (but on the whole ineffectually) self-menacing nature.

Ulysses substitutes for the interpretive ordeals posed by such writers as Lawrence, Mallarmé, and Bataille a kind of affectless busyness, the comfortable if heavy work of finding all the connections in the light of which the novel can be made intelligible but not interpreted. The experimentalism of *Ulysses* is far from the genuine avant-gardism of *Women in Love, Le Bleu du ciel,* or almost any of Beckett's fictions. The intertextual criticism invited by *Ulysses* is the domestication of literature, a technique for making familiar the potentially traumatic seductions of reading. Even more: *Ulysses* eliminates reading as the ground of interpretation; or, to put this in other terms, it invites intertextual elucidations as a strategy to prohibit textual interpretations. In much contemporary criticism, reading no longer provides a hermeneutical ground of interpretive constraint. This is not to say that there should be or ever was one legitimate interpretation of each text, but rather that—in what we might call the critical progeny of *Ulysses*—texts are made intelligible only by the intra- and intertextual clues they drop. *Ulysses* is a text to be deciphered but not read. Joyce's schemas already provide a model of interpretive nihilism. They propose, with a kind of wild structural neatness, meanings so remote from our textual experience as to suggest that there is no other basis for sense than the "line" that can be drawn between two textual points. The exegetical work to be done is enormous, but it has already been done by the author and we simply have to catch up with him.

If criticism always rewrites the texts to which it somewhat deceptively adheres, Joyce minimizes the losses inevitably incurred by literature in its critical appropriation by directing the appropriating process. In a sense, the unhappy destiny of the literary work is that it cannot avoid being read. However much the writer may work to create the ideal reader for his text, a certain inattentiveness in the reading of texts defeats that work, thus saving us from such totalitarian projects. We perhaps sensitize ourselves to effects that the author is either unwilling or unable to include among those to which he would have us respond by the uneven rhythm of our reading, by a certain laxity in our responses, a willingness to miss things that can become an escape from the image into which the text would transform us. *Ulysses* allows for no such laxity, and rather than bother—as, say, Stendhal does in his anxious and intricate effort to forge the sensibility worthy of reading him—with seductive conversionary tactics, the Joycean text escapes from the reader's dangerous freedom merely by insisting that it be read with an excruciatingly close attention and a nearly superhuman memory. It asks that we be nothing but the exegetical machine necessary to complete its sense. *Ulysses* is constantly proposing homework, work we can do outside the text (checking Dublin geography, rereading Homer, Dante, Goethe, Shakespeare, Arnold, the theosophists, Gaelic legends), and in thus insisting on how much it needs us, it also paradoxically saves itself from us. The texture of Joyce's novel is entirely remarkable in that it is at once dense and empty; it imprisons us by the very moves that eject us from the text, and it insists on an uninterrupted attention not exactly to itself but to its instructions for its own further elaboration. *Ulysses* promises a critical utopia: the final elucidation of its sense, the day when all the connections will have been discovered and collected in a critical Book that would objectively repeat *Ulysses,* which, in being the exegetical double of its source, would express the quidditas of Joyce's novel, would be *Ulysses* replayed as the whole truth of *Ulysses.*

*　　　　*　　　　*

Finally—and perhaps not so strangely—the very nihilism I have referred to goes along with a promise of salvation. Not only does *Ulysses* keep its conservative ideology of the self distinct from its increasing emphasis on the finality of language's productiveness; not only does it display a perspectival technique that brings to psychological realism the prestige of a Thomistic confidence in art's ability to radiate with the essence of things; Joyce's novel also refers us to a mind purified of "impossible ordeals" or "struggles" and elevated to the serene and redemptive management of its cultural acquisitions. Where *Ulysses* really leads us is to Joyce's mind; it illuminates his cultural consciousness. At the end of the reader's exegetical travails lies the promise of an Assumption, of being raised up and identified with the idea of culture made man. Joyce incarnates the enormous authority of sublimation in our culture—of sublimation viewed not as a nonspecific eroticizing of cultural interests but as the appeasement and even transcendence of anxiety.

Ulysses is modernism's monument to that authority, although—in what I take to be the most authentic risk Joyce takes in producing this monument—it also alludes to the anxiety from which we escape in our exegetical relocation of the work itself within the authorial consciousness at its origin. I am referring to certain moments in the representation of Bloom's solitude—not to his social solitude as a Jew in Ireland, or even to his estrangement from Molly, but rather to a kind of cosmic lack of linkage, a singleness that can be rendered only by images of his floating in interplanetary space. In one of the moral clichés to which this presumably revolutionary novel has given rise, Stephen's coldness and inability to love are often opposed to Bloom's warmth and concern for others. But Stephen's solitude is psychological (it includes his estrangement from his father and his unshakable sense of a crime against his mother); Bloom's aloneness is metaphysical. Furthermore, Stephen is as sociable and loquacious a boozer as all the other characters we meet in the editorial offices of the *Freeman* or in Barney Kiernan's pub; he too spends his day in talk and even plots his oratorical effects (in "Scylla and Charybdis"), and (in "Aeolus") he blushes with pleasure ("his blood wooed by grace of language and gesture") as he listens to the rhetorical flourishes in J. J. O'Molloy's recitation of the lawyer Seymour Bushe's "polished period" describing "the Moses of Michelangelo in the vatican." If, in "Ithaca," both Bloom and Stephen are said to be comforted by the spectacle of "the heaventree of stars hung with humid nightblue fruit" when they move from the house to the garden, it is Bloom who meditates on "the parallax or parallactic drift of socalled fixed stars, in reality evermoving wanderers from immeasurably remote eons to infinitely remote futures" and who, alone after Stephen leaves, feels "the cold of interstellar space, thousands of degrees below freezing point on the absolute zero of Fahrenheit, Centigrade or Reaumer: the incipient intimations of proximate dawn." And in the de Quincy passage from "Oxen of the Sun," which J. S. Atherton rightly sees as "a most remarkable example of Joyce's "power of combination," "Bloom gazes at the triangle on the label of the bottle of bass until it becomes a 'triangled sign upon the forehead of Taurus'—combining lingam and yoni in one symbol, which itself replicates the underlying symbol of the chapter, and placing it in the depths of space."[23]

It is the relentlessly tedious "Ithaca," with its nearly unreadable scientific expositions of such things as the many uses and virtues of water and the recent restrictions on water consumption in Dublin (when Bloom turns on a faucet), which, precisely because of the impersonality of its technique, becomes a kind of Pascalian meditation on the lack of connectedness not only between human beings but also between the human and the cosmos. We might of course also be tempted to see in the lostness of Bloom an image for the historical situation of Ireland itself: a country with no consensus about its past, little hope for its future, and cut off, both physically and culturally, from the rest of Europe. The anxiety that *Ulysses* massively struggles to transcend—however we choose to understand its origins—is that of disconnectedness. It is perhaps here that Joyce's dependence on his readers is most pronounced, for it is *their* intra- and extratextual work that reconstitutes his mind as the serene repository of the resources of our language and culture. From this perspective it hardly matters if the Homeric correspondences are, to say the least, not always exact or that the pastiches of "Oxen of the Sun" are not always very close to their originals.[26] *Ulysses* is composed as a model of the cultural fragmentation it represents in various ways. Furthermore, Joyce's authority depends on the idiosyncratic nature of the culture he reconstructs; *Ulysses* gives us back our culture as *his* culture.

For authors, the anguish of paternity is experienced as an uncertainty about the property of their work, about who owns it and if it is indeed their own. "Fatherhood, in the sense of conscious begetting," Stephen announces in "Scylla and Charybdis," "is unknown to man." It is "on that mystery and not on the madonna which the cunning Italian intellect flung to the mob of Europe the church is founded and founded irremovably because founded, like the world, macro and microcosm, upon the void. Upon incertitude, upon unlikelihood" (170). In our tireless elucidation of *Ulysses*, we certify Joyce's paternity, we bring his work back to him, we eliminate what Stephen describes as the natural enmity between father and son by showing how the book gives birth to its author. Exegesis reveals that *Ulysses* signifies Joyce's multitudinous stylistic and structural intentions; it demonstrates that the work glorifies its creator just as Christ—concentrating and purifying in his person a universal human truth—glorifies the Father. And for the worthy disciples of *Ulysses*—which we should now be able to recognize as modernism's most impressive example of the West's long and varied tribute to the authority of the Father—there are of course enormous rewards. *Ulysses* does not restore cultural continuities presumably broken by the modern age. Indeed, in a manner consistent with its nihilistic indifference to any relation between our experience of reading it and those concealed structures it signifies, Joyce's novel asks only that we reconstruct the structurally coherent fragments of Joyce's own cultural consciousness. It is not Western culture that matters, but the coherence of a particular broken version of it. Joyce is faithful to our humanist tradition at a deeper level, in his reenactment of its assumptions and promise that the possession of culture will transcend anxiety and perhaps even redeem history.

Intertextual criticism is the practical activity that testifies to our espousal of a cultural ethos of the redemptive authority and mastery of art; it is, in the case of *Ulysses,* the imitatio that allows us to join Joyce in a community built on identifications and recognitions. Verbal consciousness in *Ulysses* is not—as it is in Lawrence or Bataille—a process of clarification repeatedly menaced by the personal and social pressures antagonistic to all clarifications; rather it is a conquest the multitudinous forms of which are disguised but never threatened by the novel's textures. The community of *Ulysses* and its exegetes is redemptive in its failure to acknowledge any operative relation between experience—of this text or of reality—and the forms of intelligibility it proposes. It is the Vita Nuova in which Joyce thrillingly proposes that we spend our life with him. The call is very hard not to heed. Even in writing "against *Ulysses,*" we can only feel a great sadness in leaving it—to stop working on *Ulysses* is like a fall from grace.

CHAPTER 8

Pynchon, Paranoia, and Literature

Any novel that uses the word "paranoia" as frequently as *Gravity's Rainbow* does is likely to make the reader somewhat paranoid about the very frequency of its use. Not only is it the narrator's most cherished word and concept (it even gives birth to a new English verb: Tyrone Slothrop "paranoids from door to door" in a hotel[1]); the characters in Pynchon's work also repeatedly refer to themselves as paranoid. There is the hitch: since when do paranoids label themselves paranoid? When they do, they are of course speaking for others, using the label for themselves before it can be used against them. "You must think I'm really paranoid about people's opinion of what I write" can be given to us as: "I'm really paranoid about people's opinion of what I write," but the judgment of that anxiety as paranoid can only come from others. These others can also exist in me, and I can make a clinical joke of my own worries, but I wouldn't have them if I wasn't also convinced of their rightness. "I" can never be the subject of "I am paranoid" as an uncontested, undivided judgment.

The word "paranoia" has had an extraordinarily complex medical, psychiatric, and psychoanalytic history. I have been using it (as Pynchon also tends to use it) as if it were synonymous with something like unfounded suspicions about a hostile environment, but the fear of persecution is only one aspect of a symptomatological picture that has included such things as delusions of grandeur, schizophrenic dissociation, and erotomania. The concept has been at the center of considerable classificatory turbulence, especially with respect to whether it should be counted as one of the schizophrenic psychoses.[2] More than any other psychoanalytic term, "paranoia" has been the focus of a nosological disarray not unlike the symptomatic panic of paranoia itself. There is, in both cases, interpretive distress. Freud explained paranoia as a defense against a desired homosexual attack, a defense depending on the success of a strenuous interpretive effort. The potential benefits of interpretive control are dramatically illustrated by the ease with which Dr. Schreber, the subject of Freud's most celebrated analysis of paranoia, transcends his paranoid anxiety and even changes a plot of cosmic hostility into an epic of cosmic self-centering. God's desire to use Schreber as a "wife" in order to engender a new race rewrites catastrophe as apotheosis; the dreaded attack will still take place, but in its idealized, divine form it can finally be recognized as an object of desire. Schreber ends exactly where he began: anticipating the pleasure of being destroyed as a result of taking a passive homosexual role. But he must first analyze the components of "I love him" in ways that will allow a homosexual desire to be satisfied without danger. In the paranoid's case, "I love him" is equivalent to "I love being attacked by him"; only if this is reformulated as "I hate being attacked by a hostile world" can a megalomaniacal defense against persecution become powerful enough to make Schreber desirable to God himself. It is as if a defensive self-love were contagious or perhaps even operated as an argument that "convinces" God of Schreber's irresistible appeal. The paranoid stage of Schreber's illness allows the original masochistic wish to become conscious by creating the conditions in which it can be reformulated as a triumphant narcissism. The original (and repressed) interpretation of a "feminine" passivity as self-annihilation is—in a move that a biological realism perversely authorizes—reinterpreted as self-perpetuation.

More interesting to us is Freud's recognition of Schreber's interpretive acuity. At the end of his analysis of the case, Freud notes a striking similarity between Schreber's delusions and his own theory about those delusions. The Senatpräsident's "rays of God," for example, "which are made up of a condensation of the sun's rays, of nerve-fibers, and of spermatozoa, are in reality nothing else than a concrete representation and projection outward of libidinal cathexes"; they may be what Freud calls "endopsychic perceptions" of the very processes that he himself has proposed to explain paranoia. With just a hint of paranoia about the possibility that he may be accused of having lifted his theory of paranoia from Schreber's book, Freud protests, in advance of any such accusation, that he can "call a friend and fellow-specialist to witness that [he] had developed [his] theory of paranoia before [he] became acquainted with the contents of Schreber's book. It remains for the future," Freud concludes, "to decide whether there is more delusion in my theory than I should like to admit, or whether there is more truth in Schreber's delusion than other people are as yet prepared to believe."[3]

The delusion, however, may be inherent in the move that predicts some future sorting out of truth from delusion in either Schreber's fantasies or Freud's theories. What else could the truth of paranoia be than a replication, on a different discursive register, of the paranoid's delusions?

Freud's concluding remarks bizarrely suggest that there is some ordering truth of paranoia—of paranoia as distinct from the classificatory and theoretical discourse that constitutes it—different from both paranoid ravings and theories of paranoia. This is precisely how Pynchon defines paranoia itself: it is the "reflex of seeking other orders behind the visible" (219). The paranoid restlessness in the theory of paranoia—evidenced in Freud's insistence that he had the theory before studying the case as well as in his uneasy perception of the specular relation between case and theory—is expressed as a mistrust of the symptomatic language of paranoia. The theoretician distrusts the theorizing activity of paranoia—as if the "truth" of paranoia might turn out to be that theory is always a paranoid symptom. But Freud has perhaps already accepted this conclusion in continuing to hope for a truth by which the value of theory can be measured, a truth that would finally rescue psychoanalytic discourse from the theorizing that, it is feared, may be nothing more than a manifestation of paranoid behavior. The theoretician's distrust of theory—the sense that what theory seeks to signify is hidden somewhere behind it—repeats the paranoid's distrust of the visible.

But the Schreber case also points to a wholly different alternative: the embrace of theory as final and the renunciation of any hope that truth will finally render theory obsolete. The customary distinction between delusions and truth *too accurately* replicates the illusional structures we may wish to understand. If nonparanoid theorizing is a contradiction in terms, there may be—and Pynchon will help us with this—a way to crack the replicative mirror so that the theory of paranoia will send back a partially unrecognizable image of paranoia. Knowledge—but do we even need that word?—would then have to be redefined in terms of the inaccuracy of a replication.

*   *   *

For all the shifts of interpretive perspective on paranoia, the word, faithful to its etymology (a Greek word designating a distracted or deranged mind), has always designated a mental disorder. At least until *Gravity's Rainbow*. All the paranoid thinking in the novel is probably justified, and therefore really not paranoid at all. I say "probably" because Pynchon is less interested in vindicating his characters' suspicions of plots than in universalizing and, in a sense, depathologizing the paranoid structure of thought. Were he content to certify that all the imagined plots are real plots, he would be making merely a political point, a point for which he has frequently been credited and which undoubtedly helps to explain the popularity of his immensely difficult work. This is what we might call the sixties' side of Pynchon, Pynchon as defender of such lovable slobs as Slothrop and, in *V.,* Benny Profane the schlemiel against the impersonal efficiency of information systems and international cartels. The narrator of *Gravity's Rainbow,* true, does lend his authority to his characters' paranoid suspicions; in fact he frequently passes on information that justifies their worst fears. Thus the wildest paranoid imagination would probably not come up with the incredible but true story of IG Farben's surveillance of Slothrop right back to his infancy. The Pavlovian Lazlo Jamf's conditioning of baby Tyrone's hardons (more on this later) has to be seen in the light of Jamf's complex business deals between the two world wars, involving supercartels that were themselves perhaps involved in efforts to ruin the mark as part of a strategy to get Germany out of paying its war debts. Was Slothrop "sold to IG Farben like a side of beef," did they finance Jamf's experiments on him, has he been "under their observation—m-maybe since he was born? Yaahhh" (333). None of this is absolutely certain (except for Jamf's work with Slothrop's infant hardon, which has been described much earlier in the novel as historical fact), and the business deals and connections elliptically referred to are mind-boggling in their intricate interconnectedness. But if IG Farben's sinister interest in Slothrop is not unambiguously confirmed, Pynchon clearly does not expect us to find Slothrop's most paranoid scenarios implausible. Pynchon himself certainly has no problem with the cartel-conspiracy ideas. War, he writes, is just a coverup, a "spectacle" or "diversion from the real movements of the War." "The true war is a celebration of markets," as its "real business . . . is buying and selling, the murdering and the violence are self-policing, and can be entrusted to non-professionals" (122). An "outfit like Shell" has "no real country, no side in any war, no specific face or heritage: tapping instead out of that global stratum, most deeply laid, from which all the appearances of corporate ownership really spring" (283).

The paranoid reflex, we remember, seeks "other orders behind the visible." Speaking in another passage of the paranoia often noted under the hallucinatory drug Oneirine, Pynchon writes: "Like other sorts of paranoia, it is nothing less than the onset, the leading edge, or the discovery ["discovery," not "suspicion"] that *everything is connected,* everything in the Creation" (820). And, as the Jesuit Father Rapier preaches during some undefined Convention in the Zone: "Once the technical means of control have reached a certain size, a certain degree of *being connected* one to another, the chances for freedom are over for good" (627). The paranoid intuition is, then, one of an invisible interconnectedness. Technology can collect the information necessary to draw connecting lines among the most disparate data; and the very drawing of those lines depends on what might be called a conspiratorial interconnectedness among those interested in data collection. To put things into relation is already a conspiratorial move, or at the very least a gesture of control. In *Gravity's Rainbow* the discovery of connections is identical to the discovery of plots. The plotters get together—they "connect"—in order to plot the connections that will give them power over others.

The orders behind the visible are not necessarily—are perhaps not essentially—orders different from the visible; rather they are the visible *repeated as structure*. Paranoid thinking hesitates between the suspicion that the truth is wholly obscured by the visible and the equally disturbing sense that the truth may be a sinister, invisible design in the visible. To have "a paranoid structure worthy of the name," you have not only to "show some interlock" among individuals, events, and companies you assumed were unrelated, but also to establish different or parallel lines of connectedness (678). Paranoia repeats phenomena as design. What you thought was a chance juxtaposition may turn out to be a deliberate coupling. If that possibility inspires panic, it is also desired. Would we ever want a life without paranoid terror? "If there is something comforting—religious, if you want—about paranoia, there is still also anti-paranoia, where nothing is connected to anything, a condition not many of us can bear for long" (506). Not only that: to escape from paranoia would be to escape from the movement that is life. Slothrop, on the run in the Zone, thinks how nice it would be to lie still for a while with the heartbeat of the young woman who shelters him one night: "isn't that every paranoid's wish; to perfect methods of immobility?" (667). Only by freezing things can we prevent them from connecting, from coming together to form those invisible designs that may include us within them without our knowing it. For all the paranoid scares in *Gravity's Rainbow,* it would be even scarier if we began to *stop* suspecting hidden orders behind the visible. "Either they have put him here for a reason," Slothrop speculates during "the anti-paranoid part of his cycle," "or he's just here. He isn't sure that he wouldn't, actually, rather have that *reason*" (506).

Not that there's much danger of running short of reasons—or of imagining that our being anywhere can be a wholly plotless event. Paranoia is a necessary and desired structure of thought. It is also a permanent one, which means that there is nothing substantially new in the latest version of it. To put this in the contemporary jargon with which *Gravity's Rainbow* is obsessed: paranoia is a necessary product of all information systems. The Pynchonian opposition between They (IG Farben) and We (Slothrop, Roger Mexico, Pirate Prentice) is a replay of the opposition of Slothrop's Puritan forefathers' polarity of the Elect and the Preterite. Information control is the contemporary version of God's eternal knowledge of each individual's ultimate damnation or salvation; and both theology and computer technology naturally produce paranoid fears about how we are hooked into the System, about the connections it has in store for us.

Can we escape being manipulated—perhaps even destroyed—by such systems? Familiar tactics of protest and subversion create local disturbances that are easily forgotten and leave the most menacing paranoid structures perfectly intact. We should be suspicious of some of the appealing alternatives that *Gravity's Rainbow* offers to its own paranoically conceived apocalypses. I am thinking especially of love, anarchy, and randomness, all of which bring us back to Pynchon's credentials as a hero of the counterculture. Perhaps nothing is treated with a more tender seriousness in *Gravity's Rainbow* than Roger Mexico's love for Jessica Swanlake. Simply by existing, that love opposes the war ("They are in love. Fuck the war."), but the opposition, as the parenthetical quote suggests, is more rhetorical protest than anything else. Their love is the idealized version of Roger's pissing on the shiny table and on all the bigwigs sitting around it in Mossmoon's office (an act reminiscent of such engaging antics of the early seventies as Jerry Rubin's occupation of the New York Stock Exchange). Pynchon's work generously, and ambiguously, recapitulates the saintly assumptions of Rubinesque subversion: profound social change will not result from head-on assaults (terror is ineffective and unacceptable, revolution is unthinkable in the West, and even revolutionary regimes have shown themselves to be changes of personnel unaccompanied by changes in assumptions about the legitimacy of power), but rather from a kind of aggressively seductive subversion of the *seriousness* with which networks of power conduct their business. But, as we shall see, oppressive seriousness can be corrupted only if it is recognized that paranoid thought itself is inherently unserious, and not by violent *or* nonviolent opposition to the plots of power. The counterculture style of the sixties can provide nothing more than the always appealing historical inspiration for more complex models of nonoppositional resistance. Roger and Jessica's love is both venerated and discredited in *Gravity's Rainbow*. The love is a kind of "secession" from war, "the beginnings of gentle withdrawal . . . both know, clearly, it's better together, snuggled in, than back out in the paper, fires, khaki, steel of the Home Front. That, indeed, the Home Front is something of a fiction and lie, designed, not too subtly, to draw them apart, to subvert love in favor of work, abstraction, required pain, bitter death" (47). On the contrary: their snuggled state, their gentle withdrawal is the fiction (with its sentimental apotheosis on the evening their hearts are buoyed as they listen to Christmas songs in a church somewhere in Kent), a marginal, harmless fiction that Jessica will drop in order to return to her husband and the securities of "work, abstraction, required pain, bitter death."

Is randomness a more effective route of escape? Power depends on the control of information, on the ordering of data; what happens when data resist the ordering process? This is presented as a particularly seductive possibility in *Gravity's Rainbow* (as is anarchy, the political corollary of unprogrammed events and acts), although Pynchon also presents the random as nothing more than a momentary malfunctioning of the cybernetic machine, one which the machine is fully equipped to take account of. Thus the messed-up pinball machines sent by Chicago gangsters to "one Alfonso Tracy, Princeton '06, St. Louis Country Club, moving into petro-chemicals in a big way," and stored in a gigantic masonic hall in "the green little river town of Mouthorgan, Missouri" (678–679): has it happened "at real random, preserving at least our faith in Malfunctioning as still something beyond their grasp," or is there somewhere "in the wood file cabinets . . . a set of real blueprints telling exactly how all these pinball machines were rewired—a randomness deliberately simulated?" (683). The control of randomness has been mentioned before, and not merely as a possibility. Rocket-City "is set up deliberately To Avoid Symmetry, Allow Complexity, Introduce Terror (from the Preamble to the Articles of Immachination)—but tourists have to connect the look of it back to things they remember from their times and planet—back to the wine bottle smashed in the basin, the bristlecone pines outracing Death for millennia, concrete roads abandoned years ago, hairdos of the late 1930s" (346). The random itself can easily be programmed.

There is, however, something else—something more sinister but perhaps more promising—in the passage just quoted. As part of an "immachinating" strategy, They duplicate mnemonic images originally outside their control. The novel is full of references to enigmatic and frequently eerie replications. Lyle Bland comes back from his "transmural" voyages through space and time "raving about the presences he has found out there, members of an astral IG, whose mission . . . is past secular good and evil: distinctions like that are meaningless out there"(187). Or: people who get hit by lightning are carried off by bareback dwarves to places that look like the world they left, "but it'll be different. Between congruent and identical there seems to be another class of look-alike that only finds the lightning heads. Another world laid down on the previous one and to all appearances no different. Ha-*ha!* But the lightning-struck know, all right!" (774) Slothrop, walking with Katje on the esplanade along the beach at Nice, suddenly feels that the brilliant whitecaps can't be getting their light from the real sky above them. "Here it is again, that identical-looking Other World—is he gonna have *this* to worry about, now? What th'—lookit those *trees*—each long frond hanging, stung, dizzying, in laborious drypoint against the sky, each *so perfectly placed*" (262). Finally, the entire Zone may be a spectral double of the real world, a collection of images simulating scenes from all over the universe:

> In the Zone, in these days, there is endless simulation—standing waves in the water, large drone-birds, so well-known as to have nicknames among the operators, wayward balloons, flotsam from other theatres of war (Brazilian oildrums, whisky cases stenciled for Fort-Lammy), observers from other galaxies, episodes of smoke, moments of high albedo—your real targets are hard to come by. (570)

How are we to understand all these references to simulations and doubling? The hidden double can inspire the most panicky paranoid suspicions. Am I being given the real thing or an ontological look-alike? Thus doubling would seem to be merely one aspect of the pattern of events in *Gravity's Rainbow* that gives rise to the paranoid compulsion or "reflex of seeking other orders behind the visible." But we should look at that reflex more closely in order to determine if it is an appropriate response to phenomena of doubling and simulation. Enzian, the leader of the Southwest African natives transplanted by the Germans to Europe and now in pursuit of the rocket's secret and site, comes to wonder if he's pursuing the wrong object. Are the Hereros "supposed to be the Kabbalists out here . . . the scholar-magicians of the Zone, with somewhere in it a Text, to be picked to pieces, annotated, explicated, and masturbated till it's all squeezed limp of its last drop?" They had of course assumed that the rocket was "this holy Text," their Torah. "What else? Its symmetries, its latencies, the *cuteness* of it enchanted and seduced us while the real Text persisted, somewhere else, in its darkness, our darkness" (606).

Is the rocket the real Text? This question is an urgent one not only for Pynchon's characters but also for us. What if, as Enzian suggests, the rocket-text has seduced and blinded us to an even more important text, something in the work that it is even more necessary to read correctly than the rocket, something that would be the real key to its sense? Indeed, as we have seen, Pynchon teases us with this possibility in more than one way. The rocket and the war for which it was built are just coverups of the true war, which is "a celebration of markets" and whose "real business . . . is buying and selling." But if something like international cartels is the real text that the paranoid imagination should be reading, then we, like Enzian, are being deceived by all the prime time and space being given to the rocket. We cannot resolve the issue simply by saying that Pynchon's real subject is how his characters are victimized by the deception, and that in order to read *that* text the reader has to be set straight about the true center of historical power. For in fact the presumed real text is as obscure to us as it is to Enzian. Pynchon outlines some of the extraordinarily complex moves of international buying and selling, the durable financial connectedness among nations from which wars would merely divert us, but he also raises the possibility of a plot for which the cartelized state itself is merely a screen. The use of war to establish "neither Red communism nor an unhindered Right, but a rational structure in which business would be the true, the rightful authority" would, in comparison with *that* plot, be nothing more than "a damned parlor game," which "even the masses believe." Are cartels the ultimate plotters? International business interests may be providing just another front, behind which lie still "other orders," orders that might involve ("if one were paranoid enough" to believe this) a collaboration between the living and the dead, "between both sides of the Wall, matter and spirit" (192–193). But is it even necessary to go that far, to evoke, as Lyle Bland does after his transmural voyage, "an astral IG?" What exactly are the earthly Shell and IG Farben? How are we to understand the historical referentiality of those names when, in the novel, they refer to cartels obsessed with the predictive power of Slothrop's erections? Is there an actual place—on earth or in space, in life or in death—where paranoid suspicion can finally be satisfied, put to rest?

If such a place exists, the reader of *Gravity's Rainbow* will never enjoy its comforts. Compared to Pynchon's novel, Joyce's *Ulysses,* for all the work it requires, is play for a child-detective. Certainly Joyce wants us to suffer, but there will also be a term to our suffering. The puzzles of *Ulysses* are like stations of the cross; they are ritual agonies through which we must pass in order finally to be at one, far above the consciousness of any character in the novel, with Joyce's remarkably cohesive consciousness. Nothing could be more different from *Gravity's Rainbow.* Far from holding out the promise of a postexegetical superiority to the world it represents, Pynchon's work permanently infects us with the paranoid anxieties of its characters. Just keeping track of all the plots—and their incredible interconnectedness—is a near impossibility. The most important facts about the rocket are either shrouded in impenetrable secrecy or simply ignored. What exactly is the Schwarzgerät? Were the infant Tyrone's hardons conditioned by the smell of Imipolex G (even though the experiments took place years before Jamf developed the plastic for IG Farben), a smell that somehow precedes the arrival of the rockets themselves over London? More important, what does this casualness mean? Is it even important to get all the information straight?

Such questions can generate the most extreme anxieties, and yet the information we do get—such as the account of Jamf's experiments with little Tyrone—do little to allay them. For the major anxiety provoked by *Gravity's Rainbow* is ontological rather than epistemological. The characters themselves frequently worry about what they know and don't know; but they too, as we have seen in Slothrop's uneasiness on the esplanade at Nice, begin to wonder about their world's identity. Is the Zone a part of Europe, and if not what is it? For the reader, the characters themselves become part of the question. We have enough information about Slothrop to say who he is, but as the novel progresses, especially as he begins "to thin" and to scatter into the Zone, the much more disturbing question is raised of what he is. More generally, realistic passages are casually juxtaposed with such surrealist tidbits as Slothrop's excursion into, among other things, a kind of homosexual western when he follows his mouth harp down a toilet, and the by now celebrated adventures of Byron the Bulb. Is *Gravity's Rainbow* serious about history? Are the categories of serious and nonserious even relevant to it? What is *Gravity's Rainbow?*

And whose side is Pynchon on? Could he be one of Them? To the extent that such questions are justified, they testify to Pynchon's success in making us move on the same field of paranoid anxiety as his characters. Pynchon willingly accepts a writer's unavoidable complicity with the plots that torture his characters. If literature is to have a potential for political resistance, that potential will have to be disengaged from literature's very collaboration with the systems it would oppose. In making literature continuous with both the creation and the suspicion of orders in other areas of life—in systems as diverse as Puritan theology, Captain Marvel comics, international cartels, and computer technology—Pynchon denies literature its status as a privileged form maker *and* insists on its inescapable complicity with the most sinister plotmaking activities and strategies of control. By taunting us with the secrets of its own hidden (or inexistent) orders, *Gravity's Rainbow* places us in a predicament not too different from Slothrop's. To say this is to see how far we are from the comforting image of Pynchon the good guy (a sort of authorial version of Roger Mexico), anxious to work out some humane alternative to the impersonal and dehumanizing technique of control made available to the unscrupulous few by modern technology. Such alternatives can be nothing more than fantasy resting points within paranoid trains of thought. And it is not only because Pynchon is a plotmaking novelist that we are bound to suspect that he is working against us. Although it is obviously not a question of Pynchon's being on the side of the oppressors in the sense of sympathizing with their ambitions, he is on their side in a sense that is true for all of us. We cannot, that is, help being an object of suspicion for others. To inspire interest is to be guaranteed a paranoid reading, just as we must inevitably be suspicious of the interpretations we inspire. Paranoia is an inescapable interpretive doubling of presence.

If, then, there is no escape from the paranoid structure of thought, there may also be no escape from the murderous opposition generated by that structure. The polarity of We and They in *Gravity's Rainbow* is a paranoid polarity, and They are all the more threatening in that We can "know" them only through our suspicions about them. And, as I have suggested, that polarity may even be repeated in the relation between the reader and the text. The latter mystifies us not so much because of the information it may be hiding, but above all because of the success with which it hides its own nature. It is as if we could know everything and still not know what kind of text *Gravity's Rainbow* is. It would not exactly be a question of something missing, but rather of the text's real nature as a kind of superior intelligible double of the text we read. Pynchon's novel would signify nothing but itself, without, however, letting us move beyond the opaque surface of the signifying narrative. And that opacity would constitute Thomas Pynchon as the reader's They; he *is* the enemy text.

*   *   *

There may, however, be another way to think about this. It is a peculiarity of the paranoid structure to combine opposition with doubling; the former is, in fact, a function of the latter. The paranoid sees the visible as a simulated double of the real; it deceptively repeats the real. Or, more accurately, it deceitfully repeats the real: such doubleness would not occur if there were no intention to deceive. Otherwise, so paranoia reasons, we would have the Real Text. Thus the paranoid imagination operates on precisely that assumption its enemies—*if they existed*—would wish it to operate on: the assumption that simulations belong to the other side, that doubles have no reason to appear or to exist except to prevent us from seeing the original. The self-protective suspicions of paranoia are therefore already a defeat. The paranoid We must lose out to the enemy They, and this by virtue of the fact that it authorizes or creates the condition of possibility of Theyness by a primary, founding faith in the oneness of the Real. On the basis of that faith, all appearances risk being seen as treacherous simulations and other people have merely to fill the slot, or take the structural position of a dissimulating They in order to have us, at once, in a position characterized by anxiety-ridden suspicions and permanent subordination. In paranoia, the primary function of the enemy is to provide a definition of the real that makes paranoia necessary. We must then begin to suspect the paranoid structure itself as a device by which consciousness maintains the polarity of self and nonself, thus preserving the concept of identity. In paranoia, two Real Texts confront one another: subjective being and a world of monolithic otherness. This opposition can be broken down only if we renounce the comforting (if also dangerous) faith in locatable identities.

Only then, perhaps, can the simulated doubles of paranoid vision destroy the very oppositions they appear to support.

So only within the paranoid structure itself—and not in some extra-paranoid myth such as love or anarchic randomness—can we begin to resist the persecutions that paranoia both imagines and, more subtly, authorizes. Paranoid doubles dissimulate their source. Can they also be thought of as eliminating origins by disseminating targets? Let us consider the mysterious relation between Slothrop's hardons and the V-2. Slothrop's penile sensitivity to the rocket is an object of both military and scientific interest. His erections seem to be a response to an imminent rocket attack, a response, however, that happens from two to ten days before the stimulus. That this is a stimulus response is strongly suggested to Pointsman the Pavlovian and his colleagues by the amazing identity between the patterns on the map of London that Slothrop uses to mark (and to date) his sexual conquests and those that record rocket strikes on Roger Mexico's map of the city. How is this possible? Slothrop is apparently responding to a stimulus before it is presented. Furthermore, the normal order of the stimuli themselves is reversed with the V-2 rocket, which hits before the sound of its coming in can be heard. Pointsman speculates that Laszlo Jamf originally conditioned tiny Tyrone's hardons to occur in response to a loud noise. Having failed to extinguish Slothrop's hardon reflex at the end of the experiment, Jamf guaranteed the survival of the reflex right up to the present. There would be no problem if Slothrop were reacting to the V-1 rocket, whose sound precedes its strike. Then, Pointsman reasons,

> any doodle close enough to make him jump ought to be giving him an erection: the sound of the motor razzing louder and louder, then the cutoff and silence, suspense building up—then the explosion. Boing a hardon. But oh, no. Slothrop instead only gets erections when this sequence happens *in reverse*. Explosion first, then the sound of the approach: the V-2. (99)

In other words, Slothrop's hardon is separated from its stimulus by an event that has not yet taken place, which, so to speak, makes his hardon a logical impossibility. Maybe, Pointsman wonders, Slothrop has his predictive erections in what Pavlov called a "transmarginal" or "ultra-paradoxical" phase, that is, a phase in which the idea of the opposite has been radically weakened. A dog in the ultraparadoxical phase, for example, responds to a food stimulus when it is not there, just perhaps as Slothrop no longer recognizes the binary opposition between the presence and the absence of his hardon stimuli, thus making possible the apparent reversal of normal cause-and-effect sequence. But, with what may be less than ideal consistency, Pointsman also holds on to a modified version of Pavlovian cause and effect, "the true mechanical explanation" that Pavlov believed to be "the ideal, the end we all struggle toward in science" (102). Slothrop may be responding to "'a sensory cue we just aren't paying attention to.' Something that's been there all along, something we could be looking at but no one is" (56). Everyone has a theory for Slothrop's penile anomalies (Roger thinks it's "a statistical oddity," Rollo Groast calls it "precognition," and the Freudian Edwin Treacle calls it "psychokinesis": he makes the rockets fall where they do, thus satisfying a subconscious need "to abolish all trace of the sexual Other" [98]). But in a way the most intriguing one remains the orthodox Pavlovian reading, which the narrator reformulates in the following terms:

> But the stimulus, somehow, *must* be the rocket, some precursor wraith, some rocket's double present for Slothrop in the percentage of smiles on a bus, menstrual cycles being operated upon in some mysterious way—what *does* make the little doxies do it for free? Are there fluctuations in the sexual market, in pornography or prostitutes, perhaps tying into prices on the Stock Exchange itself, that we clean-living lot know nothing about? Does news from the front affect the itch between their pretty thighs, does desire grow directly or inversely as the real chance of sudden death—damn it, what cue, right in front of our eyes, that we haven't the subtlety of heart to see? (99)

By the time we get to these speculations, we may be prepared to find them rather plausible; we have been made ready for a state of interpretive raving. The crazy story of Jamf's experiment has been told in such a matter-of-fact way that we are inclined to accept it as the realistic underpinning of Slothrop's current penile behavior. The problem can then seem to be to figure out where the stimuli are: rocket preparations across the channel may affect menstrual cycles in a way that increases women's sexual receptivity to Slothrop, just before each rocket strike, or desire may grow when death is imminent. All this is not just a joke, but it would be a joke *on us* if we read its seriousness in terms of the cause-and-effect sequences that Pointsman hesitates to give up. Let us try to define that "seriousness" (without knowing what this word will now mean) in terms that have nothing at all to do with cause-and-effect narrativity or with the realistic probabilities that such narrative lines tend to produce.

We can take our cue from the phrase "some rocket's double." What Slothrop responds to is a climate of being, a rocketness that manifests itself in different ways in Germany and in London. And Slothrop's response is a further manifestation: his erections are replicative mutations of the rocket. *Gravity's Rainbow* can be very explicit about the rocket's phallic significance (Katje, for example, "has understood the great airless arc [followed by the rocket] as a clear allusion to certain secret lusts that drive the planet and herself, and Those who use her—over its peak and down, plunging, burning, toward a terminal orgasm" [260]), but I doubt that the rocket is meant merely to symbolize repressed sexuality. The "secret lusts that drive the planet" cannot be reduced to psychological lusts, although they can certainly recur as psychology. No single recurrence, however, should be given priority as the founder of the series. Rockets are not fired because of unsatisfied phallic lusts, and we must remember that if the rocket is a double of the phallus, it also doubles—and is doubled by—the rainbow. On the day Slothrop becomes a crossroad in the Zone, he "sees a very thick rainbow here, a stout rainbow cock driven down out of pubic clouds into Earth, green wet valleyed Earth" (729). The series rocket-cock-rainbow may be intelligible mainly in graphic terms: the rocket's rise and fall, the line from the base of the erect cock to the place on the ground where its semen might fall, and the curve of the rainbow all trace a parabola, a figure that can itself be taken to chart a kind of erotic relation of resistance and abandonment to gravity. The rocket's murderous power is, then, somewhat deemphasized by the way it replicates itself inaccurately (but the only *accurate* replications are fantasy-denials of the simulations that constitute the real) as exuberant phallic sexuality and a visual spectacle of radiant calm in nature. This is not to say that the novel denies the rocket's destructiveness; in *Gravity's Rainbow* Pynchon subordinates political and historical seriousness to certain deployments of being that can in turn affect the way we think about history and conceive our resistance to power.

Rocket power is everywhere, and its violence can take many forms, including the appeased violence of the rainbow's stilled parabolic curve. Slothrop, with his hardons and his vision of a "rainbow cock" (after which he "stands crying, not a thing in his head, just feeling natural" [729]), is the principal carrier of this cracked ontological mirror. Consequently he is also the principal threat to a projected Theyness that would reserve rockets for destruction or allow us to analyze them, with incurable melancholy, as mere substitutes for an equally destructive phallic drive. Slothrop must be pursued, and he will fight back by disappearing into roles that are themselves simulations of comic-book stereotypes and folklore heroes. He wanders through the Zone as Rocketman and in the suit of Plechazunga the Pig-Hero "who, sometime back in the 10th century, routed a Viking invasion, appearing suddenly out of a thunderbolt and chasing a score of screaming Norsemen back into the sea" (661). Slothrop loses his "personal density," begins "to thin, to scatter" (593), thus becoming *unfindable*. But, at the same time, the rocket itself loses some of its awesome prestige by virtue of its debilitating repetition in Slothrop as both his comical horniness and his metamorphosis into the rocket's legend. Such replications don't of course prevent real rockets from being fired in historical time. But *Gravity's Rainbow,* as we should now realize, takes place in a different kind of time, a nonhistorical time in which the rockets and the murderous forces behind it are denied the ontological privileges that make them possible. Slothrop as a novelistic personality is sacrificed to this operation, and the extraordinary poignancy of his robust yet menaced presence in *Gravity's Rainbow* is the premonitory sign that he is condemned to be lost. Through Slothrop we mourn the loss of personal presence, of a myth of personality that may, after all, be the only way in which our civilization has taught us to think about ourselves (to think our selves), a loss that must nonetheless be sustained if we are also to disappear as targets, and therefore as conditions of possibility, of rockets and cartels.[4]

*   *   *

In *Gravity's Rainbow,* the paranoid double—the Real Text behind visible orders—is inaccurately and subversively replicated as serial doubles that ruin the very notion of Real Texts. The story of Slothrop narrativizes a more general process of replicative positioning throughout the novel. If we have such trouble keeping track of what's going on in *Gravity's Rainbow,* it is perhaps less because of the multiplicity of characters and events than because so much of what happens has almost happened already. When Thanatz is quizzed by Hereros about the Schwarzgerät, is it the realization of Närrisch's fearful anticipation, much earlier in the novel, that he will be interrogated about the S–Gerät by the Russians? Psychological and dramatic particularities are blurred by parallelisms. Pökler loses Ilse. Thanatz loses Gottfried and then Bianca, and Slothrop loses Bianca. The thematic depth that such repetitions might create—say, an obsession with the loss of a young girl—is forestalled by their psychologically thinning effect. For the repetition works here not to open up depths, but to cast doubt on the singularity of character. Thanatz comes to realize that "the two children, Gottfried and Bianca, *are the same*" (783). And Slothrop, having lost Bianca, understands that "Ilse, fathered on Greta Erdmann's silver and passive image, Bianca, conceived during the filming of the very scene that was in his thoughts as Pökler pumped in the fatal charge of sperm [into Leni]—how could they not be the same child?" (672). And even before Slothrop begins to thin and scatter, he is already difficult to locate. Who, or what, is Pirate Prentice, with his talent "for getting inside the fantasies of others: being able, actually, to take over the burden of *managing* them" (13)—a talent that will be made nothing of in the novel except as an anticipatory double, an annunciation of Slothrop and *his* special divining talent? Finally Slothrop learns that Roosevelt has died when he, Slothrop, "was living on the Riviera, or in Switzerland someplace, only half aware of being extinguished himself." After he gets the news, "the wide necropolis" of Berlin "begins now to draw inward, to neck down and stretchout into a Corridor, one known to Slothrop though not by name, a deformation of space that lurks inside his life, latent as a hereditary disease." In that space, Roosevelt's doctors move toward the man who—if indeed they were the same—in his black cape at Yalta "conveyed beautifully the sense of Death's wings" and prepared a nation "for the passing of Roosevelt, a being They assembled, a being They would dismantle" (435). But what is Slothrop himself if not an assembled and then dismantled being, "extinguished" at the same instant as the president whose last moments he relives in that strange Corridor outside historical space and time? Is Slothrop FDR?

No matter how much we work on *Gravity's Rainbow,* our most important interpretive discovery will be that it resists analysis. To talk about Bianca is to talk about Ilse and Gottfried; to describe the Zone is to enumerate all the images of other times and places repeated there. Pynchon's novel is a dazzling argument for shared or collective being—or, more precisely, for *the originally replicative nature of being.* Singularity is inconceivable; the original of a personality has to be counted among its simulations. Being in Pynchon is therefore not a question of substance, but rather of distribution and collection. Slothrop is consecrated (and sacrificed) as a collectible of sense the day he becomes a crossroads. "At last, lying one afternoon spread-eagled at his ease in the sun, at the edge of one of the ancient Plague towns he becomes a cross himself, a crossroads, a living intersection where the judges have come to set up a gibbet for a common criminal who is to be hanged at noon" (728). Before the hanging, Slothrop takes the criminal's place, is executed for him, or rather merely before and with him, since there is no redemptive sacrifice in *Gravity's Rainbow* that might become the Ultimate Sacrifice exempting the rest of us from a similar fate. Slothrop is immolated to his own lack of originality, to his thinning or scattered nature, to his being, for example, an anticipatory replay of a common criminal's execution.

And *nothing* is original here. The very scene of the sacrifice is itself a serial element: the cross that his spread-eagled body makes is also the cross made by all the churches he passes on his wanderings, which in turn repeats the shape of the A-4 rocket ("apses out to four sides like rocket fins guiding the streamlined spires")—to which we must also add "other fourfold expressions" such as "swastikas, gymnastic symbols FFFF in a circle symetrically upside down and backward, Frisch Fromm Frohlich Frei over neat doorways in quiet streets, and crossroads," and finally the mandala shape of Herero villages in Südwest. All these images speak to Slothrop, as do the heterogeneous images from his own American past that also cross his mind—make him by crossing through —now that he has been consecrated as a crossroads:

Crosses, swastikas, Zone-mandalas, how can they not speak to Slothrop? He's sat in Saure Bummer's kitchen, the air streaming with kif moires, reading soup recipes and finding in every bone and cabbage leaf paraphrases of himself . . . news flashes, names of wheelhorses that will pay him off for a certain getaway . . . He used to pick and shovel at the spring roads of Berkshire, April afternoons he's lost, "Chapter 81 work," they called it, following the scraper that clears the winter's crystal attack-from-within, its white necropolizing . . . picking up rusted beer cans, rubbers yellow with preterite seed, Kleenex wadded to brain shapes hiding preterite snot, preterite tears, newspapers, broken glass, pieces of automobile, days when in superstition and fright he could *make it all fit,* seeing clearly in each an entry in a record, a history: his own, his winter's his country's . . . instructing him, dunce and drifter, in ways deeper than he can explain, have been faces of children out the train windows, two bars of dance music somewhere, in some other street at night, needles and branches of a pine tree shaken clear and luminous against night clouds, one circuit diagram out of hundreds in a smudged yellowing sheaf, laughter out of a cornfield in the early morning as he was walking to school, the idling of a motorcycle at one dusk-heavy hour of the summer . . . and now, in the Zone, later in the day he became a crossroad, after a heavy rain he doesn't recall, Slothrop sees a very thick rainbow here, a stout rainbow cock driven down out of pubic clouds into Earth, green wet valleyed Earth, and his chest fills and he stands crying, not a thing in his head, just feeling natural. (729)

Slothrop is, then, a sacrificial condensation of the scattered nature of sense. And nothing is stranger than that feeling of naturalness at the very moment of his own disappearance. Not only does Slothrop's sacrificial pose make him a mere replication of numerous other crosses; his most personal history is a collection of scenes from the outside, of imprints made by the human and natural landscape of his New England home. Slothrop is so glutted with otherness as to render superfluous the very notion of otherness. Slothrop is no one; he is a certain position on—to use another favorite Pynchonian term—the "interface" between himself and the world ("Could Outsider and Insider be part of the same field?" Pointsman wonders [168]), or between his individual existence and his doubles (between his erections and the V-2, between his crossroad state and "other fourfold expressions"). Rather, Slothrop *moves* in that space between inside and outside, between one simulation and another, which defeats polarities. Seen from the interface, the loci of oppositions have become vaguely delimited, even blurred marginal areas; they can no longer organize relations. Thus the very replications that characterize paranoid doubling in *Gravity's Rainbow* attack the binary paranoid structure of We opposed to They. There is no escape from that doubling, no alternatives that would put to rest once and for all our paranoid suspicion of invisible repetitions of what we see. But there is a horizontalizing of the replicative process, a displacement of the hidden double from its privileged position as the original reality behind the deceptive appearance to serial positions along phenomenal "lines" that have neither endings nor beginnings. Rather than Real Texts imperfectly designated by ontologically inferior signs, we have a replicative series of underived simulacra.

Resistance must therefore be thought of as an inaccurate synonym for conformity. Not only is paranoid terror defeated by replicative processes that both conform to paranoid structures and yet eliminate the They and the We that give rise to terror; the very excessiveness with which images are duplicated may also work to defeat networks of power. Paranoid terror asks: how can we escape incorporating the images by which They would control us? A paranoid resistance, far from confronting apparatuses of control with the impenetrable fortress of a unique selfhood, opens the subject up, makes of the subject a helplessly passive recipient of alien images. And in this apparently docile doubling of the multitudinous forms of information by which a self might be programmed, the subject can perhaps also disappear as a target of the program.

The most striking aspect of Slothrop's apotheosis as an intersection of identities is the reappearance of the random as an effect of (and not in opposition to) his having been so massively programmed. Slothrop is now everything but an interiority: a swastika, the fins of a rocket, a Herero village, snot-filled wads of Kleenex, a pine tree luminous against night clouds, the idling of a motorcycle, variations on Franz van der Groov's cosmic windmill. But, to articulate still another inaccurate replication: just as the effects of Jamf's experiments far exceed the purpose of his original work with tiny Tyrone's hardons, Slothrop is reconstituted as a free if unlocatable subject by the incommensurability of his stored images with any controlling designs. If modern technology has made it possible for human beings to be bombarded with more types of information than ever before in the world's history, and if this means that we are mainly constituted not as private selves but as collections of alien images and discourses, it is also true that we are thereby conditioned beyond any uses that such conditioning might be made to serve. In his absolute, indeed mythic, otherness, Slothrop manifests the constitutive (and not merely reflective) nature of his massive absorptions. By the very extravagance of his acquiescence in the plots around him, the paranoid is thus saved—at least intermittently—from his conviction that his interpretive suspicions about the real merely correspond to designs already there. In the paranoid's reenactment of given plots, he constitutes a kind of shallow subjectivity exceeding them.

This peculiar selfless freedom depends on both the richness and the triteness of plots in the modern world. Pynchon is especially sensitive to the media that create such plots: comic books, the encapsulated romances on billboard posters, and above all movies. More than any other literary work I know, *Gravity's Rainbow* receives and ironically replicates the alluringly corny plots of popular culture. Unlike the orders of high culture, the comic book and movie plots in Pynchon's work can never seduce us into accepting them as reflections of our Real Nature. The very aspect of popular culture that perhaps most offends its detractors—its superficial and frivolous images of human character—allow for mobile self-identifications perhaps too slippery to be coerced into fixed psychological or moral positions. More exactly, the plots of popular culture are overwhelmingly coercive without constituting anything more definite than a readiness to be seduced by other plots. Comic books and movies provide the mode of *Gravity's Rainbow's* seriousness, which is the mode of ontological comedy.

The novel's ungraspability is both a resistance to our attempts to take possession of it and a model of freedom. *Gravity's Rainbow* moves us from a world of measurably effective action on human and natural environments—a world we recognize, and which is perhaps made possible, by relatively stable identifications of its actors—to a world of ontological play. It allegorizes a substratum in personal and historical narratives, a substratum where the human and the nonhuman are no longer related as subject and object, but rather in the mysterious and nonnarrative "unity" of inaccurate replications. If it is both natural and inevitable that we should center an idea (and an ideal) of human rationality within the narratives that organize the real for us, Pynchon's work—while occasionally paying nostalgic tribute to such ideas and ideals—restructures the relation between human beings, their artifacts, and the natural world in which they live in terms of doubles, parallelisms, and simulacra. The forms of being constitute a planetary community in which rockets are parallels of erections and rainbows. From this perspective, the privilege of the human extends no further than its perception or consciousness of a relational mode that ignores the *hierarchical* privileges of humanity. The contribution of popular culture to this perspective is its preciously reductive view of the human; as Rocketman, Slothrop has the paradoxical freedom of a cardboard being, a being no longer constrained by the targetlike singleness of a rich and unique selfhood.

We must, however, not exaggerate these benefits. I have been suggesting that *Gravity's Rainbow* does not merely refer to such things as the heroes of comic-book adventure, but that its own nature cannot help being affected by the cultural forms it incorporates. At the same time,

Pynchon's novel signals its distance from those forms by its worried complicity with paranoid suspicions about the Real Text. Not only that: literature, far from saving us from the controlling designs served by information systems, is itself an information system that threatens its readers' freedom by the very elusiveness of the demands it makes on them. The unreadability that is the sign of the novel's escape from the excessively readable oppositions of plotters and victims (They and We) necessarily reconstitutes an opposition between Pynchon the plotter and his reader-victims. Literature is never merely an agent of resistance against networks of power-serving knowledge; instead it is one of that network's most seductive manifestations. It can never stand outside the oppressive manipulations of social reality and negate those manipulations by a willed alienation from history. Literature is on a continuum with those forces by which it has habitually proclaimed itself to be menaced.

If there is a menace, it is not to literature as a guardian of cultural and ethical values, but rather to literature as a preeminent plotmaker. Social history has probably always been made by forces that, if they took the trouble, could easily demonstrate how little they need literature. Encyclopedism has frequently been literature's defense against its marginal place in information systems, the political, economic, and scientific networks of power and even the symbolic orders by which a society defines itself. Thus the encyclopedic work in the modern period would demonstrate, first of all, that even in a culture saturated with scientific knowledge, art can reassert its claim to be thought of as the privileged medium that processes and "humanizes" this knowledge—integrates it into those symbolic discourses where, from the beginnings of history, human beings have ordered and sought to master their experience. At the same time, in a technological world whose ordering capacities seem to owe even less to art than did prescientific cultures, a world in which the work of art is no longer epistemologically central but merely the occasion for epistemological leisure, art can aspire toward what we might call a redemptively dismissive encyclopedism, an annihilating absorption of its culture's most ambitious projects into the superior "atmosphere" of art. Such redemptive intentions naturally leave history intact (thus even more radically marginalizing art), while art itself becomes the sublime We in paranoid opposition to a dehumanizing They, denying its own perennial if largely unnoticed participation in the exciting uses of knowledge for purposes of mastery. Nothing could be further from Pynchon's fiction, which participates—exuberantly—in an insanely industrious plotting that is also the object of his characters' anxious and probably justified suspicions. The exuberance is perhaps the sign of that participation—as if we could not help being thrilled by our interpretive ingenuities, how-

ever little they may correspond to what exists outside them and in spite
of the violence with which they reinvent the lives of others.

Slothrop, who is both the central agent of suspicion in *Gravity's Rainbow* and the major victim of its plots, follows a course similar to that of
Oedipus. Like Sophocles' hero, he learns with astonishment of all the
connections in his past and that his life has, since infancy, in all likelihood
been plotted by those modern agents of malevolent fate, Shell and IG
Farben. Also like Oedipus, he assumes the plots he has been in terror of
living, although Pynchon never offers us a cathartically maneuvered ex-
emption from his hero's fate as an awesome scapegoat for the crimes of
our paranoid imagination. Slothrop assumes his fate by disappearing into
a pop version of the (already pop) role created for him; and his annuncia-
tory virtue with regard to the rocket is erased by his very assumption of
his Rocketman identity, by a sacrificial similitude in which the cause-
and-effect logic of military planning is inoperative. No wonder Shell is
furious when Slothrop gives them the slip and gets lost in the Zone. Far
from coercing him into self-knowledge (as Oedipus is coerced by his
inexorable fate), their designs allow Slothrop to slip into an identity so
parodistically clear as to be unreadable. But he is of course on the run
from us too, from the interpretive babbling he sets off and never satisfies.
But why should it be satisfied? In our paranoid criticism we will, after
all, be running parallel to Slothrop, thus providing, if we are lucky
enough, another model of unreadability, a convincing failure of self-
knowledge, a defiant act of Slothropian Oedipalism.

George Segal, *Abraham's Farewell to Ishmael*

Epilogue

Like death, Sarah patiently waits. The mocker has become serious.

Apparently she was not always so grim-looking. Although we must assume that she was at least sixty-five years old when Abraham came into Egypt, Sarah was, so her husband tells her, such "a fair woman to look upon" that other men would be willing to kill him in order to get to her. This tribute to Sarah's seductive appeal, we quickly learn, is by no means the blindness of a doting husband:

> And it came to pass, that, when Abram was come into Egypt, the Egyptians beheld the woman that she was very fair.
>
> The princes also of Pharaoh saw her, and commended her before Pharaoh: and the woman was taken into Pharaoh's house.
>
> And he entreated Abram well for her sake: and he had sheep, and oxen, and he asses, and menservants, and maidservants, and she asses, and camels.[1]

We don't know how Sarah felt about these transactions, but we do know that she has a mocking, ironic spirit, and we can guess that she may not have been indifferent to sex. When she hears an angel tell Abraham that his wife will have a son (and we are immediately reminded of the couple's great age and that "it ceased to be with Sarah after the manner of women"), Sarah "laughed within herself, saying, After I am waxed old shall I have pleasure, my lord being old also?" God, as we might expect, hears this inner mockery and reproves Sarah (who denies having laughed, "for she was afraid"; 18:11–15). Her skepticism expresses itself not as a doubt about whether she will conceive, but rather as a doubt—not entirely relevant to what God is predicting—about whether she will have pleasure. (Is she thinking mainly of Abraham's sexual potency? Perhaps she could still have pleasure if her lord were not so old.)

In any case, once God cures her of barrenness and Isaac is born to the hundred-year-old Abraham and his ninety-year-old wife, Sarah gets a chance to laugh again. But this time it can be in public, and everyone will laugh with her:

> And Sarah said, God hath made me to laugh, so that all that hear will laugh with me.
> And she said, Who would have said unto Abraham, that Sarah should have given children suck? for I have born him a son in his old age. (21:6–7)

This is the laughter of a self-satisfaction at once individual and collective. Not only has Sarah overcome the curse of barrenness (and to have conceived at ninety can only increase her pride); more important, it is as if a curse on Abraham's race had also been lifted, for now he can indeed become, as God promised, the legitimate father of many nations. So the family and the clan rejoice: nature itself has suspended its laws so that Abraham and Sarah's seed may be as numerous as the stars of heaven, and so that the great nation born of this union will have had, at its origin, the authority of legitimacy.

There is, however, another mocking presence to be rid of. Sarah, despairing of producing a child herself, had fifteen years earlier sent Abraham to her Egyptian maidservant Hagar, and out of that union Ishmael was born. It is this bastard child (born from what was a sanctioned but second-class union with a concubine wife)—now an adolescent—whom, at the feast made by Abraham on the day Isaac is weaned, Sarah sees "mocking" (21:9). The notation is tantalizing, and the Hebrew verb has been the subject of much speculation and dispute. It has been translated recently as "playing," but more accurately it appears to denote laughter or mockery. Partly because of the resemblance between the Hebrew verb and Isaac's name, it was even assumed in late antiquity that Ishmael was fooling around sexually with his infant half-brother. This suggestion is hard to resist, but I am more intrigued by Ishmael's unexplained mocking laughter. Is he defensively mocking the ancient Sarah, who at ninety can hardly be as appealing as his own mother, Hagar, but who has nonetheless stopped him from being Abraham's heir? Is he expressing skepticism about who Isaac's parents really are—in particular, whether the centenarian Abraham is really the infant's father? Or is this now discarded son—who, God predicted earlier, would grow to be "a wild man" (16:12)—simply incapable of taking such feasts, such ceremonies of collective self-congratulation, seriously? Ishmael may, in short, be "Isaac-ing" it in three possible senses of the word: in his sexual dalliance with his half-brother, in "giving himself airs of being the true heir" (the activity of laughing is the root of Isaac's name), and finally in mocking the true heir.[2]

If nothing in the text unambiguously justifies any of these interpretations, we can at least note a curious resemblance to Sarah's first laughter.

That laughter, like Ishmael's, was unauthorized; indeed, they might both be thought of as secret mocking comments on the predictions and ceremonies of legitimacy. Sarah had inwardly laughed at nothing less than God's promise to make nations and kings come from her union with Abraham; the "wild" Ishmael is perhaps laughing at that pride of lineage, the satisfaction at having produced an heir from the first-class union with Sarah, which has made Abraham gather all his people together to celebrate the weaning of Isaac. In Ishmael's case, we have laughter *at* laughter; a dismissive, reflective irony mocks what is really the deadly serious laughter of Sarah and of the community, a laughter that says: now our future is assured, our power is assured, because the future of many kings and nations has been given its most lawful paternity. The lack of any lighthearted irresponsibility in this laughter is clearly enough indicated by Sarah's reaction when she catches Ishmael mocking. She doesn't really stop laughing. Instead her brutal reaction interprets her laughter for us:

> And Sarah saw the son of Hagar the Egyptian, which she had born unto Abraham, mocking.
> Wherefore she said unto Abraham, Cast out this bondwoman and her son: for the son of this bondwoman shall not be heir with my son, even with Isaac. (21:9–10)

All Sarah can see in Ishmael's laughter is a reflection of the seriousness of her own (second) laughter: the now superfluous child of the servant mocks because he is jealous of the power being passed to Isaac, because he is furious at losing his inheritance. Such laughter is no laugh; there is too much at stake. The community's rejoicing at its own high legitimacy must not be threatened. And, interestingly enough, that legitimacy is most passionately defended not by the patriarch himself but by the lawful mother, the once barren woman who had the courage to laugh a little at God himself and who—now that she has a son whose rights to his inheritance must be protected—is fiercer than God himself. For poor Abraham has grown attached to his bastard son, and God consoles him:

> And the thing was very grievous in Abraham's sight because of his son.
> And God said unto Abraham, Let it not be grievous in thy sight because of the lad, and because of thy bondwoman; in all that Sarah hath said unto thee, hearken unto her voice; for in Isaac shall thy seed be called.
> And also of the son of the bondwoman will I make a nation, because he is thy seed. (21:11–13)

It is the scene of expulsion that George Segal's extraordinary sculpture depicts, a scene narrated in a single verse of Genesis: "And Abraham rose up early in the morning, and took bread, and a bottle of water, and gave it unto Hagar, putting it on her shoulder, and the child, and sent her away: and she departed, and wandered in the wilderness of Beer-sheba"

(21:14). Segal's work at once centers and excludes the two women. On
the one hand, as his title indicates, they are somewhat irrelevant to his
subject: Abraham's farewell to Ishmael. Sarah is hidden from the others'
view behind a massive stone wall; Hagar, with her back to the others
(and ignored by Abraham, who seems not even to see her as he embraces
his son), has already started on her way, holding herself as if she were
already lost in the wilderness. On the other hand, in the perspective from
which our photograph is taken, Abraham and Ishmael are partly hidden
by Hagar; it is almost as if they were secondary to the sharply contrasted
figures of the two women. But like all sculpture, Segal's work shares *our*
space, the space outside the work of art, and in walking around Segal's
group we can of course alter the relations between the figures. We can
move toward the upper left area represented in the photograph, where
we would have directly in front of us Ishmael's head resting on his father's
shoulder; from this position, Sarah is invisible and we see only Hagar's
back. There is, in other words, no necessary foreground or background.
Certain angles of vision emphasize the two presences ignored by the
work's title, and we can move behind that slab of stone and not even see
Abraham and Ishmael; but we can also eliminate Sarah from our field of
vision. Our attention can and should be mobile, and in moving around
and within this group, we try out various subjects: the grief of father and
son, Hagar's abandonment and isolation, Sarah's surveillance of the scene
(but what does she see or where is she looking?—with Segal's eyeless
figures, we can never be sure, and it is possible that only Hagar is visible
to her).

Paradoxically, however, Sarah is the center of Segal's work. The Old
Testament says nothing about Sarah's being present at this scene of departure, and indeed it might seem more appropriate to have God, or one
of his angels, watching over things from behind the wall, standing guard
to make sure that his orders are carried out. But God, in a sense, is
merely carrying out Sarah's orders, and in placing her within his work,
Segal at once pays tribute to her commanding role in the story and at the
same time almost manages to escape from her. She has arranged everything, but is now only part of a group. Segal's sculpture allows us to
reread the biblical story from various perspectives, even including a perspective from which Sarah is absent. For Sarah, the incident has a ruth-
lessly unequivocal sense; the threat to legitimate inheritance must be
eliminated. She is the servant—and a beneficiary—of God's promise to
Abraham; everything else fades into insignificance when compared to the
divinely appointed mission of fathering (and mothering) nations and
kings. But what if Abraham's grief at losing Ishmael is just as important?
Segal's work unsentimentally asks this question. It doesn't really make of
father and son the new center of the story; it merely—and more radi-

cally—eliminates the possibility of centering anything, of unequivocal sense itself. Sarah knows *what counts,* but Segal's work places her in a scene where what supremely counts may get nothing more than a moment of our mobile attention, may depend on something as aleatory as where we happen to be standing as we ourselves move within this scene.

And yet the work also pays homage—disturbingly—to what is after all the unmistakable sense of the biblical story, the need to guarantee Abraham's promised lineage. Sarah the fierce guardian of that promise, Sarah who is almost absent from the scene, who might appear to be its negligible background, Sarah nonetheless, by something like the very weight of her remoteness, dominates everything. The bare-armed, full-lipped, deceptively centered Hagar is an immensely appealing rebuke to the withered, heavily clothed Sarah with her deathlike hood and narrow slit of a mouth, and yet Hagar's more human appeal is doomed to insignificance by the wholly unengaging absent presence of a divinely sanctioned fatality. Everything else but Sarah is mere anecdote, anecdotes of past sexual desires, of family feelings, of anxious isolation. Sarah, like God, knows that all that will become mere footnotes in the authorized narrative of history. The unthreatened transmission of power from generation to generation depends on keeping such footnotes in their place, on God's (and Sarah's) allowing that embrace to take place because it doesn't count, because Abraham's grief will pass, because Abraham himself will pass, because he is condemned to be nothing but the origin of a glorious collective destiny. Only death can have that kind of patience and indifference, and once death (almost imperceptibly) enters the scene, we really see nothing but its ignored presence, and we can no longer read anything but the grand historical narrative that only our dying makes possible.

Ishmael's expulsion in chapter 21 of Genesis is a major resolution to a crisis of legitimacy that begins almost at the very moment when, in chapter 12, the Lord blesses Abraham and promises to make his name great. Isaac's birth and the departure of Hagar and Ishmael are an at least momentary triumph over the threat to legitimacy and order, a threat represented, between chapters 12 and 21, by astonishing accounts of sexual misconduct. First of all, the glorious narrative is in danger of never getting started because of Sarah's barrenness; how can Abraham be the father of many nations if he can't even be a father? We might, however, choose to think of that barrenness as a compositional convenience that, by delaying Isaac's birth, allows for the deployment of *other* threats to legitimate succession, threats derived from the perversity of human desire. Abraham himself initiates the series. To save himself, he passes the desirable Sarah off as his sister, and he does this twice, first when they go into Egypt and later in Gerar. The Pharaoh and Abimelech, the king of Gerar, are happy enough to have the irresistible Sarah, although they are held at bay by God's wrath. Abimelech "had not come near" Sarah (20:4); the Pharaoh does not "take her to him to wife," although he certainly had time to enjoy her without ceremony while plagues were falling upon Egypt "because of Sarai Abram's wife" (12:17–19). We even learn that Abraham had asked Sarah to show him the "kindness" of saying she is his sister at "every place whither we shall come" (20:13); how many unrecorded times did poor Sarah get handed over to the local potentate?

But it turns out that the lie is only half a lie. Abraham explains to the justifiably irritated Abimelech that Sarah is really his sister: "She is the daughter of my father, but not the daughter of my mother" (20:12). Thus the sacred bond that the Pharaoh and Abimelech almost violate (at great cost: Egypt is visited with plagues, the king of Gerar is threatened with death) is an incestuous union, and it is not the only one in this section of Genesis. Only Lot and his daughters survive the destruction of Sodom and Gomorrah; the daughters, anxious to "preserve seed of our father," get him drunk two nights in a row and "lay with him" (the eldest on the first night, her younger sister the second night). From these incestuous revels are born the Moabites and the children of Ammon. Although he obviously manages to perform sexually, Lot, we are told, didn't even perceive when his daughters "lay down, nor when [they] arose" (19:32–35). Was it necessary to make him drink that much? He has after all not exactly been a model of sexual respectability. Earlier in Sodom, to protect the two angels sent to destroy the city from the men of Sodom, "both old and young, all the people from every quarter," who have flocked to his house and demand that he deliver his visitors over to them ("bring them out to us, that we may know them"), Lot tries un-successfully—in a gesture of ambiguously heroic hospitality—to offer the Sodomites his daughters instead: "Behold now, I have two daughters which have not known man; let me, I pray you, bring them out unto you, and do ye to them as is good in your eyes: only unto these men do nothing; for therefore came they under the shadow of my roof" (19:8).

Incest, adultery, possible homosexuality,[3] the prostitution of a spouse: the accumulation of sexual deviance in these few pages is impressive, although readers of the Old Testament know that the lurid tale is fre-quently the narrative and moral rule rather than the exception. The in-terest of such tales in this section of Genesis is, I suggest, as allegories of resistance to the divine intention of sexuality in the service of lawful suc-cession. They delay the establishment of Abraham's proper line. Indeed, they break the narrative line just as they endanger Abraham's lawful pa-ternity. The story of Sodom and Gomorrah interrupts the main plot that begins with God's promise to Abraham in chapter 12 and is resolved with

Isaac's birth and Ishmael's expulsion in chapter 21. There is a continuous swerving away from that inescapable yet also menaced line: Sarah moves away toward the Pharaoh and Abimelech, Abraham consorts with Hagar, the Sodomite men reject women, the husbands of Lot's daughters refuse to leave the city and the daughters must bear their father's children, and Sarah's very barrenness functions as a kind of biological stalling of God's plan.

It is not simply a question of the conflict between legitimacy and illegitimacy. The illegitimate, the unauthorized, do not merely disrupt the straight line; they establish another line, a *possible (unfaithful) double*. This short section has several curious doublets. The "she is my sister" strategy occurs twice, with the Pharaoh and with Abimelech. Sarah's skeptical laugh (19:12) is a repetition of Abraham's laugh in a preceding chapter when, upon hearing from God that his aged wife will be a mother of nations, "Abraham fell upon his face, and laughed, and said in his heart, Shall a child be born unto him that is an hundred years old? and shall Sarah that is ninety years old, bear?" (17:17). Hagar is sent off to the wilderness twice, once (in chapter 16) when Sarah ragefully sees that, having conceived, the servant now despises her barren mistress, and later—this time not to return—when Sarah sends her away with the mocking Ishmael. There is, finally, the recurrence of incest and perhaps of homosexuality: Lot and his daughters, Abraham and his half-sister, the Sodomites, Ishmael's possible "Isaac-ing."

All this might be taken as a structural invitation to think in terms of repetitions with more or less significant differences. And a kind of differential repetition is of course what the principal plot of this section is all about. God's promise to Abraham is held in suspense for nine chapters even as it is fulfilled during that same time—but fulfilled in a second-class way, by a birth that at once establishes Abraham's progeny and itself belongs to the series of incidents that stage a resistance to historical lineage founded on the most highly authorized sexuality. Ishmael's birth is not an ahistorical—therefore utopian and perhaps ultimately dismissible—protest against history itself as it has been appropriated by God for Abraham and Sarah's rightful heirs. Rather, Ishmael is the possibility of history as *unauthorized continuity*. It is true that he is also coopted by God's narrative. God consoles Hagar by promising her that she too will be a mother of nations, that God will make Ishmael "a great nation" (21:18), that he will "multiply [her] seed exceedingly, that it shall not be numbered for multitude" (16:10). In short, Hagar will be a minor Sarah, with her own divinely insured inheritance. But Hagar's line will produce a people of nomads, ideologically (and anachronistically) judged by the authors of Genesis when they characterize that line's patriarch, Ishmael, as "a wild man," one whose "hand will be against every man, and every man's hand against him" (16:12). And the last we hear of Ishmael is that he "dwelt in the wilderness, and became an archer" (21:20). The Ishmael story resists being coopted, is never deprived of its potential for resistance. For what is a wild man and who, exactly, is the mysteriously mocking Ishmael, the one who laughs at ceremonies and authorized identities?

Most profoundly, Isaac's birth deprives Ishmael of an identity, or it sets him afloat among different identities, none of which wholly belongs to him. He will have a line, but not the line for which he was conceived; his promised inheritance is a function of his loss of inheritance; he will continue to represent Abraham in history only because he has been expelled from Abraham's home. Indeed, the instances of sexual deviance to which Ishmael belongs in this section of Genesis are also instances of deviant identities. The maidservant is summoned to play the role of wife; the wife presents herself as a sister; the father becomes husband to his daughters. In a text so obsessively concerned with legitimation through naming (the famous naming of generations in Genesis takes place in chapters 10 and 11), the proper, the right, name is also violated (or hidden, confused, stolen), and this is a crucial element in the text's persistent subversion of authority. Ishmael is essentially homeless and nameless (and, perhaps on the basis of such intimations, Melville used him as a parable of "incomparable America"). Genesis (like *Moby-Dick* and several of the other texts considered in this study) leaves magnificently open the question of a place for deviance within history, of the fate, in time, of unauthorized desires and identities.

Notes
Index

Notes

1. Death and Literary Authority

1. Marcel Proust, *Remembrance of Things Past,* trans. C. K. Scott Moncrieff and Terence Kilmartin; and Andreas Mayor, 3 vols. (copyright © 1981 by Random House, Inc., New York, and Chatto and Windus, London; quotations by permission of the publishers), 2:783–784. The original French is from Proust, *A la Recherche du temps perdu,* ed. Pierre Clarac and André Ferré, 3 vols. (Paris: Gallimard, 1954), 2:756–757. All further references to this work (the translation and the original in that order) are included in text.
2. Moncrieff and Kilmartin translate this phrase as "an annihilation that had effaced my image of that tenderness." My own translation—somewhat less probable grammatically—is, as it were, solicited by my interpretation of the entire passage and more specifically by the narrator's remark, quoted next in my text, that he "was and would be nothing" both "before and after" the death of that "mere stranger" his grandmother had now become (2:785; 2:115).
3. Gilles Deleuze, *Proust and Signs,* trans. Richard Howard (New York: Braziller, 1972), pp. 41, 43.
4. Melanie Klein, "Early Analysis," *"Love, Guilt, and Reparation" and Other Works, 1921–1945* (New York: Dell, 1975), p. 77. All further references to this essay, abbreviated EA, are included in text.
5. In the sharp distinction that Klein makes in this essay between neurotic fixations and sublimations, the crucial point appears to be what happens to suspended libido. "In hysterical fixation . . . phantasy holds so tenaciously to the pleasure situation that, before sublimation is possible, it succumbs to repression and fixation." One page later Klein writes: "In my opinion we find that a fixation which leads to a symptom was already on the way to sublimation but was cut off from it by repression." And, in her brief account of Freud's essay on Leonardo da Vinci, Klein concludes: "In Leonardo the pleasurable situation [gratification through fellatio] did not become fixated as such: he transferred it to ego-tendencies." It is true, however, that Klein sometimes speaks of this process as a transfer of an already defined, even already fixated, pleasurable situation; she will also write that the step from

identifications to symbol formation—a developmental step obviously crucial for cultural sublimation—takes place when "repression begins to operate" (EA, 86–89). The ambiguities here may have to do with Klein's failure (or unwillingness) to recognize how radical her position in "Early Analysis" is. This suggestion seems all the more probable in the light of her later, and more "official," views of sublimation.

6. Klein, "On the Theory of Anxiety and Guilt," *"Envy and Gratitude" and Other Works, 1946–1963* (New York: Dell, 1975), p. 41.

7. Klein, "The Early Development of Conscience in the Child," *"Love, Guilt, and Reparation,"* p. 254.

8. Klein, "The Importance of Symbol-Formation in the Development of the Ego," ibid., pp. 220–224.

9. Klein, "A Contribution to the Psycho-Genesis of Manic-Depressive States," ibid., p. 270.

10. Klein, "Some Theoretical Conclusions Regarding the Emotional Life of the Infant (1952)," *"Envy and Gratitude,"* p. 64.

11. Klein, "Envy and Gratitude," ibid., p. 193.

12. For two quite different views of the relation between sublimation and idealization, see Guy Rosoloto, *Essais sur le symbolique,* (Paris: Gallimard, 1964), pp. 170–80, and Donald Meltzer, *Sexual States of Mind* (Perthshire: Clunie Press, 1973), pp. 122–31.

13. See Jean Laplanche, *Problématiques III: La Sublimation* (Paris: Presses Universitaires de France, 1980).

14. In Chapter 2 I develop these ideas in the context of the ambiguous positioning of narcissism in Freudian thought.

15. In an important essay (originally published in German in 1937) on the segregation of culture within bourgeois society, Herbert Marcuse defines the role of culture in a civilization anxious to divert human beings from their real material situation, and to suggest that the private realm of the soul, where high culture is enjoyed, somehow makes up for debased and unjust social conditions: "Culture should [according to the modern bourgeois view of it] ennoble the given by permeating it, rather than putting something new in its place. It thus exalts the individual without freeing him from his factual debasement. Culture speaks of the dignity of 'man' without concerning itself with a concretely more dignified status for men. The beauty of culture is above all an inner beauty and can only reach the external world from within. Its realm is essentially a realm of the *soul.*" This cultural ideal, Marcuse argues, has best been exemplified by art, and for good reason, since "only in art has bourgeois society tolerated its own ideals and taken them seriously [even while segregating them] as a general demand." Marcuse, "The Affirmative Character of Culture," in *Negations: Essays in Critical Theory* (Boston: Beacon Press, 1968), pp. 103, 114.

2. Erotic Assumptions

1. *The Standard Edition of the Complete Psychological Works of Sigmund Freud,* ed. James Strachey, 24 vols. (London: Hogarth Press, 1953–1974), 9:175. Vol-

ume and page references for all further citations from Freud in the Standard Edition are given in text.

2. Jean Laplanche emphasizes the notion that the sublimation of sexual impulses takes place before repression in his analysis of Freud's study of Leonardo da Vinci. See Laplanche, *Problématiques III,* especially pp. 109–115. In a 1964 seminar Jacques Lacan, in a discussion of Freud's "Instincts and Their Vicissitudes," also defines sublimation as the satisfaction of a sexual drive, "without repression"; *Le Séminaire, livre VI: Les Quatre Concepts fondamentaux de la psychanalyse* (Paris: Editions du Seuil, 1973), p. 151. For an interesting discussion of the possibly complementary relation between sublimation and sexuality, see Kurt Eissler, *Leonardo da Vinci: Psychoanalytic Notes on the Enigma* (New York: International Universities Press, 1961). I discuss this question at greater length in *The Freudian Body: Psychoanalysis and Art* (New York: Columbia University Press, 1986), chap. 2.

3. That effort and argument have frequently been made, often with interesting results, in the context of speculations on the relation between art and the primary process. I am thinking, for example, of Ernst Kris's notion of controlled or regulated regression, in which the ego, instead of being overwhelmed by the primary process, creatively uses it; see his *Psychoanalytic Explorations in Art* (New York: Schocken, 1952). Anton Ehrenzweig goes further than Kris in arguing for "the eminently constructive role of the primary process in art." For Ehrenzweig, "what is missing in Kris's concept . . . is the insight that creativity does not merely control the regression toward the primary process, but also the work of the primary process itself"; *The Hidden Order of Art: A Study in the Psychology of Artistic Imagination* (Berkeley: University of California Press, 1967), pp. 31, 261–262. Finally, Jean-François Lyotard has made an extremely stimulating argument for what he calls the *double renversement* (the double reversal) of unconscious processes in art. To the extent that art merely repeats the contents of unconscious desires, it can be read symptomatically. More interesting for Lyotard (and for us) is *the nonrealization of desire in art.* By repeating the movements of desire rather than its hallucinatory contents, the work of art prevents desire from settling into any constituted, definitive meanings; it is as if unconscious desire were emptied of its specific representations by becoming the object of its own characteristic mode of operation. See Jean-François Lyotard, *Discours, figure* (Paris: Editions Klincksieck, 1971), and "Oedipe juif," *Dérive à partir de Marx et Freud* (Paris: Union générale d'éditions, 1973).

Within the psychoanalytic community, there has of course been considerable discussion of art. An issue of *American Imago* from several years ago, devoted to "Genius, Psychopathology and Creativity" (Spring–Summer 1967), gives a fairly good idea of the problems that have generally seemed important to psychoanalysts in their attempts to give a Freudian account of aesthetics. This issue was inspired by Kurt Eissler's work on Leonardo and Goethe, and it pointed to some lively debate on such questions as: Is narcissism the maturational force behind the reparative energy that goes into artistic creation? Do the motives for creativity derive their strength from aggressive and libidinal derivatives or, predominantly, from "deaggressivization" and "delibidinization?" What is the role of ego synthesis in the creation of a new gestalt? Are the regressions of creative personalities in the service of the ego, or do they aim at ego restoration, even ego survival? Should we think of sublimation as synonymous with creativity? Is artistic activity "autonomous"—that is, detached from the original sphere of conflict—or does the entire process of creativity proceed side by side with the underlying conflict, a conflict by which it is constantly nurtured? Some of these questions certainly merit attention, but the attention that psychoanalysts (especially in America) have given to them almost always seems intellectually naive. This may be the result of what often seems to be these psychoanalysts' royal indifference to nearly everything that has happened in esthetic theory and literary criticism since Kant. At a much higher level of professional psychoanalytic interest in art, there is of course the work of Jacques Lacan. Malcolm Bowie has recently made a good case for Lacan's ambivalent, troubled efforts to appropriate literature for psychonalytic truth; Bowie speaks of "the rhythm of admiration, envy and aggresion, that marks [Lacan's] handling of literary materials." See his *Freud, Proust and Lacan: Theory as Fiction* (Cambridge: Cambridge University Press, 1987), p. 158.

In the context of my attempts to outline a theoretical approach to art inspired by speculations on the Freudian hypothesis of primary narcissism (see especially the discussion of Baudelaire and Nietzsche in Chapter 3), Heinz Kohut, given his work on narcissism and his interst in art, seemed like a promising reference. Unfortunately he gives us little more than the usual psychoanalytic clichés. In an essay entitled "Observations on the Psychological Function of Music," he speaks of "the psychoeconomic efficacy of musical activity for the relief of pregenital libidinal and aggressive tensions," and he suggests that art can be a useful substitute to schizophrenics who don't have a therapist, since, as we all know, art allows "a controlled and limited regression." See *The Search for the Self: Selected Writings of Heinz Kohut, 1950–1978*, vol. 1, ed. Paul H. Ornstein (New York: International Universities Press, 1978), pp. 249–251.

4. Laplanche seems to be suggesting something consistent with the idea I develop here when he writes, in summing up Freud's thesis in the 1914 essay on narcissism: the "libidinal cathexis of the ego is inseparable from the very *constitution* of the human *ego*." Jean Laplanche, *Vie et mort en psychanalyse* (Paris: Flammarion, 1970), p. 116; *Life and Death in Psychoanalysis,* trans. Jeffrey Mehlman (Baltimore: Johns Hopkins University Press, 1976), p. 67.

5. *As if:* I qualify here in order to indicate that such terms as "fascinated" and "self-reflection" have to be phenomenologically inaccurate to describe that consciousness, although our—and Freud's—metapsychological speculations assume a certain form of persistence in consciousness of its own primitive states. Such states are inferred from their inaccurate replication in far more developed mental structures. In the essay on narcissism, the "evidence," quite properly, comes after the speculative assertion instead of leading up to it, and this very sequence highlights the paradox that the evidence is massive for that which, strictly speaking, there can be no evidence.

6. Kohut presents a wholly different view of the relation between sexuality and the self. For him—and this has led to much resistance on the part of drive-oriented Freudians—the "bedrock" of early development is not castration anxiety but rather the threat to the nuclear self. The sexual is inherently secondary to self-formation and self-confirmation. What Freud called instinctual vicissitudes are, for Kohut, esentially *responses to* how the self was treated, whether or not it was confirmed by "the mirroring self-object." Nonpathological sexuality is a "firming up" of the sense of the bodily self. This is of course wholly at odds with the idea, argued for in this chapter, of sexuality as constitutive of ego formation. See Heinz Kohut, *The Restoration of the Self* (New York: International Universities Press, 1977).

Perhaps closer to that idea is Kernberg's thesis of primary narcissism and primary object investment as coincidental. He postulates a primary undifferentiated self-object representation out of which narcissism and object investment develop simultaneously. This is, he points out, different from both Kohut's theories and classical thought. See Otto F. Kernberg, *Borderline Conditions and Pathological Narcissism* (New York: Aronson, 1975), especially chap. 10. An interesting "classical" objection to Kernberg's work can be found in Milton Klein and David Tribich, "Kernberg's Object-Relations Theory: A Critical Evaluation," *International Journal of Psychoanalysis*, 62, part 1 (1981).

For some valuable theoretical essays on narcissism, see the issue entitled "Narcisses" of *Nouvelle Revue de psychanalyse*, 13 (Spring 1973).

3. Boundaries of Time and Being

1. "The Work of Art in the Age of Mechanical Reproduction," in Walter Benjamin, *Illuminations,* ed. Hannah Arendt, trans. Harry Zohn (New York: Schocken, 1968), pp. 231, 221, 234. Further page references to this collection of Benjamin's writings are given in text.

   Which is the real Benjamin? Gershom Scholem deplored the dialectical materialism of the later writings as a betrayal of the metaphysical-theological determinations of the earlier writings. Others—including Adorno and Brecht, who had very different ideas of what this should mean—encouraged Benjamin's interest in Marxism and dialectial materialism. Should we think in terms of periods, or of a permanent opposition in his thought, or of parallel and persistent intellectual tracks?

2. Benjamin did not of course invent the difference between *Erlebnis* and *Erfahrung.* I am principally interested in his characteristic historicizing of the distinction. It should also be pointed out that, especially in the 1930s, *Erlebnis* was a highly valorized term in Nazi ideology.

3. Richard Wolin, *Walter Benjamin: An Aesthetic of Redemption* (New York: Columbia University Press, 1982), p. 31.

4. This attention was to lead to the "Pariser Passagen," or the Arcades Project. In this massive, unfinished work, Benjamin wished to do for the modern age what his *Trauerspiel* study had done for an earlier period: illustrate the pro-

found meaning of the modern through an allegorical reading of details of city life, especially of Paris, "the capital of the nineteenth century."

5. Walter Benjamin, *The Origin of German Tragic Drama,* trans. John Osborne (London: New Left Books, 1977), p. 29.

6. Theodor Adorno, *Minima Moralia: Reflections from Damaged Life,* trans. E.F.N. Jephcott (London: New Left Books, 1974), p. 247. In three letters of 1935, 1936, and 1938, Adorno responded in detail to some of Benjamin's principal writings: "Paris, Capital of the Nineteenth Century" (the Arcades Project), "The Work of Art in the Era of Mechanical Reproduction," and "The Paris of the Second Empire in Baudelaire." The letters show Adorno's impatience with what he considered to be the antidialectical influence of Brecht on Benjamin's thought. See Adorno, *Aesthetics and Politics,* trans. R. Taylor (London: New Left Books, 1977), pp. 110–133. In an interesting essay, Jürgen Habermas has argued that "Adorno never noticeably hesitated to attribute to Benjamin the precise intention of ideology critique that he followed in his own work, and in this he was wrong." Habermas recognizes in Adorno "the better Marxist," but perhaps because of this the latter "did not see that his friend was never prepared to give up the theological heritage, in as much as he always kept his mimetic theory of language, his messianic theory of history, and his conservative-revolutionary understanding of criticism immune against objections from historical materialism." Benjamin cannot be looked to for "a theology of revolution": "The liberation from cultural traditions of semantic potentials that must not be lost to the messianic condition is not the same as the liberation of political domination from structural violence." "Walter Benjamin: Consciousness-Raising or Rescuing Critique," in *On Walter Benjamin: Critical Essays and Recollections,* ed. Gary Smith (Cambridge: MIT Press, 1988), pp. 115, 117, 120. I agree with Habermas' view of the truly important emphases in Benjamin's work, although he is considerably more sympathetic than I am to their effects on Benjamin's views of art and of history.

7. In a note to his brief commentary on "Correspondances," Benjamin describes correspondences in mimetic terms: "Beauty in its relationship to *nature* can be defined as that which 'remains true to its essential nature only when veiled.' The *correspondances* tell us what is meant by such a veil. We may call it, in somewhat daring abbreviation, the 'reproducing aspect' of the work of art. The *correspondances* constitute the court of judgment before which the object of art is found to be a faithful reproduction—which, to be sure, makes it entirely problematic" ("On Some Motifs in Baudelaire," p. 199). Obviously the most problematic aspect of these remarks is their relation to Baudelaire.

8. For a brilliant critique of the "modernist myth" of originality and of the original work behind all copies of it, see Rosalind E. Krauss, "The Originality of the Avant-Garde," in *The Originality of the Avant-Garde and Other Modernist Myths* (Cambridge: MIT Press, 1985). Furthermore, Benjamin is naive about what he seems to see as the sudden emergence of technological factors in artistic composition. Adorno complained: "You under-estimate the technicality of autonomous art [the individual master works of classical and

bourgeois art] and over-estimate that of dependent art [art dependent on technology for its production]" (*Aesthetics and Politics*, p. 124).

9. As Habermas rightly notes, "Benjamin was always ambivalent about the loss of aura" ("Consciousness-Raising or Rescuing Critique," p. 106). I am interpreting this celebrated Benjaminian concept in the light of what I take to be his profound distrust not only of modernity but also of history itself, although I realize that "The Work of Art in the Age of Mechanical Reproduction" can be read as an almost enthusiastic announcement of the work of art's emancipation, "for the first time in world history . . . from its parasitical dependence on ritual" (*Illuminations*, p. 224). Such a reading would of course underline such remarks as: "We do not deny that in some cases today's films can also promote revolutionary criticism of social conditions, even of the distribution of property" (*Illuminations*, p. 231), although with regard to such hopes Adorno's sarcastic comment may not be entirely out of place: "the idea that a reactionary is turned into a member of the avant-garde by expert knowledge of Chaplin's films strikes me as out-and-out romanticization" (*Aesthetics and Politics*, p. 123). "The Work of Art in the Age of Mechanical Reproduction" is, for all its fame, surely one of Benjamin's least satisfactory performances, although its incoherences, hasty judgments, and ambiguous emphases reflect—and make painfully visible—fundamental characteristics of his thought.

   For an extremely acute and sympathetic reading of Benjamin's film theory, see Miriam Hansen, "Benjamin, Cinema and Experience: 'The Blue Flower in the Land of Technology,'" *New German Critique*, 40 (Winter 1987), 179–224. Recognizing Benjamin's attitude toward the decline of the aura as "profoundly ambivalent," Hansen defines the "redemptive" function that Benjamin assigns to film in terms of its "registering sediments of experience that are no longer or not yet claimed by social and economic rationality, making them readable as emblems of a 'forgotten future.'" Cinema raises the possibility of "the discontinuous return of the auratic mode of experience through the back door of the 'optical unconscious'" (pp. 187, 209, 212).

10. "On Language as Such and on the Language of Man," in Walter Benjamin, *Reflections: Essays, Aphorisms, Autobiographical Writings*, ed. Peter Demetz, trans. Edward Jephcott (New York: Harcourt Brace Jovanovich, 1978), p. 318.

11. Ibid., pp. 323, 321.

12. The fascist use of art is closer than the communist use of art to art's role in religious rituals. Communism, Benjamin writes, responds to fascism by "politicizing art." That is, it insists that certain practices already going on in a society (artistic production) *have* a political value (and the insistence is of course both descriptive and prescriptive). This is different from what is either a kind of invention of art for political purposes or an aesthetic reworking of political expression—which can be thought of as characteristic of both modern fascism and of social groups in which what we now recognize as art is, or was, used in cultic contexts. Strictly speaking, and unlike the communist appropriation of art, the aestheticizing of politics in ritual does not depend on the prior existence of an art independent of ritual.

13. "Theologico-Political Fragment," in *Reflections*, pp. 312–313. For some significant distinctions between human and divine violence, see "Critique of Violence," in *Reflections*, pp. 277–300.

14. Wolin, *An Aesthetic of Redemption*, p. 39. As we might expect, Benjamin is much better at drawing our attention to images of decay and deadness than at locating moments of transcendental eruption. He acutely notes, for example, Baudelaire's "empathy with inorganic things," and he writes suggestively, again in connection with Baudelaire, about the intoxicating effect of a city's masses on the very commodities (including human bodies) the city offers ("only the mass makes it possible for the sexual object to become intoxicated with the hundred stimuli which it produces"). Benjamin, "The Paris of the Second Empire in Baudelaire," in *Charles Baudelaire: A Lyric Poet in the Era of High Capitalism*, trans. Harry Zohn (London: New Left Books, 1973), pp. 55–57. In contrast to this, Benjamin's idealist bias leads him to identify Baudelairean correspondences with the experience of the *idéal*, with "the data of remembrance—not historical data, but data of prehistory" ("On Some Motifs in Baudelaire," 182), and this blinds him to the way in which the proliferation of correspondences in modern life work to break down the very opposition between *spleen* and *idéal*.

    It should be pointed out that Benjamin—for example, in the 1929 piece on "Surrealism"—came to insist on "a *profane illumination*," a materialistic anthropological inspiration, one even conceived of as "the true, creative overcoming of religious illumination" (*Reflections*, p. 179). This strikes, it is true, quite a different note from the judgment of "natural life" in the 1922 essay on "Goethe's *Elective Affinities*." In the earlier piece, Benjamin spoke of human life's remaining innocent "only as long as it is connected to a higher life . . . When supernatural life disappears from man's existence, even if he does not commit any immoral acts, man's natural life is burdened with guilt"—*Essais*, vol. 1, 1922–1934, trans. into French by Maurice de Grandillac (Paris: Denoël/Gonthier, 1971–1983), p. 43. But whether the *source* of the illumination be profane or divine, it is in both cases an assault on historical time, and the "Theses on the Philosophy of History," with its meditation on a *Jetzzeit* "shot through with chips of Messianic time," was completed in 1940, the year of Benjamin's death.

15. *The Origin of German Tragic Drama*, pp. 178, 182.

16. Charles Baudelaire, *The Painter of Modern Life and Other Essays*, trans. Jonathan Mayne (London: Phaidon Press, 1964), p. 3; *Oeuvres complètes*, 2 vols., ed. Claude Pichois (Paris: Bibliothèque de la Pléiade, Gallimard, 1976), 2:685. Page references to this essay are given in text, first to the English edition and then to the French.

17. Benjamin, *Charles Baudelaire*, p. 82.

18. "This is in fact an excellent opportunity to establish a rational and historical theory of beauty"; "I defy anyone to point to a single scrap of beauty"; "Consider, if you will, the eternally subsisting portion as the soul of art" (3).

19. The failure of certain periods to represent the material side of their modernity is excusable only "in the case of a masquerade prescribed by fash-

ion." Also, "the goddesses, nymphs and sultanas of the eighteenth century are still convincing portraits, *morally* speaking" (13; 695).

20. "The Salon of 1846," in *The Mirror of Art: Critical Studies by Charles Baudelaire*, trans. Jonathan Wayne (London: Phaidon Press, 1955), p. 84; *Oeuvres complètes*, 2:455–456.

21. Ibid., pp. 84–85; 2:455.

22. My translation; *Oeuvres complètes*, 1:692.

23. The use of body positions and penetrations as a pretext for sexist ideologies of power is thus implicitly set aside by Baudelaire's recognition that the other can just as easily be substituted for the self in a move of penetration as in the acquiescence to being penetrated. But this still leaves us with Baudelaire's misogyny, to which I will be coming back.

24. Freud, *The Ego and the Id*, in *Standard Edition*, 19:25–26; and Leo Bersani, *The Freudian Body: Psychoanalysis and Art*, (New York: Columbia University Press, 1986), p. 95.

25. Freud, *Three Essays on the Theory of Sexuality*, in *The Standard Edition*, 7:203.

26. See Bersani, *The Freudian Body*, pp. 37–39, and Jean Laplanche, *Life and Death in Psychoanalysis*, trans. Jeffrey Mehlman (Baltimore: Johns Hopkins University Press, 1976), pp. 87–88.

27. The by now classical "moral" perspective on Baudelairean masochism can be found in Jean-Paul Sartre's *Baudelaire* (Paris: Gallimard, 1947). For two critical responses to the Sartrean thesis, see Georges Blin, *Le Sadisme de Baudelaire* (Paris: José Corti, 1948), and Georges Bataille, "Baudelaire," in *La Littérature et le mal* (Paris: Gallimard, 1957). In a move that has analogies to my argument here, Bataille defines the poetic as "a relation of *participation* of the subject in the object" (p. 48).

28. "The Salon of 1846," in *The Mirror of Art*, p. 85: *Oeuvres complètes*, 2: 455–456.

29. Jacques Le Rider speaks of a 1921 essay by Lou-Andreas Salomé on narcissism which, Le Rider notes, condenses an important poetic and moral debate from the beginning of the century. Le Rider finds echoes of Nietzsche, Rilke, and Freud and his disciples in Salomé's nostalgia for the lost (narcissistic) union of the self and the world. She also wrote to a skeptical Freud of the liberation of the drive toward that union as the goal of a successful analysis. See Jacques Le Rider, "Le Narcissisme orphique de Rainer Maria Rilke," *Europe*, 719 (March 1989). Indeed, in early analytic circles, there are interesting discussions of the breakdown of the barriers between the "I" and the "non-I." Paul Federn, for example, arguing against the prevalent view of feelings of estrangement from the world as accompanied by "an increase in narcissism attended by a decrease in object-cathexis," characterized estrangement as a state that ensues when "the ego boundary *loses* some of its libidinal cathexis," thus suggesting the importance of narcissism for an erotic interest in objects. "From the very beginning, the primary ego feeling also includes the external world," although this type of object cathexis "is of a purely narcissistic nature and not yet that of object libido." Federn, *Ego Psychology and the Psychoses*, ed. Edoardo Weiss (London: Maresfield Reprints, 1953), pp. 284, 294–295; see especially chaps. 2 and 15.

To put my own speculations in relation to these other texts: I have been suggesting, especially in my readings of Freud and Baudelaire, that in primary narcissism ego boundaries are *at once* constituted, "cathected," and exploded. Narcissism would be essential, as Federn proposes, to feelings of closeness to the world, but this would be because narcissism tends to dissolve (not to fortify) those boundaries separating the self from the nonself. The fantastic expansion of the ego beyond its boundaries is not a triumph of the ego, for it is only when the ego loses its identity that such an expansion is conceivable.

30. My translation; *Oeuvres complètes*, 2:133.

31. Benjamin, *Charles Baudelaire*, pp. 98–100.

32. Ibid., pp. 55–56.

33. *Oeuvres complètes*, 2:73; *Les Fleurs du mal*, trans. Richard Howard (Boston: David R. Godine, 1982), p. 75.

34. This argument is elaborated, in the context of analyses of ancient Assyrian sculpture, in Leo Bersani and Ulysse Dutoit, *The Forms of Violence: Narrative in Assyrian Art and Modern Culture*, (New York: Schocken, 1985).

35. My translation; *Oeuvres complètes*, 1:702, 700, 677. *Mon coeur mis à nu* also includes these famous lines on women: "A woman is hungry and she wants to eat. Thirsty and she wants to drink. / She is in heat and she wants to be screwed. / What admirable qualities! / Woman is *natural*, that is to say abominable." My translation; *Oeuvres complètes*, 1:677.

36. My translation; *Oeuvres complètes*, 1:678.

37. *Oeuvres complètes*, 1:150; *Les Fleurs du mal*, trans. Howard, p. 124.

38. Ibid., 1:114; p. 130.

39. My translation; *Oeuvres complètes*, 1:275–276.

40. Friedrich Nietzsche, *The Birth of Tragedy and The Case of Wagner*, trans. Walter Kaufmann (New York: Random House, 1967), pp. 36, 46. Further references to *The Birth of Tragedy* will be to this translation, with page numbers given in text.

41. As Walter Kaufmann reminds us in a note to this passage: "This conception of contemplation devoid of interest, as well as much else that is indebted to Schopenhauer, was later expressly criticized by Nietzsche" (48).

42. Here is Nietzsche's judgment of *The Birth of Tragedy* in his 1886 preface: "I consider it badly written, ponderous, embarrassing, image-mad and image-confused, sentimental, in places saccharine to the point of effeminacy, uneven in tempo, without the will to logical cleanliness, very convinced and therefore disdainful of proof, mistrustful even of the *propriety* of proof, a book for initiates, 'music' for those dedicated to music, those who are closely related to begin with on the basis of common and rare aesthetic experiences, 'music' meant as a sign of recognition for close relatives *in artibus*—an arrogant and rhapsodic book that sought to exclude right from the beginning the *profanum vulgus* of 'the educated' even more than 'the mass' or 'folk.'" (19).

43. If Dionysus belongs to nature, Paul de Man writes, "then he is forever and radically separated from any form of art, since no bridge, as metaphor or as representation, can ever connect the natural realm of essences with the textual realm of forms and values." De Man studies the "genetic pattern" and

the "imagery of filiation" by means of which Dionysus "can enter into a world of appearances and still somehow remain" Dionysus. By arguing for "the deconstruction of the genetic pattern in *The Birth of Tragedy*," de Man intends to refute Philippe Lacoue-Labarthe's claim that in his first book Nietzsche does not truly contest Schopenhauer's statement that music is the unmediated image of the will (a statement that accepts the "logical absurdity" of unmediated representation) and, more fundamentally, that Nietzsche fails to contest the will itself "as the ontological category by means of which beginning and end, origin and purpose are united in one genetic pattern." De Man, *Allegories of Reading: Figural Language in Rousseau, Nietzsche, Rilke, and Proust* (New Haven: Yale University Press, 1979), pp. 96, 100–101. See also Philippe Lacoue-Labarthe, "Le Détour," *Poétique,* 5 (1971), 53–76; the essay is reprinted in *Le Sujet de la philosophie (Typographies I)* (Paris: Aubier, Flammarion, 1979), pp. 31–74.

44. Art does not "represent" life: "Indeed, even when the tone-poet expresses his composition in images, when for instance he designates a certain symphony as the 'pastoral' symphony, or a passage in it as the 'scene by the brook,' or another as the 'merry gathering of rustics,' these two are only symbolical representations born of music—and not the imitated objects of music—representations which can teach us nothing whatsoever concerning the *Dionysian* content of music, and which indeed have no distinctive value of their own beside other images" (54).

45. Thus tragedy carries a metaphysical hope and is not, in the ordinary sense, tragic. "According to Nietzsche," as Deleuze writes, "it has never been understood that the tragic equals the joyful." Gilles Deleuze, *Nietzsche and Philosophy* trans. Hugh Tomlinson (New York: Columbia University Press, 1983), p. 36.

46. It is therefore, more radically, unthinkable. For Heidegger this meant, above all, unavailable to metaphysical thinking. Discussing "the Eternal Recurrence of the same," Heidegger writes: "That Nietzsche experienced and expounded his most abysmal thought from the Dionysian standpoint only suggests that he was still compelled to think it metaphysically, and only metaphysically. But it does not preclude that this most abysmal thought conceals something unthought, which also is impenetrable to metaphysical thinking." Martin Heidegger, "Who Is Nietzsche's Zarathustra?" trans. Bernd Magnus, in *The New Nietzsche,* ed. David B. Allison (Cambridge: MIT Press, 1985), p. 79.

4. Literature and History

1. André Malraux, *Man's Fate,* trans. Haakon M. Chevalier (New York: Random House, 1934, 1961), pp. 227–228; *La Condition humaine* (Paris: Gallimard, 1946), p. 229. Further page references, first to the English translation and then to the French, are given in text.

2. Georges Bataille, *Blue of Noon,* trans. Harry Matthews (New York: Urizen, 1978; reprint Marion Boyars Publishers, 1985), p. 12; *Le Bleu du ciel,* in *Oeuvres complètes,* vol. 3 (Paris: Gallimard, 1971), p. 385. Further page ref-

erences, first to the English translation and then to the French, are given in text.

3. The introduction to *Le Bleu du ciel* appeared separately, with the title "Dirty," in 1945, with the indication that it had been written in 1928. Bataille's manuscript also suggests that he eliminated sixteen pages from the beginning of part 2 (we go from page 17 to page 34, and Bataille notes: "manquent 16 pages supprimées"). See *Oeuvres complètes,* 3:560.

4. Denis Hollier, writing brilliantly about Bataille's use of the Don Juan tradition, speaks of two crucial transformations: the Commander's sexualization and Don Juan's necrophilia (the Commander has become Don Juan's Don Juan). See Denis Hollier, "Bataille's Tomb: A Halloween Story." *October,* 33 (Summer 1985).

5. D. H. Lawrence, *Women in Love* (New York: Viking, 1960), p. viii.

5. Flaubertian Rhythms of Knowledge

1. Gustave Flaubert, *Bouvard and Pécuchet,* trans. A. J. Krailsheimer (New York: Penguin, 1976), pp. 143–144; *Bouvard et Pécuchet,* ed. Claudine Gothot-Mersch (Paris: Gallimard, 1979), pp. 219–220. Further page references to *Bouvard et Pécuchet* (as well as to the *Dictionnaire des idées reçues,* also included in these editions) are given in text, first to the English and then to the French.

2. In his remarkable study of *Bouvard et Pécuchet,* Charles Bernheimer reaches conclusions similar to mine about the detachment of Flaubert's text from its presumed sources: "The reader is confronted by a text that purports to be the response of two fictional characters to two anterior texts, but, as he reads, the precise outlines of both texts and response are effaced and he is set adrift in a flotsam of surreal or hallucinatory images of undefined origin." Bernheimer interprets this detachment of the signifier from the signified in the psychoanalytic terms of a withdrawal of erotic investment, and the consequent operation of the death instinct. He also argues that Bouvard and Pécuchet "have no existential commitment to any of the codes they adopt," which of course runs counter to my distinction between the narrator and Flaubert's bonshommes. Bernheimer, *Flaubert and Kafka: Studies in Psychopoetic Structure* (New Haven: Yale University Press, 1982), pp. 120, 113.

3. The absence of attribution is also a way of depriving the sources of such summaries of their epistemological authority. In comparing Flaubert's notes for the novel to the published text, Claude Duchet has studied this "process of disinformation." Obscured and distorted, the texts behind *Bouvard et Pécuchet* are unable to function as reliable sources of knowledge; we have "a counter-mimesis at work on the level of the representation of ideas." Duchet, "Ecriture et désécriture de l'histoire dans *Bouvard et Pécuchet,*" in *Flaubert à l'oeuvre,* ed. Raymonde Debray-Genette (Paris: Flammarion, 1980), p. 124).

4. Making a very different argument, Eugenio Donato sees in *Bouvard et Pécuchet* an accurate representation of the "epistemological ideology"—the belief, above all, that "the implicit order of Nature and of History" can be made visible—of the Museum as that ideology was developed from approxi-

mately the time of Buffon to that of Cuvier. Donato, "The Museum's Furnace: Notes Toward a Contextual Reading of *Bouvard et Pécuchet*," in *Textual Strategies: Perspectives in Post-Structuralist Criticism*, ed. Josué V. Harari (Ithaca: Cornell University Press, 1979), p. 231.

5. Claudine Gothot-Mersch summarizes these notes, and provides excerpts from the unpublished manuscripts, in her excellent edition of *Bouvard et Pécuchet*. See also Geneviève Bollème, *Le Second Volume de "Bouvard et Pécuchet"* (Paris: Denoël, 1966), and the article by Claude Mouchard and Jacques Neefs, "Vers le second volume de *Bouvard et Pécuchet*, in *Flaubert à l'oeuvre*.

6. Incomparable America

1. Herman Melville, *Moby-Dick,* ed. Harrison Hayford and Hershel Parker (New York: Norton, 1967), pp. 545–546. Further page references to this edition are given in text.
2. Richard Poirier discusses the complications—the often conflicting energies— in American writers' perception of their relation to a cultural past in *The Renewal of Literature: Emersonian Reflections* (New York: Random House, 1987).
3. Nearly half the cetological passsages in *Moby-Dick* come from books *on* whaling, in which references to whales can hardly be taken as proof of the hold exercised by the whale, everywhere and at all times, on human attention. We also know, thanks to the work of Luther S. Mansfield and Howard P. Vincent for the 1952 Hendricks House edition of *Moby-Dick,* that while implying that he had read all the authorities he mentions, Melville's research often "went no further than his much-used copy of Beale's *Natural History of the Sperm Whale*" (editors' note, *Moby-Dick*, p. 117). Ishmael's research also parodies the research of other cetology efforts: the "long detailed list of the outfits for the larders and cellars of 180 sail of Dutch whalemen" (371) is a takeoff on a pedantically statistical passage in William Scoresby's *History and Description of the Northern Whale Fishery*. Finally, the proofs offered in "The Affidavit" chapter of the sperm whale's acting "with wilful, deliberate designs of destruction to his pursuers" consist of little more than examples of ships attacked by a whale, and the chapter ends with the contention that the sea monster whose capture in the Sea of Marmora is related by Procopius was a sperm whale, a contention supported by an astonishingly vague evidential chain:

> "*Further investigations* [what are they?] have recently proved to me, that in modern times there have been isolate instances of the presence of the sperm whale in the Mediterranean. *I am told, on good authority*, that on the Barbary coast, a Commodore Davis of the British navy found the skeleton of a sperm whale. Now, as a vessel of war readily passes through the Dardanelles, hence a sperm whale could, by the same route, pass out of the Mediterranean into the Propontis.
> "In the Propontis, *as far as I can learn*, none of that peculiar substance called *brit* is to be found, the aliment of the right whale. *But I have every*

reason to believe that the food of the sperm whale—squid or cuttle-fish—lurks at the bottom of that sea, because large creatures, but by no means the largest of that sort, have been found at its surface. *If, then, you properly put these statements together, and reason upon them a bit,* you will clearly perceive that, according to all human reasoning, Procopius's sea-monster, that for half a century stove the ships of a Roman Emperor, must in all probability have been a sperm whale." (181–182; emphasis mine).

4. Much of the recent criticism of *Moby-Dick* has been concerned with the novel's political significance. These readings have generally been of a referential nature, pinpointing moments and events in mid-nineteenth-century America to which Melville's work would be addressing itself. Alan Heimert's article "*Moby-Dick* and American Political Symbolism" is seminal in this respect. Among Heimert's major claims are that "Melville associated the quest of the 'sublime' White Whale with imperial aspirations" and that behind Moby Dick and Ahab stand, respectively, Daniel Webster and John C. Calhoun; in *American Quarterly,* 15 (Winter 1963), 498–534. More recently, Michael Paul Rogin has argued that "Melville is a recorder and interpreter of America's society whose work is comparable to that of the great nineteenth-century European realists" and, more specifically, that "*Moby-Dick* registers the dependence of America's freedom on America's slavery, and the threat of American slavery to destroy America's freedom"; *Subversive Genealogy: The Politics and Art of Herman Melville* (Berkeley: University of California Press, 1979), pp. ix, 121.

5. This argument is made in C.L.R. James's stirringly personal book, *Mariners, Renegades and Castaways: The Story of Herman Melville and the World We Live In* (New York: C.L.R. James, 1953). The *Pequod's* crew, James writes, "owe no allegiance to any body or anything except the work they have to do and the relations with one another on which that work depends" (p. 20.) "The contrast is between Ahab and the crew"; Melville endowed the crew with "the graces of men associated for common labor" (p. 30).

   I will soon be raising objections to the widespread tendency to see Ishmael as a viable alternative to Ahab. From a different perspective, Donald E. Pease has also argued against such a reading. Criticizing the tendency of F. O. Matthiessen and "forty years of Cold War critics" to turn to Ishamel as, in contrast to Ahab, "the principle of America's freedom," Pease makes a persuasive case for the structural interdependence of Ahab and Ishmael. "Ahab's compulsion to decide *compels* Ishmael *not* to decide." And: "The fate befalling Ahab's decisive conversion of work into deed determines Ishmael's need of a realm in which the indeterminate play of endless possible actions over-determines his *in*decision." Pease, "Moby-Dick and the Cold War," in *The American Renaissance Reconsidered: Selected Papers from the English Institute, 1982–83,* ed. Walter Benn Michaels and Donald E. Pease 9 (Baltimore: Johns Hopkins University Press, 1983). p. 147.

6. To mention two ends of a kind of moral spectrum of perspectives on homosexuality in *Moby-Dick:* Leslie Fiedler, in *Love and Death in the American*

Novel (New York: Stein and Day, 1966), finds Melville (and other American writers) unable to deal with adult heterosexual love. Robert K. Martin, in *Hero, Captain, and Stranger: Male Friendship, Social Critique, and Literary Form in the Sea Novels of Herman Melville* (Chapel Hill: University of North Carolina Press, 1986), reinterprets this failure as an accomplishment of the highest order. "The homosexual relationship," he writes, "is invested by Melville with radical social potential; it is through the affirmation of the values of nonaggressive male-bonded couples that the power of the patriarch can be contested and even defeated" (p. 70). Martin's argument has an engaging specificity. The patriarchal structure might be broken down by a kind of communal masturbatory narcissism: "Men coming together [in group masturbation] are not men fighting each other, or even men hurting whales" (p. 82). The pacification of the phallus through masturbation remains, however, a problematic notion.

7. I say this fully aware of what might be called the narratological problem of Ishmael. Melville doesn't take much trouble to maintain his presence throughout the novel; for several chapters in a row, Ishmael the character disappears, and a fairly conventional omniscient narrator takes over. It could also be said that Ishmael is very unlike the other members of the crew—in his understanding of Ahab, his humor, his intellectuality. If I use "Ishmael" to refer consistently to *Moby-Dick*'s narrator, it is because I think the very inconsistencies, and the apparent irreducibility of the narrative voice to a psychologically reliable narrative persona, themselves define a nearly undefinable, nearly unrecognizable persona that, mainly for the sake of convenience, we can call "Ishmael." But to use this name consistently, as I have done, does not obviously mean that a conventional psychological or moral identity corresponds to the name. Ishmael must be as elusive, even as absent, as that incomparable America he nonetheless strives to express. And if, as a character, he is different from the rest of the crew, he is, more significantly, also a philosophical articulation of their estrangement, of the *isolato* condition.

8. The distance between this America and historical America is also suggested, from another perspective, by the ship's name. The Pequod Indians, a reputedly bloodthirsty Connecticut tribe, were massacred by militia from Hartford in 1637. If Melville's *Pequod* is an image of America, it is an America expelled from America and eliminated by America. Rogin writes that in naming Ahab's ship *Pequod*, Melville paid ironic homage to a process in which "the conquest of savages and the acquisition of their power" is implicitly seen as "regeneration through violence" (*Subversive Genealogy*, p. 124). For a study of this process, see Richard Slotkin, *Regeneration Through Violence*, (Middletown: Wesleyan University Press, 1973).

9. In *Pierre* Melville himself will satirize the illusion of literary originality. A critique of the possibility of originality from the perspective of a poststructuralist ideology of textuality can be found in Edgar Dryden, "The Entangled Text: Melville's *Pierre* and the Problem of Reading," *Boundary*, 2 (July 1979). Joseph Riddell addresses the same question in "Decentering the

Image: The 'Project' of 'American' Poetics?" in *Textual Strategies: Perspectives in Post-Structuralist Criticism,* ed. Josué V. Harari (Ithaca: Cornell University Press, 1979), pp. 322–358.

7. Against Ulysses

1. James Joyce, *Ulysses, The Corrected Text,* ed. Hans Walter Gabler with Wolfhard Steppe and Claus Melchior (New York: Random House, 1986), p. 3. Further page references to this edition are given in text. The "corrected text" has, since I worked on this chapter, become the notorious text. John Kidd's by now famous attack on this version of *Ulysses,* and on the *Synoptic Edition* that preceded it (in 1984), was published under the title "The Scandal of *Ulysses*" in *New York Review of Books,* 35 (June 30, 1988), 32–39. "The *Synoptic Edition,*" Kidd argues, "is a study not of Joyce's manuscripts but of inadequate facsimiles" (p. 34). Charles Rosswann, several months later, published a piece showing that "Kidd's public criticisms of the new *Ulysses* were preceded by serious private doubts among the scholars who were chosen by the estate to advise its editors"; "The New *Ulysses:* The Hidden Controversy," *New York Review of Books,* 35 (December 8, 1988), 53–58. The record of the attention given to this quarrel will be a significant entry in the annals of institutionalized Joyceanism.
2. Perhaps the most notable expression of this complaint can be found in S. L. Goldberg, *The Classical Temper: A Study of James Joyce's 'Ulysses'* (London: Chatto and Windus, 1969). Goldberg speaks of a "precarious intellectualization of structure under which some of the later writing collapses completely." In some of the chapters from "Cyclops" on, "the gap between the formal values implicit in the techniques and organization and the values enacted by the characters progressively widens" (p. 281).
3. To certify the effects of my own nervous (and probably imperfect) vigilance, I should add that Gerty makes a cameo appearance toward the end of episode 10 ("Wandering Rocks"), p. 208.
4. John Paul Riquelme, *Teller and Tale in Joyce's Fiction: Oscillating Perspectives* (Baltimore: Johns Hopkins University Press, 1983), p. 202.
5. Hugh Kenner, *Joyce's Voices* (Berkeley: University of California Press, 1978), p. 17.
6. The "stylistic intrusions" and point-of-view discontinuities in *Ulysses* can be fairly brief, as in the following move away from (and return to) Bloom's own language to convey his thoughts about slaughtering animals for food and his inner tableau of a cattle market:

> "After all there's a lot in that vegetarian fine flavour of things from the earth garlic of course it stinks after Italian organgrinders crisp of onions mushrooms truffles. Pain to the animal too. Pluck and draw fowl. Wretched brutes there at the cattlemarket waiting for the poleaxe to split their skulls open. Moo. Poor trembling calves. Meh. Staggering bob. Bubble and squeak. Butchers' buckets wobbly lights. Give us that brisket off the hook. Plup. Rawhead and bloody bones. Flayed glasseyed sheep

hung from their haunches, sheepsnouts bloodypapered snivelling nose-
jam on sawdust. Top and lashers going out. Don't maul them pieces,
young one.

"Hot fresh blood they prescribe for decline. Blood always needed. Insidious. Lick it up smokinghot, thick sugary. Famished ghosts.

"Ah, I'm hungry (140)."

The imagined sounds of the animals ("Moo" and "Meh") usher in a change
of scene and style. With "Butchers' buckets wobbly lights" we are probably
no longer in Bloom's thoughts of the slaughterhouse but, rather startlingly,
in the slaughterhouse itself (with even snatches of direct speech from that
new scene: "Give us that brisket off the hook" and perhaps "Don't maul
them pieces, young one"). And someone else has obviously come in to take
Bloom's linguistic place for the dense impressionistic description of the
hanging flayed sheep.

Bloom's mind can also be invaded by an alien style when he himself would
be incapable of doing justice to the intensity of his own feelings. Here is part
of his memory, as he drinks wine in Danny Byrne's pub, of the time he
kissed Molly, many years before, "hidden under wild ferns on Howth":
"Ravished over her I lay, full lips full open, kissed her mouth. Yum. Softly
she gave me in my mouth the seedcake warm and chewed. Mawkish pulp
her mouth had mumbled sweetsour of her spittle. Joy: I ate it: joy" (144).
The syntactic inversions and condensations, the funny "Yum" in the middle
of the description, and the symmetrical verbal columns of "joy" which, in
framing "I ate it," give to those words a kind of ceremonial dignity, provide
a perspective at once slightly comic and slightly solemn on that moment of
fusion—of joined mouths and shared seedcake—which Bloom longingly relives as his "sense moistened [by the wine] remembered." Other intrusions
are structurally massive, as in the interruptions of the anonymous pub
crawler's speech in "Cyclops" by parodies of newspaper articles and popular
sentimental fiction. "Cyclops" even ends by violating its own intrusive principles: the last sentence of the final parody (of biblical prose), in which
Bloom ascends to heaven, ends with the jarring intrusion of the pub crawler's
style: "And they beheld Him even Him, ben Bloom Elijah, amid clouds of
angels ascend to the glory of the brightness at an angle of fortyfive degrees
over Donohoe's in Little Green Street like a shot off a shovel" (283).

7. Fritz Senn, *Joyce's Dislocutions: Essays on Reading as Translation,* ed. John Paul
   Riquelme (Baltimore: Johns Hopkins University Press, 1984), p. 141.
8. David Hayman, *Ulysses: The Mechanics of Meaning* (Madison: University of
   Wisconsin Press, 1970, 1982), p. 92. In the 1961 Random House edition of
   Ulysses used by Hayman, "Agenbite of inwit" occurs in this passage (as well
   as on the preceding page of the novel), thus making attribution of the passage
   even more difficult since, as Hayman notes, the phrase is surely Stephen's.
9. The Homeric correspondences are of course the best example of this double
   posture. Joyce wrote *Ulysses* with all these parallels in mind; he even intended to use the corresponding episode in the *Odyssey* as the title for each
   chapter. But then he withdrew those helpful chapter heads and kept the Ho-

meric reference only in the title of the book itself. And then he made sure that the correspondences would not be missed by making them explicit in the schema he sent to Carlo Linati in 1920. Finally, however, the correspondences to Homer, as *Ulysses'* readers quickly discover, are extremely casual and at times even comically unexpected or incongruous. Long sections of the *Odyssey* are simply ignored; the order of the episodes in Joyce—especially in the middle section, the tale of Odysseus' wanderings—does not follow Homer's order; and one Joycean episode, "Wandering Rocks," has no corresponding episode in Homer (since Odysseus chooses to risk the passage between Scylla and Charybdis rather than to attempt the even more dangerous Wandering Rocks).

10. Kenner, *Joyce's Voices,* pp. 69–70.

11. Here is the account of how Ignatius Gallaher seduces Little Chandler in "A Little Cloud" with his stories of continental corruption: "Ignatius Gallaher puffed thoughtfully at his cigar and then, in a calm historian's tone, he proceeded to sketch for his friend some pictures of the corruption which was rife abroad. He summarised the vices of many capitals and seemed inclined to award the palm to Berlin. Some things he could not vouch for (his friends had told him), but of others he had had personal experience. He spared neither rank nor caste. He revealed many of the secrets of religious houses on the Continent and described some of the practices which were fashionable in high society and ended by telling, with details, a story about an English duchess—a story which he knew to be true. Little Chandler was astonished." *Dubliners* (New York: Penguin, 1967), p. 78. We can imagine hearing a few echoes of actual speech ("Corruption is rife abroad," "Some things I can't vouch for," "That's a story I know to be true"), but such echoes may actually be summaries of Gallaher's speech in the style of that speech. Simply to pose this alternative is already to begin moving outside his mind without quite leaving it (which is all the more notable since the perspective is unambiguously that of a *report on* Gallaher's speech; the narrative camera is not, as in free indirect discourse, situated within the character's consciousness). The provincial and pretentious nature of Gallaher's disabused worldliness is exposed through the excessively scrupulous attention the narrator gives to his speech. It is the kind of talk that would distribute first, second, and third prizes in corruption, and so the narrator appears to be trying, in that vein, to guess which city Gallaher found most corrupt: he "seemed inclined to award the palm to Berlin." The closest we come to explicit comment is the rather dry summary of Gallaher's naive and self-serving repetition of all the rumors he has heard ("He spared neither rank nor caste"), and the casual decision not to bother *us* with any of the details in that true story about an English duchess. Someone is paying even more attention to Gallaher than Little Chandler is, to the point of knowing that he can best be replayed by a decision to omit part of what he says. We get the flavor of his speech, but that flavor comes to us not as an element of his actual speech or even as an appreciation of an external observer, but rather as a component in an objectifying point of view, a point of view that seeks ultimately not to be a point of view, to be instead the exact verbal translation of the essential Gallaher.

Joyce himself, it should be noted, would probably have preferred to speak of this sort of writing as deliberately colorless, as realizing the ideal of "a style of scrupulous meanness." See his *Letters,* 3 vols., ed. Stuart Gilbert and Richard Ellmann (New York: Viking, 1966), letter to Grant Richards, May 8, 1906, 2:134.

12. *A Portrait of the Artist as a Young Man* (New York: Penguin, 1976), pp. 212–213.

13. "The Boarding House," *Dubliners,* p. 63.

14. "Ambiviolences: Notes for Reading Joyce," in *Post-Structuralist Joyce: Essays from the French,* ed. Derek Attridge and Daniel Ferrer (Cambridge: Cambridge University Press, 1984), pp. 33, 57. For Lacan on Joyce, as well as readings of Joyce by some of Lacan's disciples, see *Joyce avec Lacan* (Paris: Navarin, 1987).

15. See Richard Poirier, "The Difficulties of Modernism and the Modernism of Difficulty," *Humanities in Society,* 1 (Spring 1978).

16. Frank Budgen, *James Joyce and the Making of "Ulysses"* (London: Grayson, 1934), p. 56.

17. In a letter to Harriet Shaw Weaver, Joyce spoke of the "scorching" effect of his writing: "each specific episode, dealing with some province of artistic culture . . . leaves behind it a burnt up field." *Letters,* July 20, 1919, 1:129.

18. The rest of this paragraph restates an argument made in my chapter on Malraux and Bataille. The earlier juxtaposition of Bataille and Lawrence has even greater force here, in coupled contrast to Joyce.

19. Joyce, *Letters,* letter to Frank Budgen, March 20, 1920, 1:139–140.

20. Richard Ellmann, *Ulysses on the Liffey* (London: Faber and Faber, 1972), p. 136–139.

21. Kenner, *Joyce's Voices,* p. 40.

22. In Leo Bersani, *The Death of Stéphane Mallarmé* (Cambridge: Cambridge University Press, 1982).

23. J. S. Atherton, "The Oxen of the Sun," in *James Joyce's "Ulysses": Critical Essays,* ed. Clive Hart and David Hayman (Berkeley: University of California Press, 1974), p. 331.

24. See Atherton's essay for some examples of how Joyce seems to have dipped into the guidebooks he apparently used most frequently for "Oxen of the Sun" (Saintsbury's *History of English Prose Rhythm* and Peacock's anthology in the World's Classics series, *English Prose: Mandeville to Ruskin*).

8. Pynchon, Paranoia, and Literature

1. Thomas Pynchon, *Gravity's Rainbow* (New York: Bantam Books, 1973), p. 295. All references will be to this edition, with page numbers in text.

2. See H. Ey, P. Bernard, and C. Brisset, *Manuel de psychiatrie* (Paris: Masson, 1978), chap. 7. There is a good summary of the history of psychiatric thought concerning paranoia, in the entry Paranoia, in Jean Laplanche and J.-B. Pontalis, *The Language of Psychoanalysis,* trans. Donald Micholson-Smith (New York: Norton, 1974).

3. Freud, "Psycho-analytic Notes on an Autobiographical Account of a Case of Paranoia (Dementia Paranoides)," *Standard Edition,* 12:78–79.
4. Pynchon's attachment to that myth, and to the presumed obligation of the novelist "to develop plot and characters," is evident in the astonishing introduction he wrote for the publication of his early short stories, *Slow Learner* (New York: Bantam Books, 1984), p. xxviii.

Epilogue

George Segal's plaster sculpture, *Abraham's Farewell to Ishmael* (1987; copyright © 1989 by George Segal/VAGA, New York), was first shown at the Sidney Janis Gallery, New York; photograph courtesy of the gallery.

1. Genesis, chapter 12, verses 14–16. I am using the King James version.
2. The fine verb "Isaac-ing" is Robert Alter's coinage, and the quoted words in this sentence are his. I am also indebted to Alter for pointing out that the rabbis who read "mocking" in a sexual sense may have done so for philological reasons: the verb suggests sexual dalliance in the words of Potiphar's wife about Joseph in Genesis 39 or in Isaac's version of the sister-wife story, when Abimelech looks out the window and sees him "playing" or "fooling around" with Rebecca (Genesis 26:8).
3. Modern biblical scholarship tends to maintain that Sodom was destroyed not for anything having to do with homosexuality, but rather for its inhospitable treatment of visitors sent by God. See especially Derrick Sherwin Bailey, *Homosexuality in the Western Christian Tradition* (London: Longmans Green, 1955). A good summary of the arguments about why Sodom was destroyed can be found in John Boswell, *Christianity, Social Tolerance, and Homosexuality: Gay People in Western Europe from the Beginning of the Christian Era to the Fourteenth Century* (Chicago: University of Chicago Press, 1980), pp. 92–97.

Credits

Sections of this book have appeared, in preliminary form, in the following journals: *Critical Inquiry* (Chapter 1), *Novel: A Forum on Fiction* (Chapter 5), *Raritan* (Chapter 7), and *Representations* (Chapter 8). My thanks to the publishers for permission to reuse this material.

Index